THREAD'S NOT DEAD

The Designer's Guide to the Apparel Industry

By Jeff Finley

www.threadsnotdead.com

THREAD'S NOT DEAD • Jeff Finley

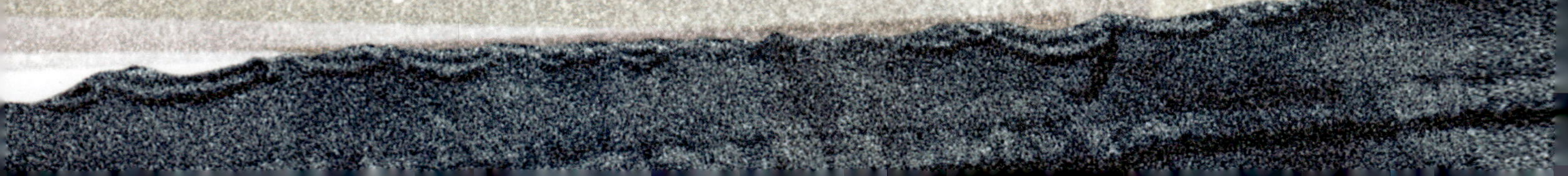

Legal Notice:

While all attempts have been made to verify information provided in this book, neither the Author or publisher assumes any responsibility for errors, omissions, or contrary interpretation of the subject matter herein. The content is based on personal experience and anecdotal evidence. This publication is not intended for use as a source of legal, business, marketing, or accounting advice. Use this information as you see fit, at your own risk. Your situation is unique and may or may not be suited to the suggestions or examples I provide in this book. Use your head and your best judgement and adjust this information accordingly.

The Purchaser or Reader of this publication assumes responsibility for the use of these materials and information. Adherence to all applicable laws and regulations, federal, state, and local, governing professional licensing, business practices, advertising, and all other aspects of doing business in the United States or any other jurisdiction is the sole responsibility of the Purchaser or Reader. The Author assumes no responsibility or liability whatsoever on the behalf of any Purchaser or Reader of these materials. Any perceived slights of specific people or organizations are unintentional.

Any trademarks, logos, and images used in this publication are property of their respective owners and are simply used as references and editorial purposes only.

Dedicated to Emptees.com (2007-2011)

On March 1st, 2011 Emptees.com closed its doors. The Emptees website had been instrumental in building a thriving t-shirt design community. It had been a major source of inspiration for this book and it is sad to see the site shut down. This book includes many references to Emptees and even links which may have been broken as a result of the closing. Fortunately, the community has come together to create a replacement that promises to archive and salvage all the content and be better than ever. This website is called Mintees.com. Every attempt has been made to relink and fix any errors that may have occurred. If you discover an error, please let us know so we can fix it.

Thank you Emptees,

Jeff Finley

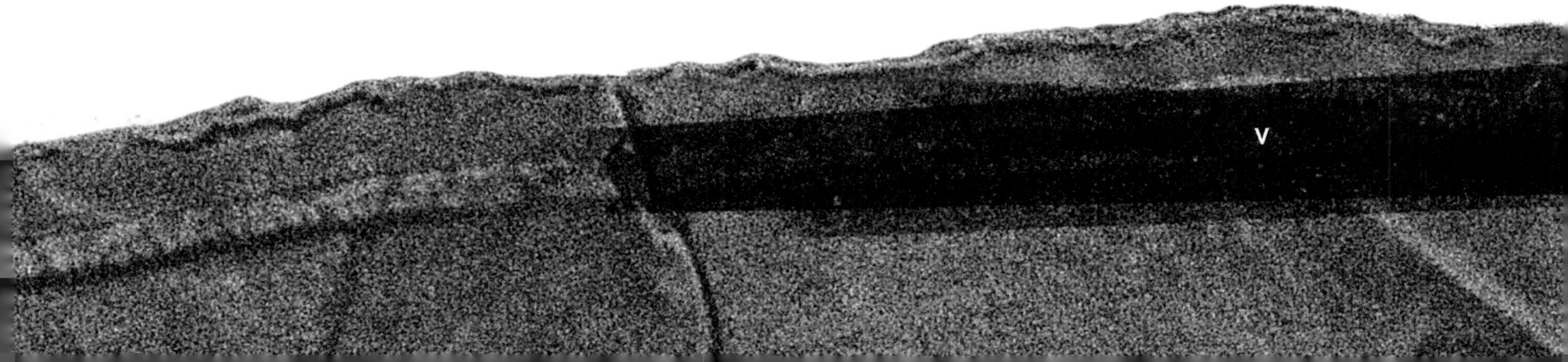

CONTRIBUTORS

Matt Wigham, founder of Indie Labs. He created Emptees, Big Cartel and Pulley.

Jeffrey Kalmikoff, VP of product at SimpleGEO. He was formerly CCO at Threadless and Director of Design & UX at Digg.

Marc Hemeon, Director of UX at Oakley. Formerly Design Lead at Digg and CTO and Partner of Design by Humans and TeeFury.

Mark Capicotto, designer and founder of Glamour Kills, one of the great success stories to arise out of the indie apparel design community.

Rob Dobi, designer and entrepreneur. Clients include Thursday, *Teen* Magazine, and Fall Out Boy. He has his own clothing brand called Fullbleed.

Maxx242, illustrator and designer with 13 years industry experience. Clients include Famous Stars and Straps, Miami Ink, Fox Racing, and Blink-182.

Angryblue, respected poster artist and t-shirt designer for over five years. Clients include Slayer, Nine Inch Nails, Harley-Davidson, and Guns N' Roses.

Jamie Tallerico, designer at Abercrombie & Fitch. He was formerly a designer at Atticus Clothing, American Eagle, and Art Director at XVLA Denim.

HorseBites, freelance illustrator currently working with The Black Axe. He has over six years experience designing for the punk and hardcore scene. Clients include Fall Out Boy, Strike Anywhere, and No Idea Records.

Ben Scrivens, founder of the horror t-shirt brand Fright-Rags. He has been a major client of countless designers in the indie t-shirt community.

Brandon Rike, freelance designer nearly ten years experience designing for bands and indie apparel companies. Clients include Linkin Park, Deftones, and Billy Joel.

Munk One, illustrator and designer with eleven years in the apparel business. He has worked for Wilson Sporting Goods, Blink-182, and KidRobot.

Kelly Kiernan, founder of Cure Apparel. Diagnosed with Type 1 Diabetes in 2005, launched Cure Apparel to raise awareness and funds for diabetes research.

Adam Hendle, designer, blogger, founder of IAMTHETREND and Shirt Launch.

Jon Kruse, designer and founder of How To Start a Clothing Company. He also has his own apparel company Mediocore Clothing.

Dave Pearson, founder of apparel brand Paint the Stars. Has worked with well-known designers in the indie apparel design community.

LT Magnotto, expert color separator for Jakprints. He has over six years experience preparing t-shirt designs for screen printing.

Rikki Burns, illustrator and designer. She curiously made a name for herself winning design contests at DesignByHümans and shirt.woot.com.

Table of Contents

INTRODUCTION

"You have to learn the rules of the game. And then you have to play better than anyone else."

— *ALBERT EINSTEIN*

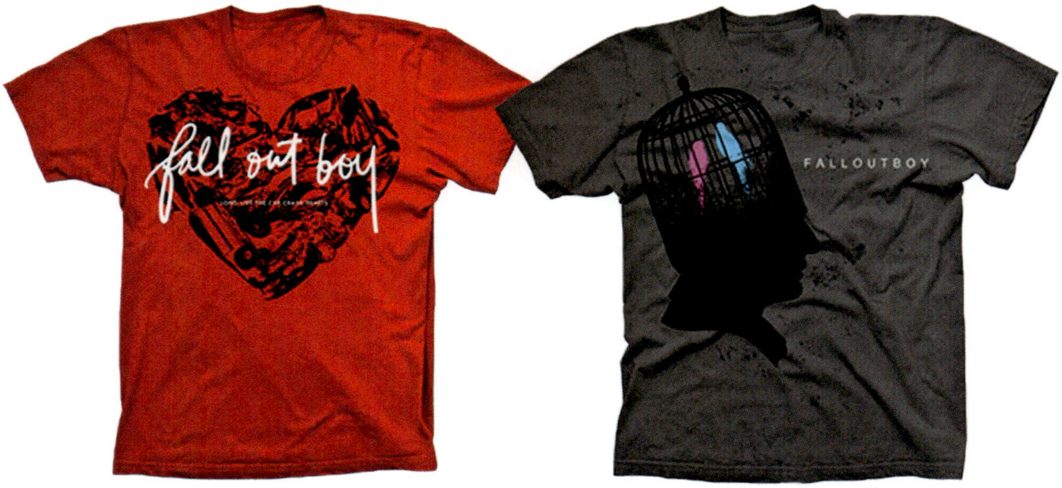

Designs for Fall Out Boy by Rob Dobi

What is This Book?

This book was written by **Jeff Finley**, that's me. I'm an artist/designer and partner at **Go Media**, a creative agency based in Cleveland, OH. Over the past six years I've done t-shirt designs for bands ranging from Jimmy Buffet to Metallica and everywhere in between. I've worked with dozens of indie apparel brands on everything from their initial line of t-shirts to their brand identity. However, lots of people reading this book know of Go Media because of the design articles and tutorials on our blog **GoMediaZine** and our "vector packs" sold at our stock art boutique **Arsenal.** For those who need numbers, here's a vain attempt to prove my credibility: Our blog is read by over 300,000 visitors per month and over 22,000 readers subscribe via rss. The Arsenal has served over 80,000 customers since 2006 and is widely considered a leader in indie stock art boutiques. It was from these years of serving my clients and fellow designers that I felt I owed it to them to write this book.

Humble Beginnings

It took a lot of work to get to this point. Six years ago I was just another art school kid trying to get good grades and graduate on time. I had no experience in t-shirt design — in fact I didn't even know such a thing existed. I was oblivious and all I cared about was getting a "real job" doing CG special effects or animation for games or film. I spent my time prepping my resume and demo reel with the hopes I would land an entry level position at a studio somewhere. Needless to say, that's not how things ended up.

The Inspiration

I was unable to find a job in my field. As I graduated I got jaded, and wasn't really interested in CG special effects or games anymore and had discovered the work of **Rob Dobi**, **Derek Hess**, and **Angryblue**. If those three artists had a dollar for every time I mention them as inspiration, they'd be rich by now.

What inspired me about those artists, aside from their sheer talent, was that they earned a living for themselves designing posters and t-shirts for bands I was into. Through their work, I discovered a whole new world of commercial art. That was the moment I decided I was going to follow in their footsteps and make a name for myself and design for my favorite bands.

The Secret Underground

In this book I will show you how I did it and reveal to you the secret underground of the apparel industry. I'll show you how other ambitious artists just like you overcame all the common stumbling blocks to become some of the most well-known designers in the indie apparel industry. You'll learn how to design for clients and how to start your own apparel line. You'll learn some of the tricks we have used to get ahead in the industry and how we have been able to transform our hobbies into careers. I think I can speak for all the experienced contributors to this book when I say "I wish this guide had been written when I started out."

So Who is This Book For?

This book is for artists and graphic designers who want to dominate the indie apparel industry. Specifically, it's for those who want to make a living, get famous or otherwise live like a rockstar designer. If you're the CEO of The Gap or looking to take your multimillion-dollar franchise to the next level, you probably don't need this book. But if you're an up-and-coming designer looking to break out in a big way and develop a clothing brand, this book is absolutely for you. If you are curious about who does the art on the shirts you wear, this book is also for you.

Why This Book?

I'm writing this book to show you how to dominate the t-shirt scene. My goal is to inform you of all the major aspects of being a designer in the t-shirt world. I'll talk about what it's like to be a designer and how to build your own apparel brand. I'll discuss design, branding, printing, marketing, sales, and e-commerce. I want you to learn from our collective mistakes and give you insight so you can quickly grow into the famous and recognized designer you want to be. I want you to go big-time!

I've also solicited the help of dozens of successful apparel industry designers and businesses who have been there and done that. They have fascinating stories of how they started in a position just like the one you are in today. I've deconstructed their stories into case studies and common practices that will get you the results you're looking for.

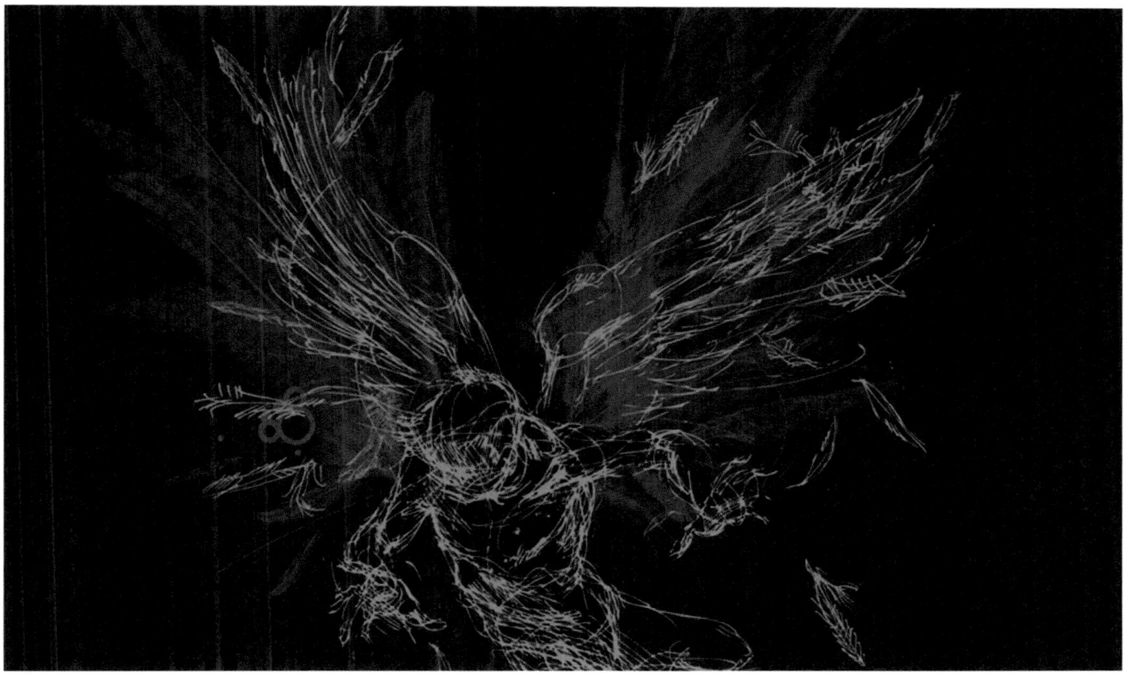

"Flying Angel" — a collab between Derek Hess and Go Media for Strhess Clothing

Defy the Hand You're Dealt

This book is a lesson in doing things yourself and taking matters into your own hands. Defying the hand you are dealt, so to speak. It will help you realize that you can turn your small side project into a full-time job and have tons of fun doing it. Been dying to quit your dreadful day job? You can, but not without determination and hard work. In fact, everyone I've interviewed can attest to that fact. It is hard work, but they all agree they wouldn't do it any different if they could.

This book will help you design better t-shirts and make a name for yourself. It will teach you how to make a decent living doing what you love. It will help you avoid making our same mistakes. It will also help you accept your own failures as learning experiences that only serve to make you better.

So without further ado, let's get started.

To view websites cited in this book, please visit www.threadsnotdead.com/links.

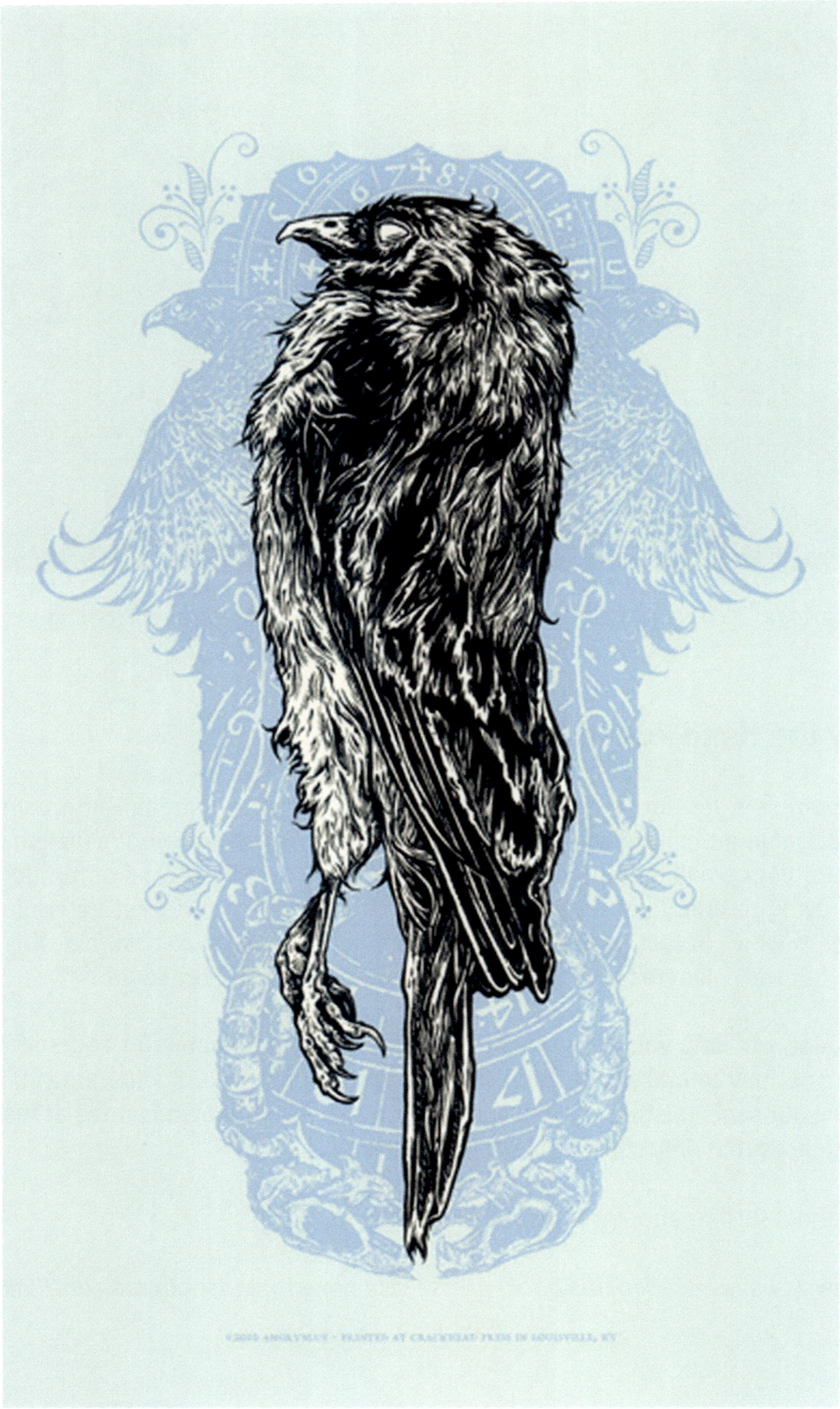

"The Strain"
by Angryblue

I

AN ARTIST WITH A DREAM

"Find a job you love and you'll never work a day in your life." — CONFUCIUS

When I Grow Up...

Growing up, I was always the art kid. As early as elementary school I was being "commissioned" by my friends to draw things for them. I allowed myself to feel warm and fuzzy when peers gave me compliments on my drawings of Mega Man or Mortal Kombat characters ripping out each other's spinal cords. One friend asked me for a drawing-a-day for a whole year and kept a binder of all my doodles. He said he would keep it until I was famous and then he could sell it and get rich. That made my 13-year-old self dream big. What if I did become a famous artist? What if I could actually earn a living doing art?

> *"I'm getting paid to create art. If that's not the craziest thing you've ever heard of as an artist, then I don't know what is."*
>
> —*RICHARD MININO (HORSEBITES)*

Fast forward to today and I am living the dream. I AM making a living doing art and getting my name out there. It's not as hard as you might think. If you look around, tons of former "art kids" are breaking out, hustling, and transforming the visual landscape of our surroundings. They are starting businesses, making unique products, and inspiring others. The one thing we all have in common is that we LOVE what we do. I'm including YOU in this because if you didn't, you probably wouldn't have bought this book!

Dealing with the Best Job Ever

How many times have you said "I can't believe someone is paying me to make art!" If you haven't had the opportunity to say that yet, you will. Getting paid while doing something you would do for free anyway is a glorious feeling! Not only do you get paid, you can often set your own hours and work from anywhere in the world. Dream job? To many, yes!

Because this is a "dream job" so to speak, the industry is very competitive. There are lots of up-and-coming artists willing to work for less money than you. It's like the

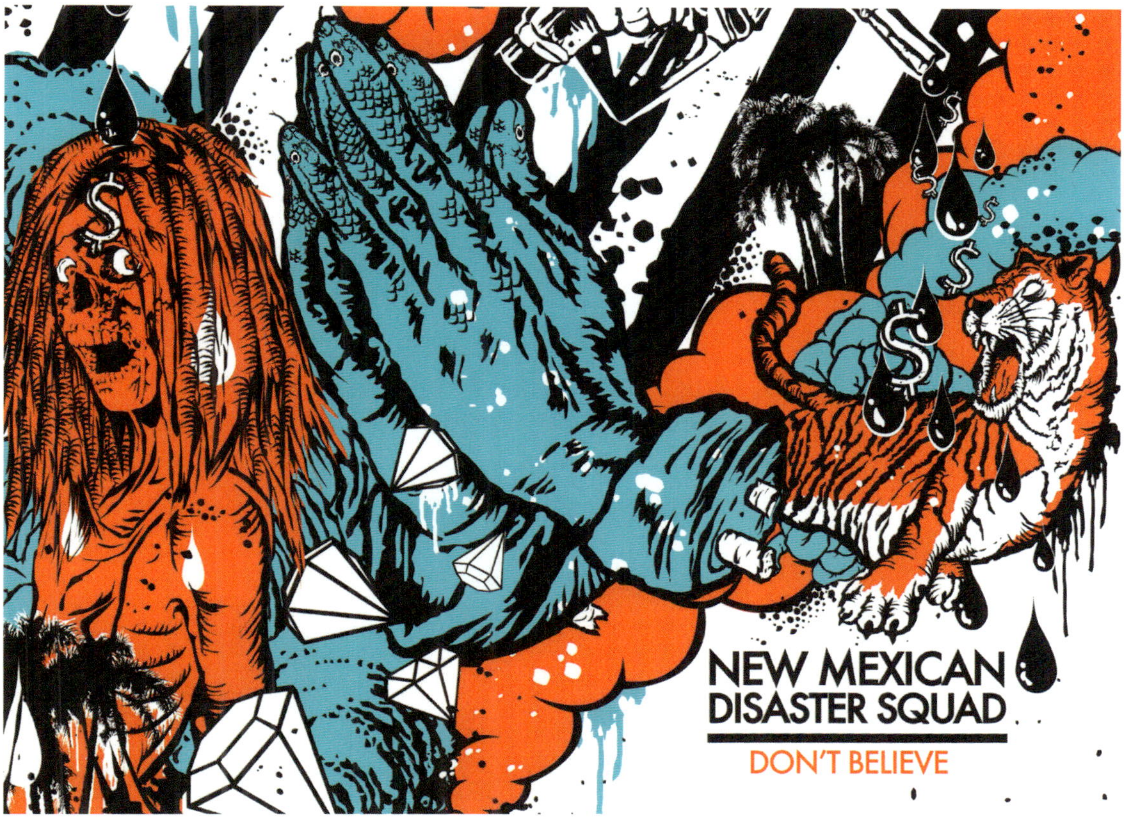

New Mexican Disaster Squad artwork by HorseBites

music or movie business where there are lots of people trying to "break in" because of the chance of making it big-time. I know because I was one of those eager ones myself.

I first started freelancing in 2004 and had the opportunity to do some designs for a record label. Oh boy, a real record label!? They weren't even that big, but I was trying to get exposure and was willing to take just about any job. I worked my butt off for free and they let me put my logo on things I designed for them. I was just starting out so I found it worth the exposure. This is how a lot of us started out.

I soon realized that I couldn't live on exposure alone and I had to start finding ways to make money at it. Of course, right? This is where it becomes more than just about art, but about business and you're going to need more than just drawing skills to succeed.

To view websites cited in this book, please visit www.threadsnotdead.com/links.

Your Three Roles: The Artist, Designer, and Entrepreneur

The Artist

According to the Wikipedia, *"Artist* is a descriptive term applied to a person who engages in an activity deemed to be an art. An artist also may be defined unofficially, as, 'a person who expresses themselves through a medium.' The word also is used in a qualitative sense of, a person creative in, innovative in, or adept at, an artistic practice."

Art has a lot to do with using your intuition; your ability to figure things out that don't always have a clear path to the solution. That's what makes us artists special.

Notice those keywords *creative, innovative,* and *adept.* I've seen the word *artist* being tossed around when referring to someone skilled at marketing, or influencing people: The "art of persuasion" or the "art of picking up chicks." By that definition, it's safe to say that...

The Designer:

As you get into commercial art, you're making art *with a purpose.* Your art is supposed to help sell a product, define a brand's identity, or evoke specific emotions in your audience. When you start making art for other people, your self-expressiveness gets put aside a little bit and now you're trying to solve a problem for someone else. This is usually where the word "design" comes in. You're crafting a solution to a creative problem and sometimes that involves drawing pictures or otherwise creating "art."

So what's the difference between artist and designer? I've heard some designers regard artists as self-indulgent and pretentious. And artists regard designers as snooty know-it-alls who lack empathy and feeling. The truth is we are BOTH. We are constantly shifting between the self-expressive artist and the critical designer. It's best to embrace the fact that these are two characteristics that make up who we are. If you want to look at it from another angle, an artist is who you are and design is what you do.

In this book I'll often use "artist" and "designer" interchangeably.

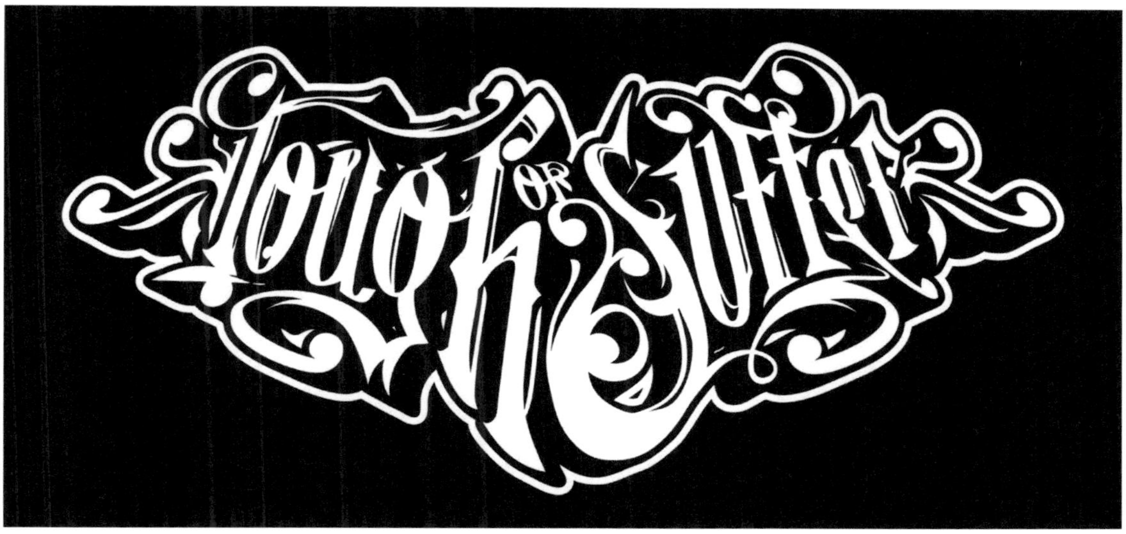

"Tough or Suffer" hand lettering by Jeff Finley of Go Media

The Entrepreneur: Embracing Your Business Side

The other characteristic is the entrepreneur. This is the dreamer. The one that allows us to fantasize about "making it big one day." If you've ever said to yourself "I want to start my own clothing line" then that's your entrepreneurial spirit peeking its head out. We all have it. And of course, if you're reading this, you are acutely aware of it.

This part of us gives us that drive. We crave to be better craftsmen, better illustrators, or better designers. But why? Because we have a goal and a vision for our success. To get the most out of this book, you must *fully embrace* the artist, the designer, and the entrepreneur. You must have a vision for yourself and an unrelenting determination to get there. You're going to need it.

I must warn you, it's not a cakewalk. It takes a ton of work and passion to get there. To move on to the next chapter you must decide right now whether you have what it takes.

To view websites cited in this book, please visit www.threadsnotdead.com/links.

11 Character Traits of Successful Designers

Over the years I've interacted with LOTS of designers. Hundreds. Thousands maybe? When you're knee deep in social media, blogs, and communities of other designers, it all becomes a blur. But certain people stand out from the crowd. I've noticed a lot in common with these standout individuals. Here are some common character traits that they all seem to share:

1. **They are a genuine fan of design.** They outwardly express their love of other people's work and follow their inspirations closely. They are "hearty in their approbation and lavish in their praise," to quote the great Dale Carnegie, author of *How to Win Friends and Influence People.*

2. **Hungry for knowledge and self-improvement.** They actively seek out feedback and have an innate desire to get better. They see themselves as a constant work in progress and enjoy the process of learning.

3. **Humble yet confident.** The designers I witness doing well know they're good but could always be better. I like the phrase, "always a student, never a master."

4. **Willingness to share knowledge.** You get more results out of helping others than by hurting them. Successful designers are often writing about their experience, sharing tips, answering questions, and helping others.

5. **Unrelenting work ethic.** Most designers become successful by busting their ass. They admit to working long days and nights to get where they are today. Not because they have to, but because they WANT to. They crave it and eat, sleep, and breathe their work.

6. **Undeniable Talent.** Let's not forget that most successful designers have a raw talent that has been honed since they were young. Talent isn't everything in this business, but it does go a long way. If you've got talent, you can get away with not having some of these other traits, but only for so long. At Go Media, we've always said that a designer with 30% talent and 70% hustle will outperform the designer with 70% talent and 30% hustle.

7. **They have some marketing chops.** Every designer in the t-shirt scene knows that you can't be afraid of self-promotion. The successful ones are constantly putting themselves out there where they can get the most eyeballs. Whether that's through advertising or simply interacting on communities like Emptees or Threadless. You can be an amazing artist but if you avoid the Internet or any sort of social engagement, you're facing an uphill battle.

8. They get lucky. Sure, some of the big name designers claim they got where they are out of luck and happenstance. It's true, I know plenty of designers who can have all these traits but are still spinning their wheels. But the truth is you need a small amount of luck to get you those big opportunities. Successful designers create their own luck. They attend events, they network, they help others who, in turn, help them. They stay in touch with their fans and clients, and they give people reasons to talk about them. In other words, they hustle and good things happen to those that hustle.

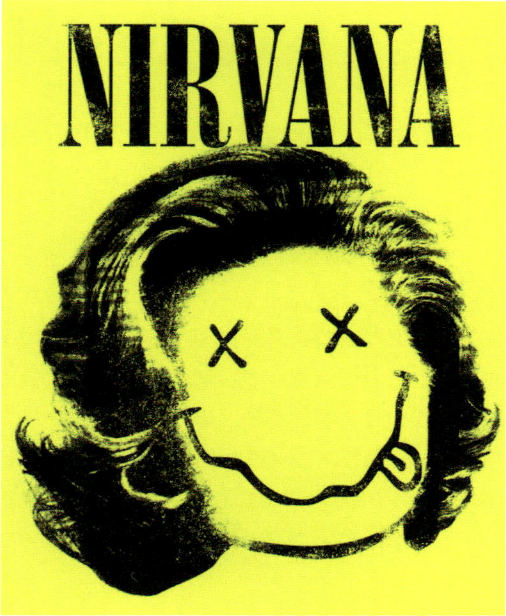

Design for Nirvana by Brandon Rike

9. They understand branding. Good designers are memorable because they have a unique style or fresh take on what other people are doing. They don't want to be like everyone else and understand how important it is to have a solid brand. They are consistent with their image and people know what to expect. Every time you interact with a customer or fan, that's branding at work — you're giving someone an impression of you that sticks with them. From having a solid logo and visual identity to the way you treat others and deliver on projects, it all adds up. The best ones are consistent across the board.

10. They have a solid website. Successful designers use their website to show off their portfolio and attract customers. A solid website is deceptively simple and most people overthink it. All you need to remember is to make it extremely easy to see your work, contact you, and learn about you. Link to your social media profiles, why not. But don't clutter up your site and try to make it "fancy" if that's not your expertise.

11. They are great communicators. They are professional and polite communicators and they put other people first. They are honest, direct, straightforward, and know when to say the right things. They respond to emails timely and make their clients feel good and pumped up about themselves.

To view websites cited in this book, please visit www.threadsnotdead.com/links.

Keys to a Great Portfolio

The most important asset you have is your personal brand. This boils down to one thing: your work. Your portfolio should speak for itself and hopefully speak loudly enough to attract new clients.

If you don't have a website with your own domain like **www.yourname.com** you need to get on that ASAP. Just go to **GoDaddy** and register your domain. Even though there are sites like Cargo, Behance, Coroflot, deviantArt, Flickr, and more where you can show your portfolio, you should definitely have your own "home base." Same goes for email. Don't use a Hotmail or Yahoo email address. It's best if you had **yourname@yourdomain.com** but if you have to, Gmail isn't so bad. In fact you could still use Gmail and **brand it with your own domain**.

Why you need your own website

- You have complete control with branding, functionality, hosting, etc. It's yours! It's more professional. It's also more trustworthy. Unless you have a .biz which looks spammy ;-)
- Who can forget about stats! Use **Google Analytics**, **Clicky**, **Reinvigorate**, etc. to see how people find you and what they're doing on your site. It's good practice to keep an eye on your stats and referrers.

It's really a no-brainer, but it's also important to have accounts on any site that allow you to upload a portfolio. **www.behance.net** and **www.flickr.com** are two of the big ones. It allows you to make contacts, get feedback, build your network and get exposure.

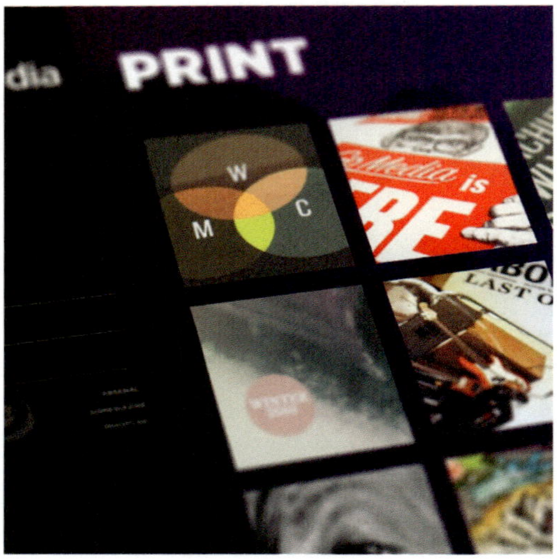

A screenshot of Go Media's Print portfolio

So what makes a good portfolio? From what I've seen, here are five traits of a rock solid portfolio.

Logos of popular sites designers use to display their portfolio.

Five Traits of a Rock Solid Portfolio

1. **Professional Presentation.** Lots of folks use the **Lightbox JS** or **Cargo** which is fine. It's not exactly unique, but that's ok. They usually have some sort of gallery to flip through work or it could be laid out all on one page. Another sign of good t-shirt design presentations are professional mockups. Cartoony cutouts look amateurish. Use real photos if possible, but if not, use photo realistic t-shirt templates. We **sell some at the Arsenal** and created **shirtmockup.com**, but there are plenty of others available if you go Googling.

2. **Simply good work.** Duh, this is obvious, but not always possible when you're starting out. That's like saying good designers are good because they're good! But the simple fact is there's not much you can do if your work isn't any good. Also, only show your best work. You don't need to show everything! If you have bad work in there, clients will find it and make judgments about you. When in doubt, leave it out.

3. **No more than one click away.** If it takes more than one or two clicks to get to your work, you're making it terribly inconvenient for people. One click to the portfolio and there should be work visible. Then maybe another click to view a specific project's details.

4. **Recognizable Clients.** I never like to admit that name dropping big name clients is key to getting more work, but it's the truth. You need to have proof that you are worth hiring! Also, new clients like to see that they are the type of client you typically work with. If you list a lot of bands, you'll likely get more band work. If you list a lot of restaurants... You get the picture.

5. **It's Targeted.** Great portfolios usually feature well-done work of a specific type, client, or genre. Like I said above, the work you show in your portfolio often dictates the work requests you actually get. The best portfolios know what they want to show off and do it well.

To view websites cited in this book, please visit www.threadsnotdead.com/links.

Examples of Great Portfolio Websites

- Rob Dobi — http://www.dobi.nu/
- Felix LeFlamme — http://www.felixlaflamme.com/
- Laurie Shipley — http://www.laurieshipley.com/
- Brandon Herbel — http://www.makebelievestudio.net/
- The Black Axe — http://www.theblackaxe.com/
- Oliver Barrett — http://ohbarrett.com/
- AJ Dimarucot — http://www.ajdimarucot.com/
- Ray Frenden — http://frenden.com/
- Glennz Tees — http://store.glennz.com/

Work for Me or Them?

This book is for designers in the apparel industry. This would include those that design shirts for other people like bands, clothing labels, universities, etc. You know, "clients." This book is also for those that run their own company and design their own tees for it. We'll call this "working for yourself."

So what should you do?

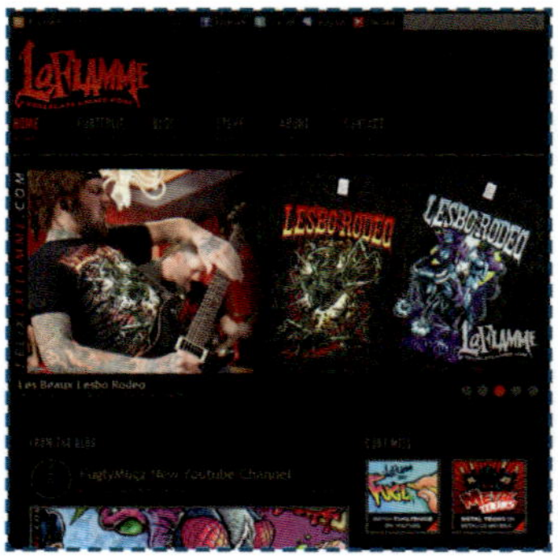

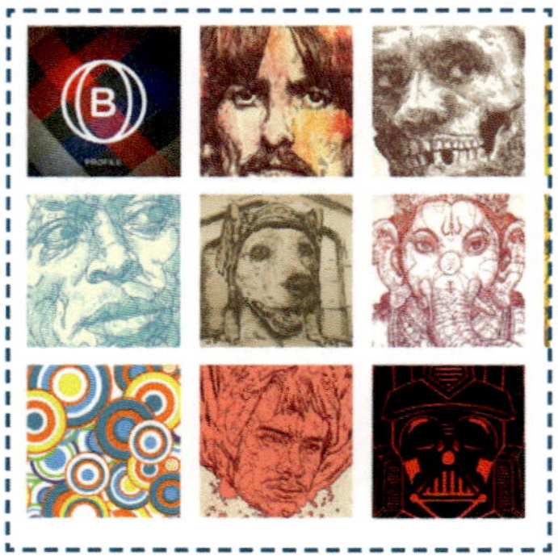
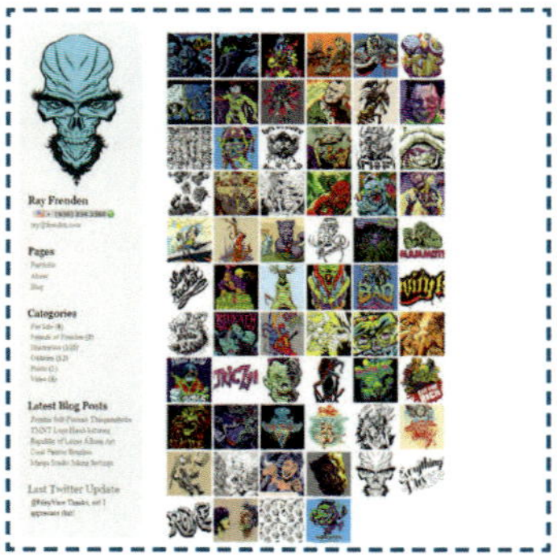
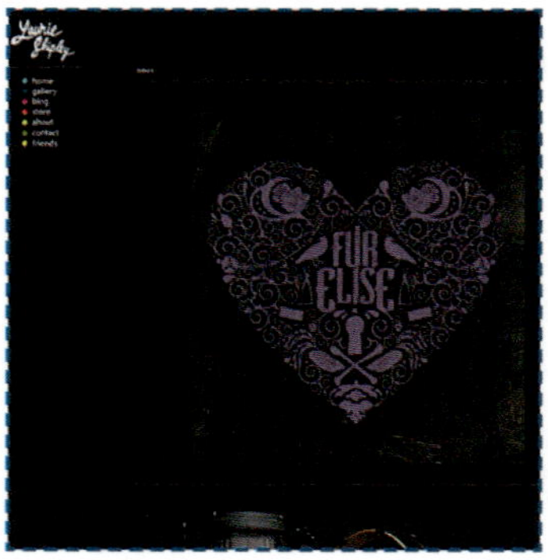
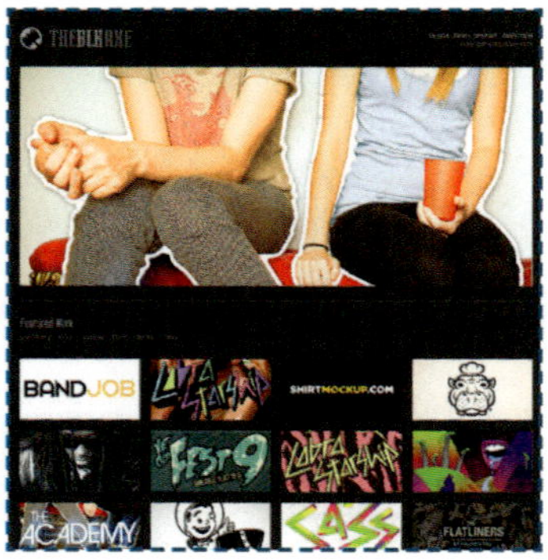

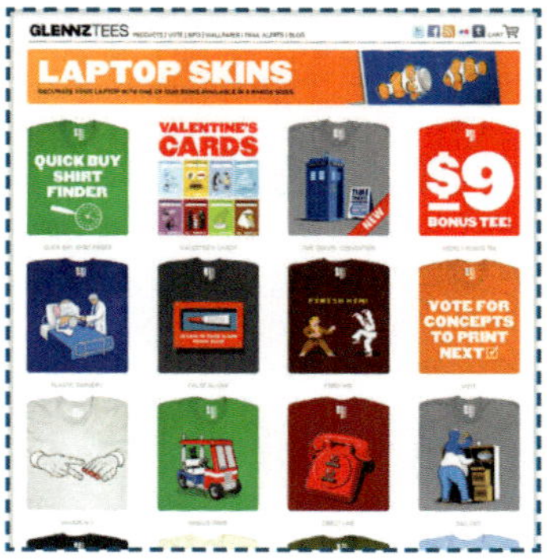

Do both. Here's why:

If you haven't gotten your feet wet designing t-shirts for other people, then you probably aren't ready to start your own line. Most successful artists spent years doing client work before they ventured off on their own.

At Go Media, we have worked for countless bands and indie clothing companies. There's a lot to be learned about what people like and what sells. Not to mention the technical hurdles that you'll overcome while getting paid by clients. It's better to learn on someone else's dime than your own, right? Of course, if you're learning "on the job" — make sure clients are aware so they don't see a massive invoice because you spent 23 hours reading Photoshop for Dummies.

Working with an Established Brand

In addition to freelancing or starting your own brand, you might consider working at an established company or brand first. Designer Jamie Tallerico has been around the block as a freelancer and in-house designer for XVLA Denim, Atticus Clothing, Abercrombie & Fitch, and American Eagle Outfitters. He's seen it all.

The experience you can gain from being on the front lines like this is priceless. If he started his own line, he would have lots of insider knowledge most startup brands lack. Look into this as these companies might offer internships or in-house positions, so keep an eye out if that's a route you want to take.

This next chapter is about working for clients and building a successful freelance design business. Shall we continue? Follow me, my friend.

To view websites cited in this book, please visit www.threadsnotdead.com/links.

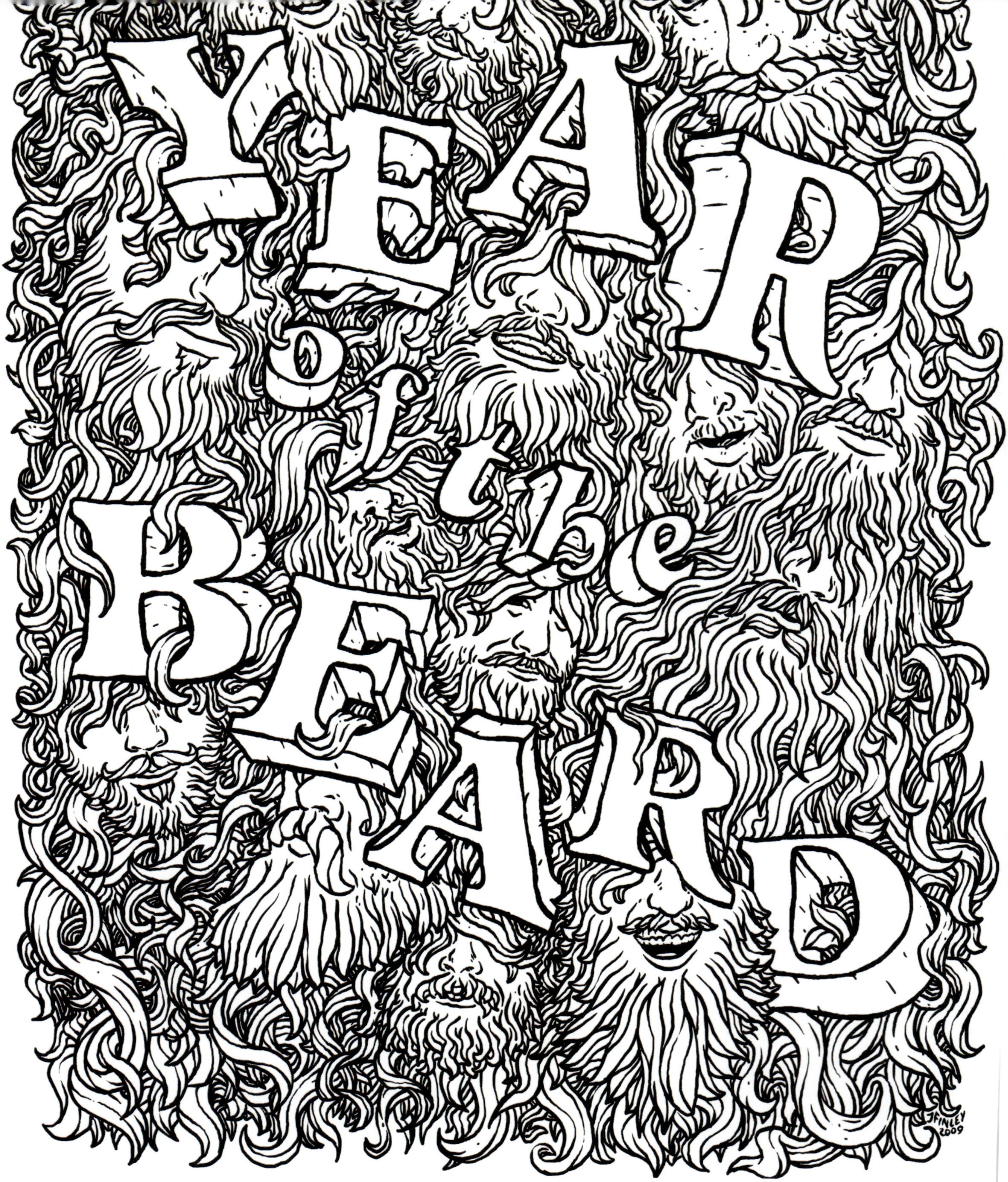

"Year of the Beard" designed by Jeff Finley

II

FREELANCING

If you're working at a full-time job, try freelancing on the side. With enough experience designing for clients, you'll be better equipped to build yourself a killer brand that stands out.

Flying Solo: Don't Be Afraid

Fear sucks, but we're all afraid. There are questions arising in the first time freelancer's head right now. How do you get someone to pay you to make art? What if you've never designed a shirt before? What if you mess up and someone gets mad at you? We all had these questions when starting out. Don't worry, it's not that hard. Here's a story of my first shirt design.

You've Got to Start Somewhere

I got my first shirt design gig back in 2004 from a start–up clothing company. They asked me to create a shirt design of a rose that morphed into a butterfly. Ok! The only way I knew how to do it was to draw on paper, scan it in, and color it in Photoshop. So I did just that. However, I had no idea how many colors to use — I just tried to copy what other artists like Derek Hess or Rob Dobi were doing. Those guys knew how to do it, right? So I fumbled around trying to color my pencil drawing in Photoshop. Things were not looking so good, but I sent the file off to the client. He loved it. To this day I laugh because BOTH of us were just starting out. Today, the company would never have accepted that design. He didn't know better and neither did I. A match made in Heaven!

There are plenty of potential clients looking to hire a hardworking and affordable novice designer.

As it turns out, he printed it, and it turned out pretty cool! Aside from an insanely thick plasticky print, he was able to somehow get my artwork onto a t-shirt. When he mailed me the shirt to see, I felt amazing. My first printed design!

Being a Noob isn't a Bad Thing

Working with this start-up clothing brand was great because neither of us had much to lose. It was a good collaboration. I didn't get paid very much — I think it was $50 for a few days of work and stress. I would never take a job like that now. Still, there are plenty of potential clients out there looking to hire a hardworking and affordable novice designer.

It's critical that you pour sweat & soul into these projects, regardless of pay. As you follow this book, you'll see that a rock solid portfolio becomes more and more important as you move up the food chain. This is your opportunity to develop one.

These indie clothing companies make great first clients. In fact, my next section is about just that.

Why Bands and Indie Clothing Brands Make Great Clients

Now that you're in the t-shirt design swimming pool getting your feet wet, it's time to move closer to the deep end and learn to swim. The best opportunity to get LOADS of experience doing t-shirt designs is working for bands and clothing companies. They are regularly looking for fresh artists to work with. It might not be the best paying gig, and there is certainly a lot of competition, but *this is your proving ground.*

How to Find Bands and Clothing Companies

Where might you start looking for these bread & butter clients? When I first started, MySpace was huge. Bands were using it to promote themselves and really, for the first time, they were easy to contact. A fan from Ohio could contact his favorite band on MySpace and there was actually a chance of getting a response. Later, clothing companies like **Glamour Kills** used MySpace to get involved with their fans and customers. The possibilities pioneered by social media helped spawn the **clothing company boom of 2006–2007**.

Bands and indie clothing brands are easy enough to find. In addition to social networking sites, try poking around on **Mintees**, **Band Job**, or **IAMTHETREND** to find fresh blood. Look at the brands that other designers are designing for. Chances are they are hiring designers just like you! You can often find their contact information on their website or social networking profiles. When you find a few companies you want to work with try these tactics to get in the door.

Four Tips When Contacting a New Client

1. **Send them a message or email directly.** Politely introduce yourself and let them know that you're a designer and you dig what they are all about. Tell them you'd like to design some shirts for them and ask how do they typically work with other designers. Keep the email simple and direct. Make sure you link to your portfolio or a place where they can see relevant work that relates to them.

2. **Maybe include sketches.** They LOVE seeing designers take initiative and present them with good ideas. However, I've heard that some bands/companies take the ideas and run without crediting you, but that has never happened to me personally.

3. **List a few previous clients.** If you have some similar companies in your client list, it doesn't hurt to name drop them in your email. It helps boost their trust.

4. **Talk about money when the time is right.** If they write back and are interested, they generally want to know how much you charge. Tell them your rates and hopefully they'll agree on the price and hire you for the job.

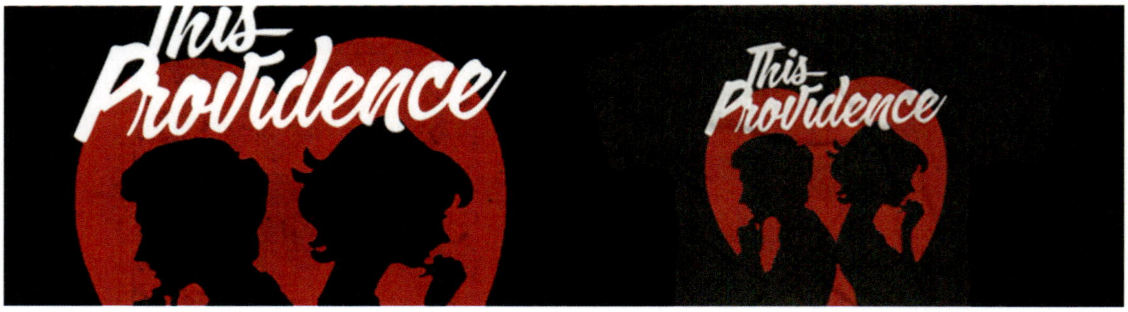

This Providence tee designed by Brandon Herbel

Pricing and Sales Strategies

If there's one question we get asked a lot at Go Media it's this one. Upcoming designers and even experienced ones aren't sure how to value their services. If you spend a few minutes Googling around, you can find a lot of ways to figure out pricing. Like **hourly rate calculators** where you input all your expenses and desired salary and then it gives you an hourly rate. But should you charge hourly or flat rate? How do I avoid getting stiffed? Would a contract make things easier? What about doing pro bono or spec work?

What should I charge?

This largely depends on how skilled you are and how many customers you have. Obviously, when you're starting out you'll be charging almost nothing. When Go Media started, founder Bill Beachy was charging flat rates. For example — he was charging $100 to design a t-shirt and would spend two days (20+ hours) doing an elaborate illustration. That worked out to about $5/hr. That sucked, but he was doing what he loved.

Now obviously, with Bill putting in so much work and charging so little, word got around fast. Soon he had all the $100 t-shirt jobs that he could handle. As a result, he raised his price... $150, $175, $200, $300. Every time he was slammed with work he would up his price. This is a really good strategy for the designer that is just starting out: start with really low rates and when you get busy enough, increase the amount you charge.

You will lose some customers when you raise your rates. But if you want to survive in the long-run you can't make it charging $5/hr. Currently Go Media charges $100/hour for print design and $125/hour for web and multimedia work.

Flat Rate vs. Hourly Billing

In the beginning we were really in love with the concept of flat rate billing. It seemed very clear and simple to us. When we are buying something we like to know what we're going to pay up-front. As long as our prices were really low, it worked out fairly well.

Let's take a logo design for instance. When Bill started he charged $300 for a logo. Most people thought this was a fair rate and he got lots of work. Some of those logo projects, however, took a really long time. As he began working with larger and larger companies they wanted more concepts, more revisions, and more discussion about their logo. Obviously — a company's brand is VERY important. Cost is not a deterrent for these larger companies. So, of course, his price kept going up. Soon he was charging $900 for a logo. This was a fair price for a big company that wanted lots of concepts and revisions. But for the little guy, he would practically knock them off their feet when he told them he was charging $900 for a logo. They would say: "900 DOLLARS??!! All I want is a little logo — it will only take you an hour!" And they were right. Bill COULD design them their idea of a logo in about an hour.

This is where the flaws in the flat rate billing system begin to surface. What does a "logo" really mean? We could spend one hour on a logo and we could also spend 50 hours on a logo. So you either create a crazy scale of products like "simple logo design," "average logo design," "complex logo design" and "ultimate logo design" OR you switch to hourly billing.

In the end we decided to switch to hourly billing. This IS how most service industry firms work. If someone asks for a flat rate we don't turn them down, we just talk about their project and get all the details before we give them a rate.

How can I avoid being stiffed?

Over the years, particularly early on, both Bill and I got stiffed a lot. Eventually, Bill found one little trick that prevented this from happening:

Require a deposit before you begin work.

It's simple: if someone wants to hire you for a $300 project, tell them you require a $150 deposit before you start. That's it. This one little step will eliminate 95% of people that will eventually stiff you.

We usually try to get a 50% deposit before we start, then clients make the final payment when we're done. If the project is really big then we will reduce the deposit to 33% or 25%. If someone wants to take advantage of you, they don't want to make any payment at all. By requiring a payment up-front you scare off the jerks. If someone balks at making a deposit, they probably never wanted to pay you a dime in the first place. Be happy they are leaving your life. You're better off for it.

Require a payment before you start and before you release your files to avoid being stiffed.

One exception to this is working with big corporations. If Pepsi says: "Bill us, we will pay you in 30 days." I would tend to believe them. If they stiff you, go get a lawyer and sue them. They have lots of money and the lawyers would love to help you sue Pepsi (for the record: Pepsi has ALWAYS paid us.) This brings me right to my next topic:

Should I have contracts?

My quick answer is: Skip the contracts for little fish and small projects, have contracts for big fish and huge clients.

A contract is only good if you can enforce what it says. Let's say, for instance, that you design a $300 t-shirt for band and you make them sign a contract. Then let's say the band stiffs you. What now? Do you wave the contract in their face and say: "Or Else!" No, you go to court — which Bill has done in exactly this scenario. And when you get to court, the very first thing the judge will say to you, as he did in this case is: "The court is not a collection agency. You have to collect this money on your own." So, the band never shows up and you win the case. Now what? Well, you can go back to the band and say: "HA! I won the court case — now pay up!" And they'll probably laugh at you. If you go to a professional collection agency they won't touch anything for less than a few thousand dollars. And if they DO succeed at collecting any money they will keep about 20–40% of it.

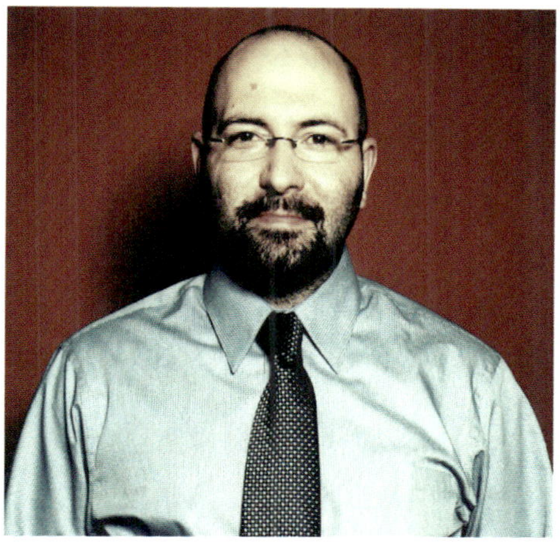

Go Media president Bill Beachy

So, now you've spent all the time writing the contract, going to court, hiring a collection agency and sleepless nights worrying about this bum, and for what? You will still probably get stiffed.

This is what happens when you're dealing with little fish. The scenario changes when you're working with bigger companies and bigger projects. Obviously, if you've been hired to do a $200,000 project — you might want to get a contract written up. You'll want this because one, you probably have a lot more at risk. You may need to devote months of your time to the project, hire more staff and buy more equipment. And two, in the event that you are stiffed, there will be lawyers willing to help you collect. They will likely be able to get good use out of a contract in a trial. Go Media will only mess with contracts for projects over 50k and those are typically web development projects, not t-shirt designs.

Other Tips for Avoiding Busters

"Busters" is the term Bill uses for people that have no money and want you to do work for them. They will do everything in their power to convince you that their idea is the next big thing. They will promise you great riches, fame and success beyond your wildest dreams. If you'll just do this first job for free they will pay you triple on the next job. Or, if you do the design — they'll pay with royalties when their product starts flying off the shelves.

Guess what? It will never happen. 99.9% of the time you will be stiffed. On the off chance that one of these busters DOES make some money — you won't see a dime. He will stop answering your calls, stop answering your emails and find himself some other sucker to work for free.

Be wary of clients that are hyperactive with energy and try to get you pumped up about their business, but have no up-front money to pay you. If they offer you part ownership in their company — but YOU do all the work, that's a bad deal. If they offer you a part ownership in exchange for your services I would say: "Why don't you pay me for a few projects so we can see if we work well together?" Anyone that is serious about having you as a business partner will think this is a good idea.

Do I Need an Accountant?

Yes. I highly recommend getting a good accountant involved in your business as soon as possible. I know that starting out you probably can't afford one. That's fine. Make do by flying "under the radar." But once you have enough money, get yourself a really good accountant. Their advice is priceless. You don't want to end up the next Enron.

What's a Kill Fee?

Sometimes a client will pay you to create concepts that they may not use. That payment is called a kill fee. If they decide to use your concepts they will pay you more money. This often happens when a company needs to pitch your work to their customer. We run into this a lot with the t-shirts we design. A merchandising company will want to pitch a line of t-shirts to Metallica. They will pay us a kill fee for some designs, pitch them to Metallica, and then pay us more for the designs Metallica likes.

Working for a kill fee is just a matter of preference. Go Media tries to avoid kill fees.

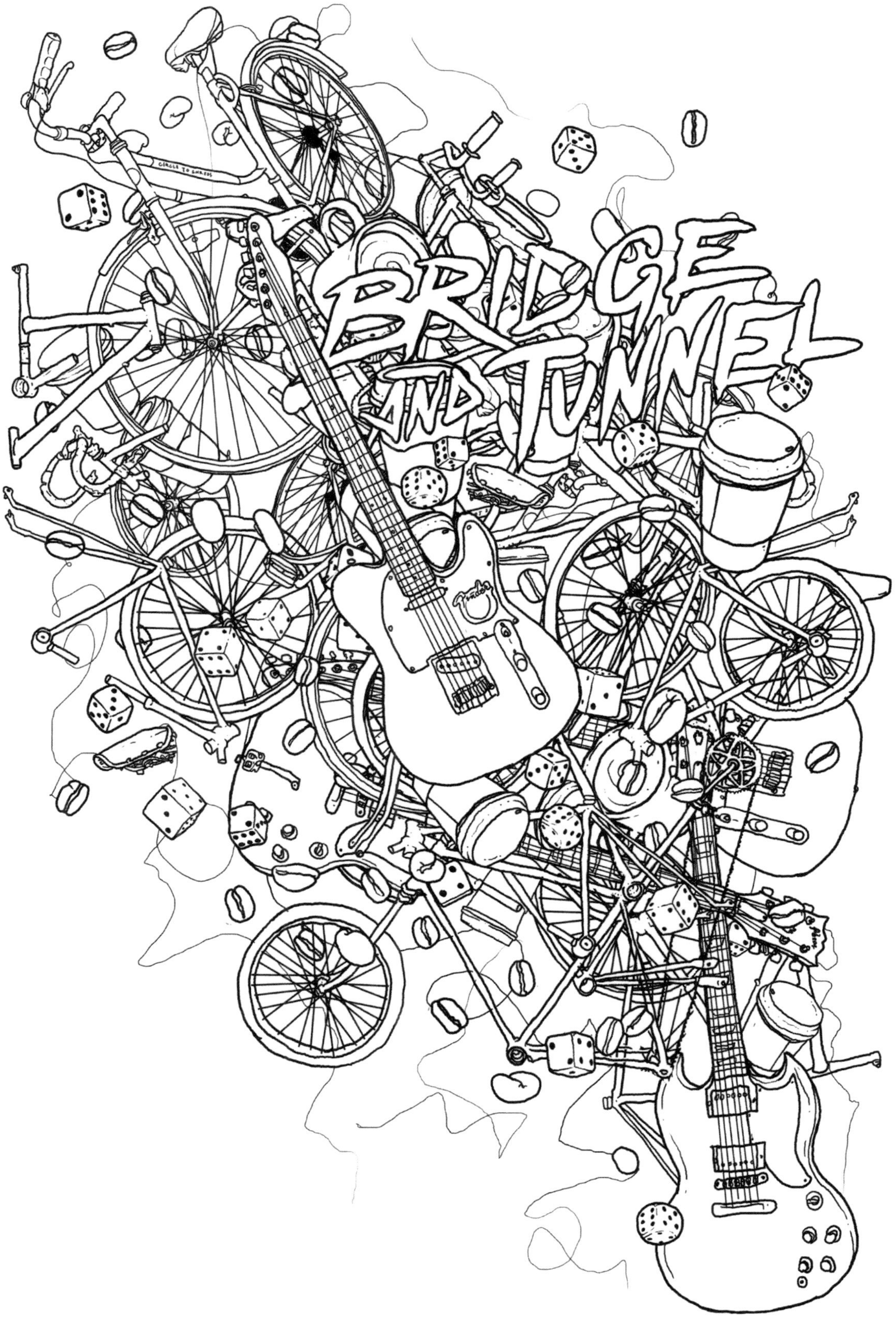

"Bridge and Tunnel" by Jeff Finley

We would rather be paid in full for our time. But if someone brings you a project that you're really excited about, you may be ok accepting the risk that the kill fee is all you'll get.

Pitching

Pitching is when you create a design for free, show it to the client and hope they'll pay you for it. In truth, Go Media does not pitch very much, but that is starting to change. I know that the large advertising companies work this way. They create entire marketing campaigns, then pitch them. These pitches are usually with large companies and winning a contract will result in MILLIONS of dollars of business. So, obviously it's worth it for them to invest the time and money to pitch.

Pitching is also a matter of preference. It's a great way to introduce yourself to a company or to break into a new industry. Obviously there are risks (that you'll not get paid for your efforts), so weigh those against the opportunity to land a savory job.

How do I send invoices and track sales?

Go Media uses **QuickBooks.** This is a somewhat complex piece of financial software, but it's great. It takes a while to learn, but it's worth it in the end. Don't try to understand all of it at once...just learn as you go. Start by focusing on how to generate an invoice. Little by little you'll learn more over time. Your accountant can help you too once you have one. QuickBooks even offers credit card processing for a small fee. There is also **FreshBooks**, an online bill app that uses PayPal and other payment methods. We have heard good things about it, so check it out.

Pricing is a Sensitive Issue

Pricing is a sensitive issue and it's really competitive in this industry. I've seen well known and extremely talented designers are losing jobs because there are more aggressive novices who charge next to nothing and are "stealing" jobs away. In a down economy, clients are really attracted to this low price and are willing to take a sacrifice in quality and experience to save money. Industry veterans complain that this drives down the overall value of design services, but that's typically how things go in a competitive industry.

To remedy this, designers are going to have to offer more value for their services if they want to stay competitive. Offering consulting or brand advice, or offering to help advertise or promote the customer are things you could do to add value to your services. You need to give the client MORE than just a Photoshop file. Think about it.

How to Snag Those Big Clients

How do some designers get to work on big-deal projects like new tees for Air Jordan? Or how do you design the merch for bands like Metallica or Miley Cyrus? Before I tell you how it's done, let's look at the pros and cons of big clients.

I'd say any designer who currently works for indie brands would certainly benefit from working with bigger fish. Of course you'll reap all the great benefits of working with a big client, but surprisingly, you'll benefit just as much from the slips & falls. Sometimes the fish are too big, the stakes are too high, and the expected output is overwhelming.

Pros of Big Clients:

- Big clients can pay you more than you are used to.
- They can open doors to new opportunities and exposure.
- They provide a relatively consistent income and almost always pay for your work.
- Large clients add credibility to your portfolio; it proves you can handle the work load.

Cons of Big Clients:

- Sometimes the opportunity is so in demand they can get away with paying you less.
- More hoops to jump through for approvals and getting paid takes longer.
- They have their own rules for working with designers that might override your current protocol for client interaction.
- If you happen to lose the client, it can be devastating if most of your income relied on that client.

Mo' Money Mo' Problems

Go Media landed a large web project for a Fortune 500 company in 2007. It was extremely stressful and deadlines were crushing, but we wanted the opportunity to prove ourselves on a big project. It was the most money we'd ever been offered and it required a skill set that we didn't quite have yet. But we accepted the job and put our nose to the grindstone. We even had to hire new staff to handle the load. The client and deadlines were so demanding, our staff was racking up tons of overtime and we even had to slave through the Christmas holiday much to the chagrin of our staff.

We toughed it out and kept a positive outlook, until things started going sour. Deadlines shifted and feedback and direction started getting foggy. They'd ask for something completely new and expect it overnight. They even flew in their own project manager to our "studio" (which was just Bill's townhouse at the time) and he kept us all in check. We started getting angry at each other and morale was at an all-time low.

In the end, the agency that subcontracted us went out of business and flaked on the final payment. We were stunned. We put in months of work and we still got stiffed! We did get lawyers involved but we couldn't make the client pay because they filed for bankruptcy and we were left holding the bag.

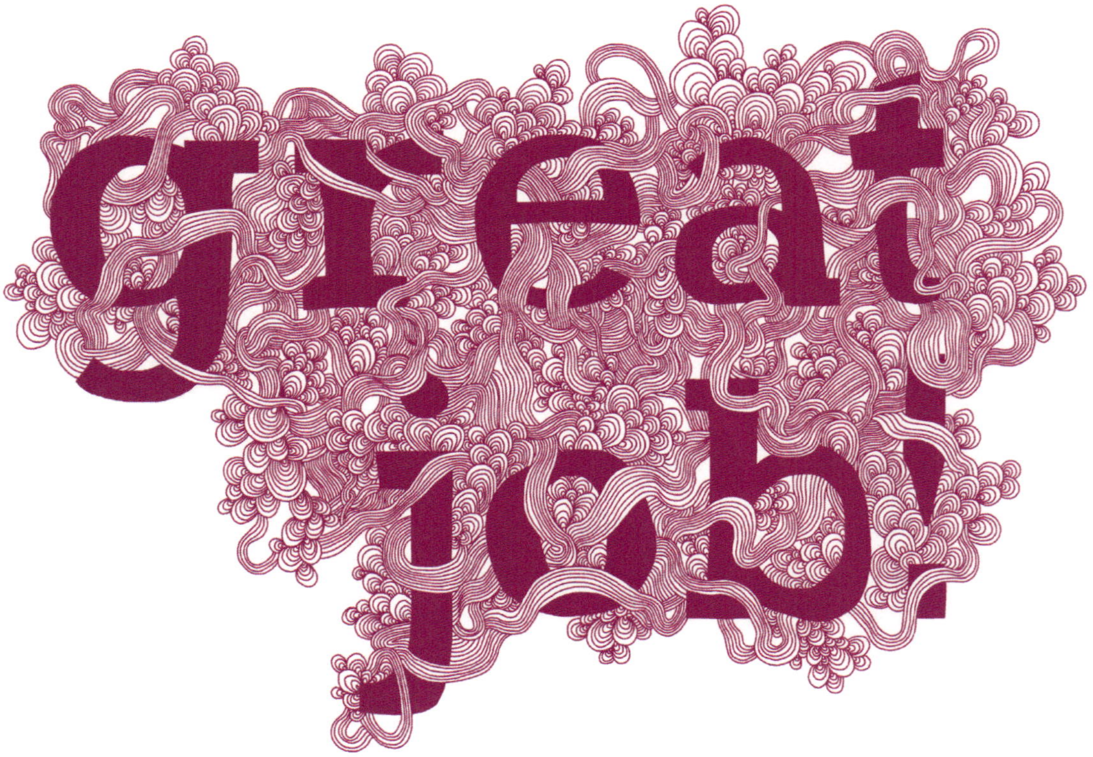

"Great Job" by RikkiB

It was devastating for us, but we toughed it out and made it through. Sometimes, things get crazy when big numbers are involved. Lots of egos and reputations are on the line and it's difficult to find that personal relationship with a client that can be so rewarding.

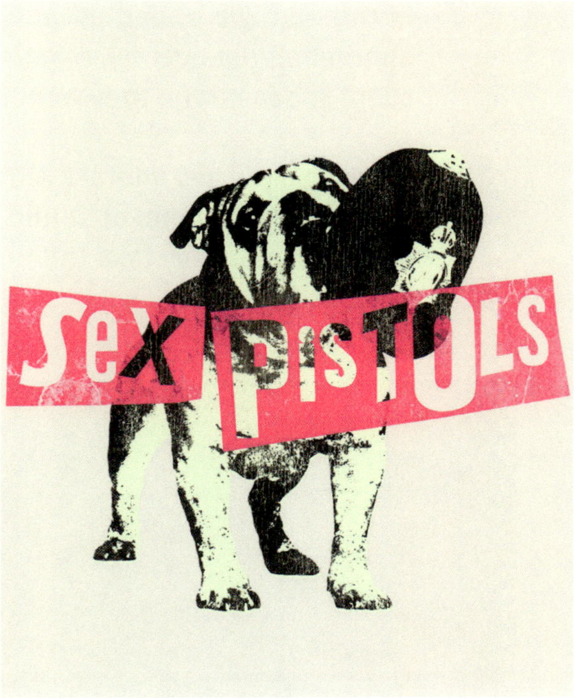

Sex PIstols tee designed by Brandon Rike

Let's Talk About HOW to Land these Big Clients

I wish there was an easy formula. If there was, we'd all be handsomely paid and working on national campaigns for celebrity clothing lines. But the truth is large companies typically play it safe and hire designers or firms they trust can get the job done. It's not often they switch from designer to designer.

But there are ways to get in.

Artist Reps & Agents

Did you think agents were only for actors, athletes, and celebrities? Think again! Artists and illustrators all over are represented by an agent or agency and that's how they get a lot of work. You are the talent and an agent's role is to find clients looking for that talent.

We have worked with repping agencies in the past and some of our biggest jobs came from them. Through them we were able to work for Pepsi, Monster Energy, Red Bull, Cambria Suites, and more. We were even offered a job to design shirts for Air Jordan and the payout was over $1,200 per design. At that time, we thought the price was crazy high! It was more than double what we typically got for t-shirt design jobs and we still thought we were charging a lot. The funny thing was, the rep told us "It's apparel, so the pay is low, we're sorry." It makes you realize SOME people are making good money doing t-shirt design while most of us have to scratch and claw our way through each month to pay our bills. Some of you reading this may have worked with major brands before and were severely underpaid by them. It all depends! It's mind-boggling how the pay can be so different.

In the end, we ended up not getting the Air Jordan job because the client chose another studio over us. Agents do that, they pitch their artists to the client and the client chooses who they want to work with. You win some, you lose some.

Repping agencies interact with clients and then look in their pool of talent to match up the right designer or studio for the job. They typically negotiate the payment with the client and they take their cut as the artist rep. Many illustrators and fine artists get jobs this way.

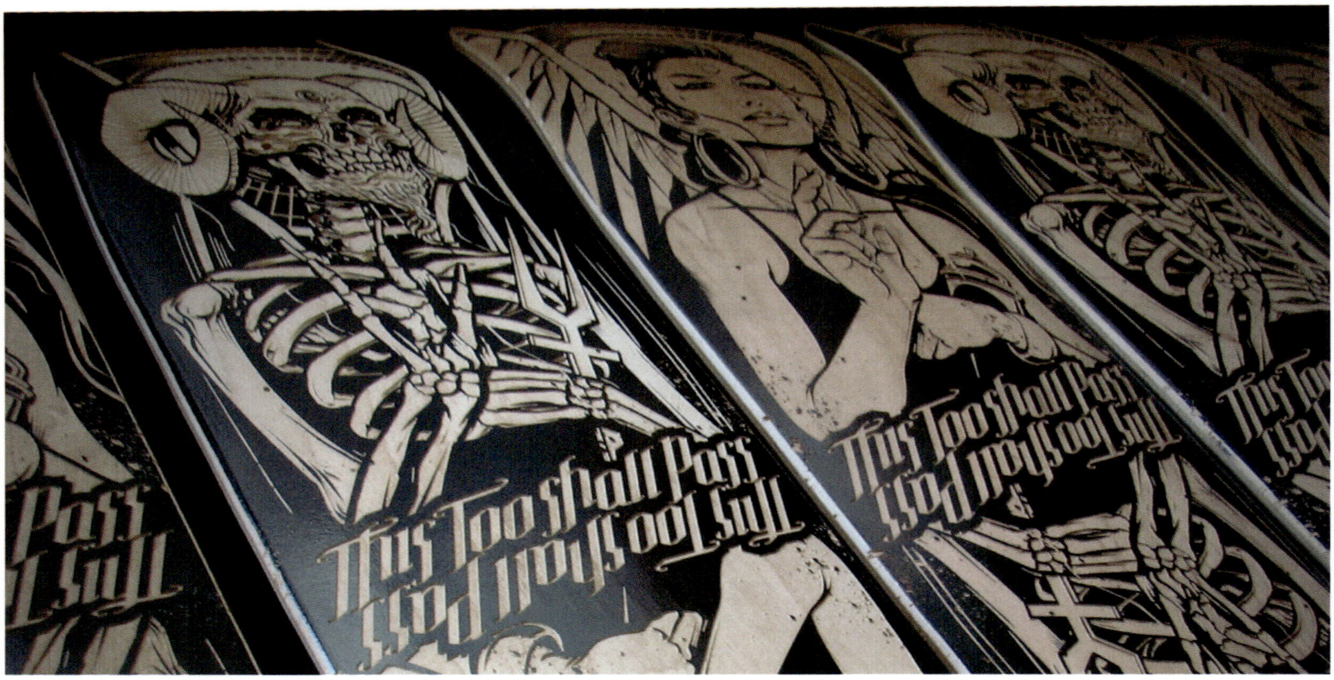

Skate decks by Munk One

There are plenty of repping agencies out there, but the barrier to entry is tough. We've knocked on the door of a bunch, and sometimes it seems like nobody is home. You've got to figure out who the right people are to talk to and how to reach them. Try reaching out on LinkedIn or other social networking sites.

They get daily submissions and requests, so you can imagine how overwhelming it becomes to sift the wheat from the chaff. They talk to the people that stand out the most. Do your research and make friends online. Be professional and follow their submission process. But make sure you stand out and give them a compelling reason to include you in their roster.

Visit www.threadsnotdead.com/links for a list **of artist repping agencies**.

The Easiest Way to Design for Major Label Bands

How do you get the opportunity to design a shirt for Korn, Metallica, Madonna, or Michael Jackson? Merchandising companies of course. It's unlikely Madonna is going to hire you herself. Instead, big celebrities get their merchandise made through merch companies.

A lot of bigger labels use merchandise companies like Bravado, FEA, or Global Merch who are good at taking all of the merch to retail. Their job is strictly to manage the band's merch and the relationships with retail buyers like Hot Topic. The band merch is officially licensed and there's quite a bit of red tape involved that I personally don't even know much about. As a designer in this situation, you're the very last person in a long chain, and often in the dark about the whole process. Once your design is sent off, who knows where it goes and what happens to it. You're about as far away from the band as you can possibly be. But these merch companies are usually the ones that consistently employ some of the best freelance designers and studios out there.

One merch company can provide a designer with a stream of band merch work. It can run the gamut from heavy metal band tees for Slayer or Slipknot to The Jonas Brothers and Taylor Swift. I'm sure Taylor Swift has no idea that the designer who did her tees likely has also done tees for Insane Clown Posse or Marilyn Manson. Most of the band tees you see in retail stores are from a small number of merch companies. If you're looking to really take the leap into band merch design, this is where it's at.

From my experience, it was fairly easy to contact a merchandise company and get forwarded to a creative director. You might have to do a project or two for no pay to "prove your worth" or maybe you'll get a job right away. It never hurts to try, but you need to have an incredible portfolio if you plan on going this far.

Pros of Working with Merch Companies:

The best thing is that you'll work on a steady stream of big name bands. This is the highest opportunity for most designers to get their designs to a mass audience. Have you ever wondered who did that new Iron Maiden t-shirt design? It was probably a freelancer working for a merch company. The pay is typically decent at best, but it's usually consistent. As you can tell, you're not going to make a lot of money doing band merch, unless you're a big name artist that Platinum selling bands are asking for by name. In that case, you'll be doing work directly for the band — but the product will be put through the pipeline into retail stores.

The Cons of Working with Merch Companies:

Due to the insane competition, there's a big pool of freelancers who are also submitting designs and approval percentages are much lower than if you worked one-on-one. Chances are even if your design is approved, you won't even know it until you see it randomly in a store somewhere. And guess what, you probably have to pay for it if you want a sample to have yourself.

Another downside — and this is a big one for new faces in the design community — is that most of the work is "undercover." Meaning you won't even be allowed to show off your work, unless it's been approved and is for sale. It could be a year before that happens. You never know. And there's a lot of hush-hush stuff going on behind the scenes that designers aren't even aware of. You can ruin a lot of people's careers (including your own) if you accidentally leak the design you did when you weren't supposed to show it. Be careful here.

Also, merch companies have their own payment policies and if you aren't willing to play their game, you don't play at all. It can be frustrating as a designer who spends years perfecting their own payment policies and structures only to have certain clients (not just merch companies) totally ignore them. Like I said, larger companies tend to do this. Fortunately, you usually get paid, but sometimes it's months after you've already done the work.

Doing major-label band merch helps you add credibility to your portfolio.

Some Tips on Attracting Big Clients:

1. You must have a solid portfolio, this is obvious. The proof is in the pudding and a big client needs to see you can handle their project.

2. Try doing some pro bono work for free, to prove your worth.

3. Don't be a flake! Answer your emails promptly, over communicate if you have to. Big clients need reliable designers.

4. Send out friendly emails to your wishlist clients. Make friends with them and don't spam. People are easier to contact than ever.

5. When you get your first big client, use it as leverage for your next. Put the name in your client list and show everyone what a bang-up job you did for them.

Legal Barriers Simplified

One of the biggest requests for this book was to clear up some of the common legal issues in the t-shirt design scene. First, let me say I'm not in a position to give legal advice. I'm not a lawyer, but I can share what I know from my own experience. Any action you take as a result of my advice is at your own risk.

Also, as my partner Bill Beachy says, "Before I get started I want to stress a few things. First and foremost, it should ALWAYS be your goal to run your business 100% legally. This means paying ALL your taxes and following ALL laws. If you truly want to achieve great success with your company, it's best to do it right (as right as possible) from the very beginning. You do NOT want to end up like Enron or Martha Stewart; cheating on your finances, getting caught and going to jail. If you start your business by cheating it will be a very hard habit to get out of."

It can be daunting thinking about lawyers, accountants, s-corps, partnerships, taxes, licenses, payroll, health insurance, etc. That stuff is important for ALL businesses, not just the apparel industry. A book could be written alone on that stuff. But fortunately, Bill **broke it all down on our blog**. But let's touch on a few of the most misunderstood legal issues in the apparel industry.

Parodies and Spoofs

Parody is the one of the most misunderstood laws out there involving art. Do you want to make fun of something famous and sell it on a t-shirt? Do you want to do a zombified illustration of Harry Potter, cool! But be careful, you could get trapped in a legal battle and that's never a good place to be.

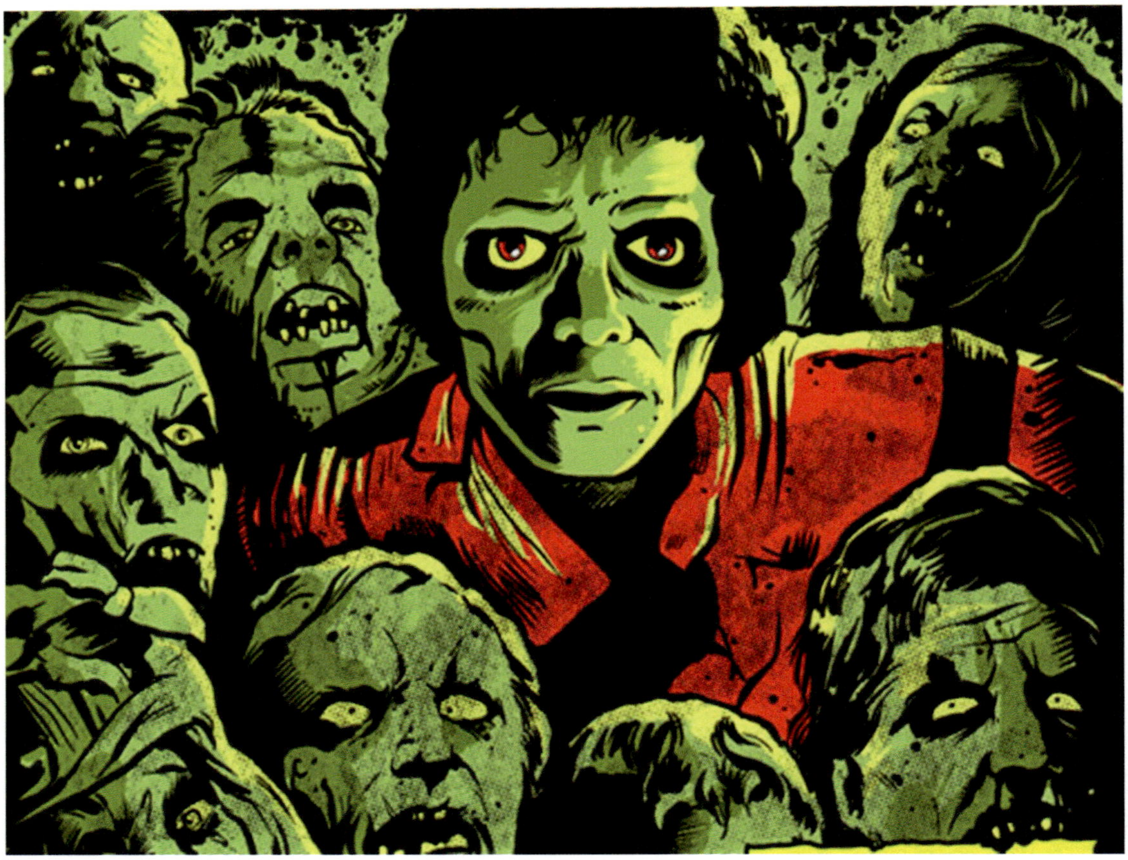

"Thriller" illustration for Michael Jackson by Rob Dobi

I've done research on this topic and everything I read says "consult your attorney" for specific answers. Not everyone is in a position to give you legal advice and that's why it's such a foggy issue. Even if your design is an original spoof or criticism of another's copyrighted work, you could still get taken to court and be forced to let a judge decide. The brand you spoofed could get offended and have a reason to take you to court. Someone once said "if the judge laughs, its ok. If not, you're screwed."

If you could get permission from the source you are parodying, then that's great. But as you might expect, not everyone would approve of you making money at their expense. It's such a touchy subject, so I'm going to have to tell you to get official legal advice if you plan on using parody to sell tees.

At www.threadsnotdead.com/links there's a **link for reference.**

Fair Use

Similar to parody, there is also the concept of "fair use." Essentially this is an effort to allow limited use of copyrighted material without requiring permission from the rights holders, such as commentary, criticism, news reporting, research, teaching, scholarship, or research. Section 107 of the United States Copyright Law sets out four factors to be considered when determining whether or not a particular use is fair:

- The purpose and character of the use, including whether such use is of commercial nature or is for nonprofit educational purposes
- The nature of the copyrighted work
- The amount and substantiality of the portion used in relation to the copyrighted work as a whole
- The effect of the use upon the potential market for, or value of, the copyrighted work

It's still a cloudy issue and difficult to know when something falls under fair use. There is no specific number of words, lines, or notes that may be safely taken without permission. Crediting the source also does not substitute for obtaining permission. When in doubt, ask the copyright holder for permission or consult an attorney.

Here is more information on Fair Use: **http://www.copyright.gov/fls/fl102.html**

Putting the Fright in Fright-Rags

Ben Scrivens from **Fright-Rags** wrote a great article about copyrights and licensing. If you're unfamiliar, he sells t-shirts with images from popular horror films. As you might expect, it's complicated. In that article, he **shares his experience and lessons learned** the hard way. It's a great read if you want to know more about what can happen if you are careless with copyrighted imagery.

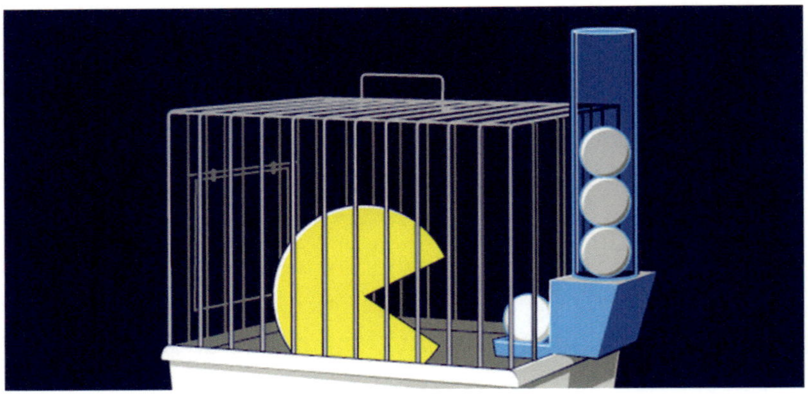

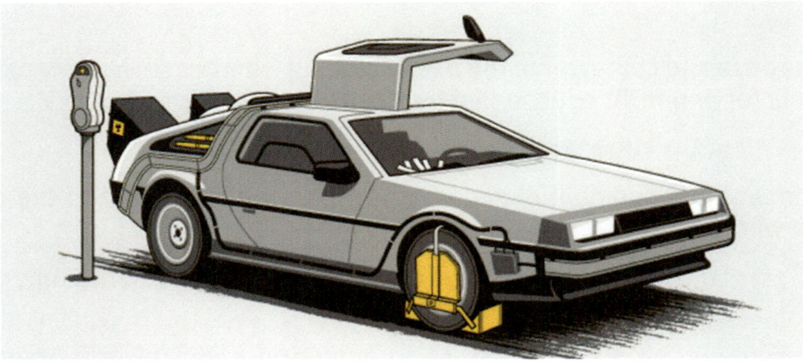

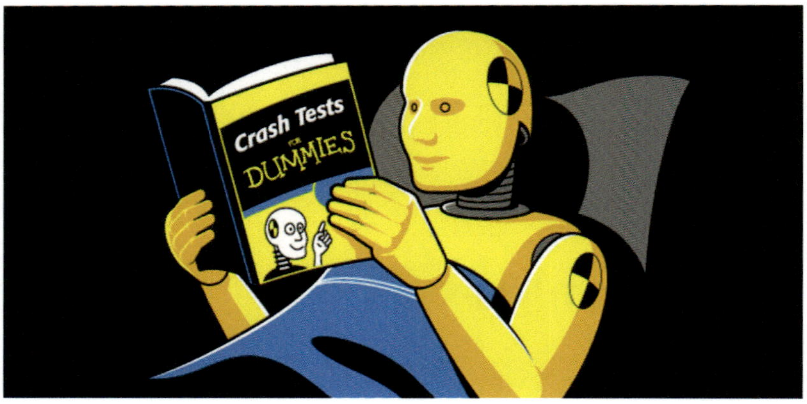

Examples of parody tees by Glennz — **http://store.glennz.com**

Work For Hire Contracts

In my interviews and research, it was obvious that the "work for hire" contract that many freelancers and studios see from clients is a scary thing. Most of us just sign it and complete the work not really knowing what it entails. But watch out, there are terms in the contract that say you lose ALL rights to the work including the ability to say that you even created the work in the first place!

You'll see these types of contracts from large companies who want to subcontract out a design from you. "Work for hire" contracts allow clients to buy your labor, all the rights to the design, and claim that it's entirely theirs and theirs alone. As the designer in this situation, you are intended to be invisible. The client might not want anyone to know they subcontracted the design, and if anyone found out, it could be detrimental to their business. I'll give an example, but first **Munk One** has some things to say about WFH contracts.

> *A "work for hire" contract is different than other contracts in that you lose absolutely ALL rights to your work including authorship rights (the ability to say you even created the work) and promotional rights (in your portfolio) in perpetuity (FOREVER). This sort of contract is not needed at all to reproduce the work and can only be considered a legal rape of the artist's rights. This sort of legal abuse is considered unethical to much of the artist community and damaging to the artist profession as whole.*

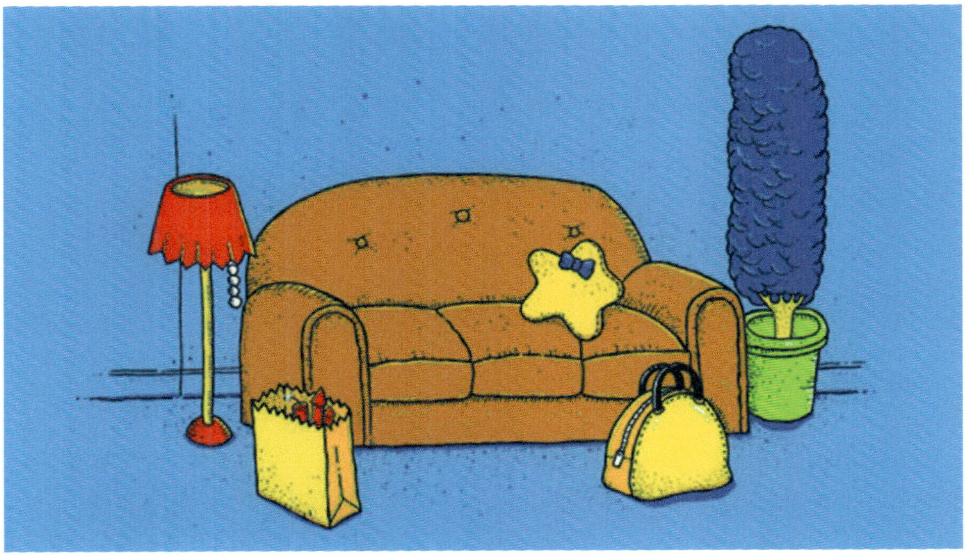

"Springfield Still Life" by Alvaro Arteaga Sabaini for Threadless

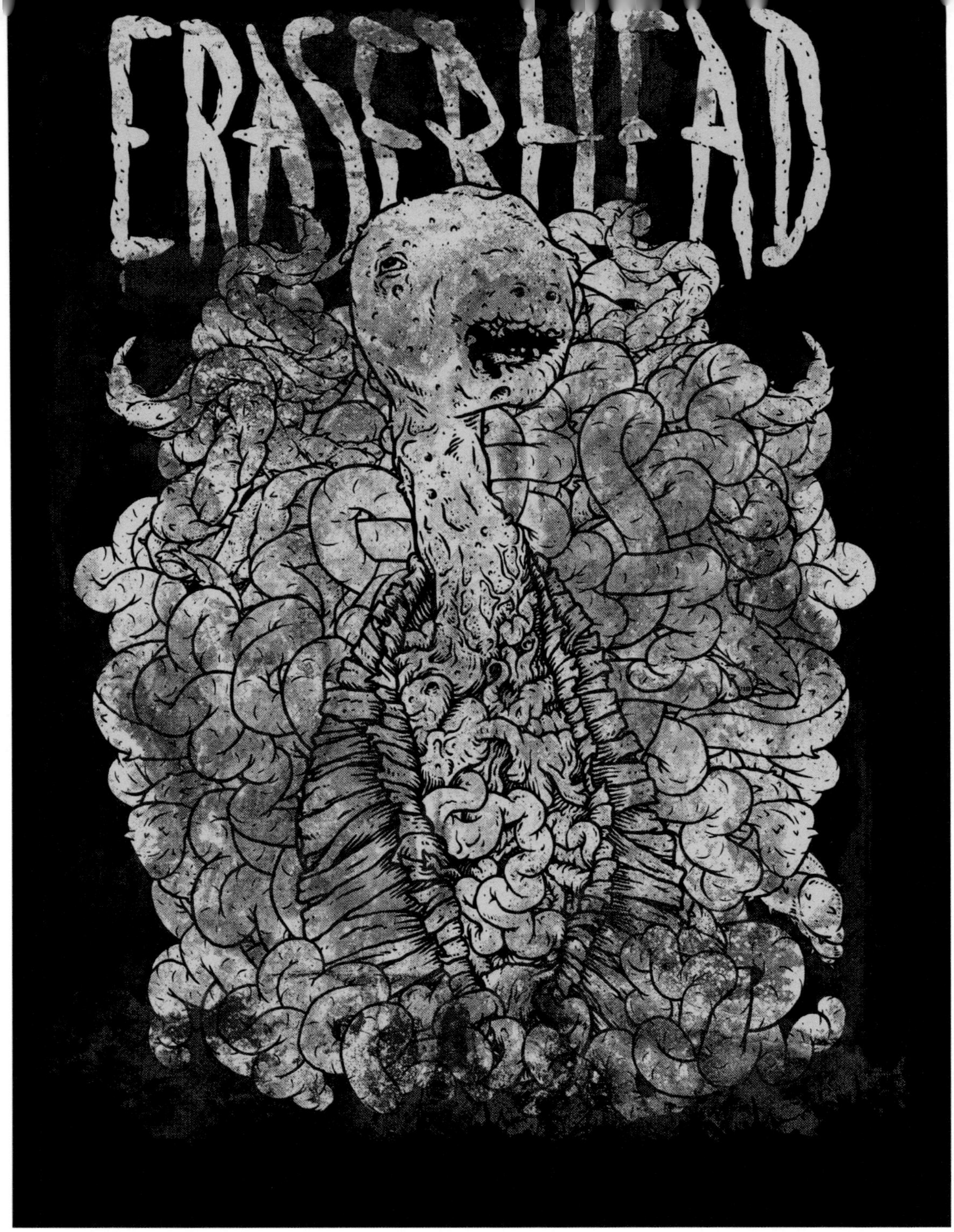

"Eraserhead" design by Jeff Finley for Fright-Rags

> *A WFH (work-for-hire) contract legally treats the artist as if they were a paid employee without providing all the perks and benefits of being an actual salaried employee like regular pay, sick pay, social security, vacation time, lunch breaks, insurance, etc.*

The best route would be to hire a lawyer to go over your contracts, but since not everyone has the funds for something like that, the next best thing is to do your own research through books and the Internet about contracts and legal terms. Try to protect your rights by watching for and removing phrases like "in perpetuity" and "work-for-hire." — Munk One

Sadly many companies try to force you to sign a WFH contact before they pay you. Protect yourself before starting any project by always asking for the contract you will be signing or better yet create your own and have it approved before starting on the project.

If for some reason you do choose to sign one of these contracts, at least make sure the price of the art is significantly higher than the usual fee in order to cover the money that could have been made off of it in the future.

Get Permission Before You Post!

Here's a story of how Go Media got in trouble for showing off our work. We've been in that "invisible" situation before but never really thought much of it. We've posted work in our portfolio and even wrote tutorials about how we did it. We didn't think we needed permission. Big mistake.

We were actually called by the manager of a legendary 80s band (I can't give the name) demanding us to remove the work from our site. Apparently the designs we were showing were not approved or even seen by the band. Word got back to them after seeing the design pop up on fan message boards who were talking about new merchandise.

From what we learned, the client that hired us was subcontracting us to create designs that they would then pitch to the band in an attempt to lure the band away from their current merchandising company. We had no idea; we were just the invisible designers. We immediately removed the designs from our sites and from now on, we get permission from the client before we promote the work we did.

Visit www.threadsnotdead.com/links for more reading on **WFH contracts.**

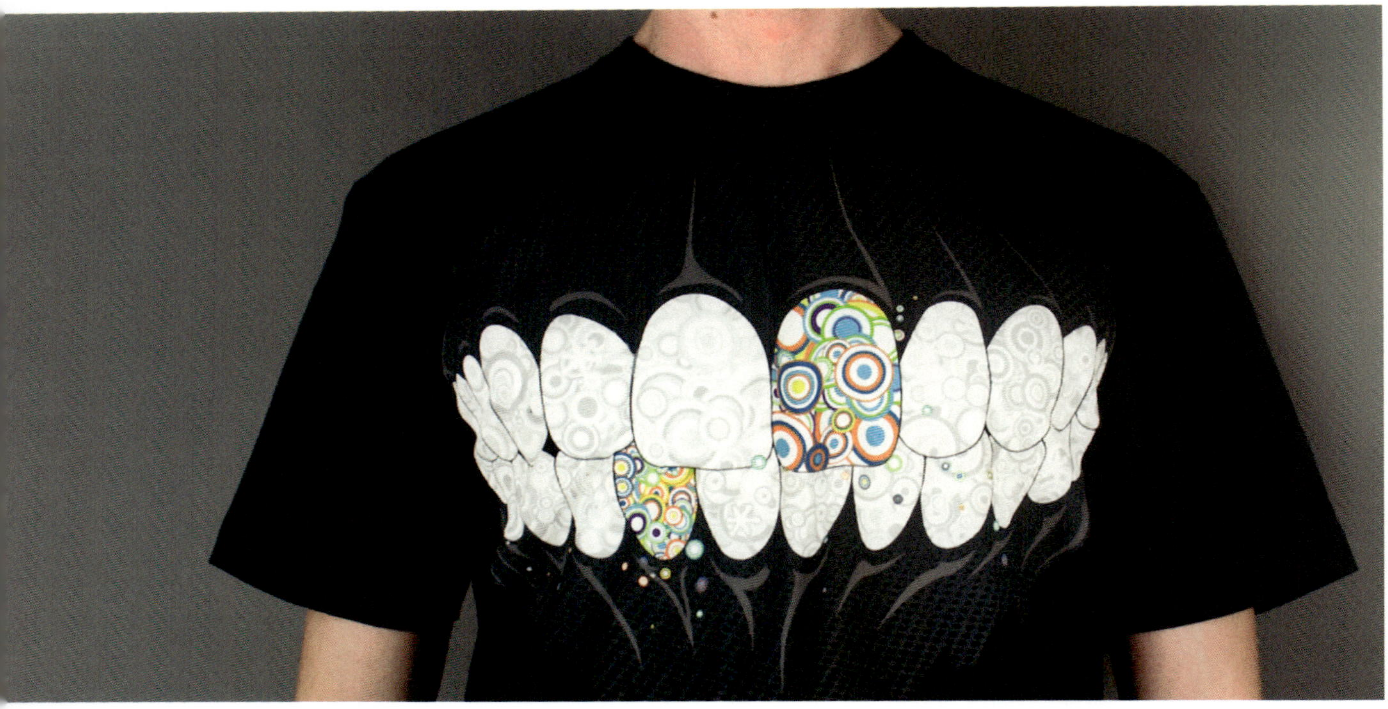

"Digi Grill" by Oliver Barrett of Go Media for Jakprints

Ripping/Stealing/Biting

This is a common problem in every creative industry, whether it's music, art, film, illustration, etc. Someone else copies another artist's work and claims it as their own. There's a fine line between being influenced by another's work and outright ripping it.

A popular site that exposes this activity is **You Thought We Wouldn't Notice**.

It goes without saying, but don't bite another artist's style. Sure it's ok to be inspired but you MUST put your own spin on things. Most successful designers known for their style get that way because they have their own unique approach to their work. This evolves over time and sometimes takes years to develop.

I've seen artists outright steal another artist's work and use it as their own. This is awful. Fortunately, communities like Emptees usually catch these crimes & **make the thief feel ashamed** for what they've done.

But what happens when YOUR designs get stolen? You can cry and throw a fit or publicly bash them (I don't recommend stooping that low). You could sue them but

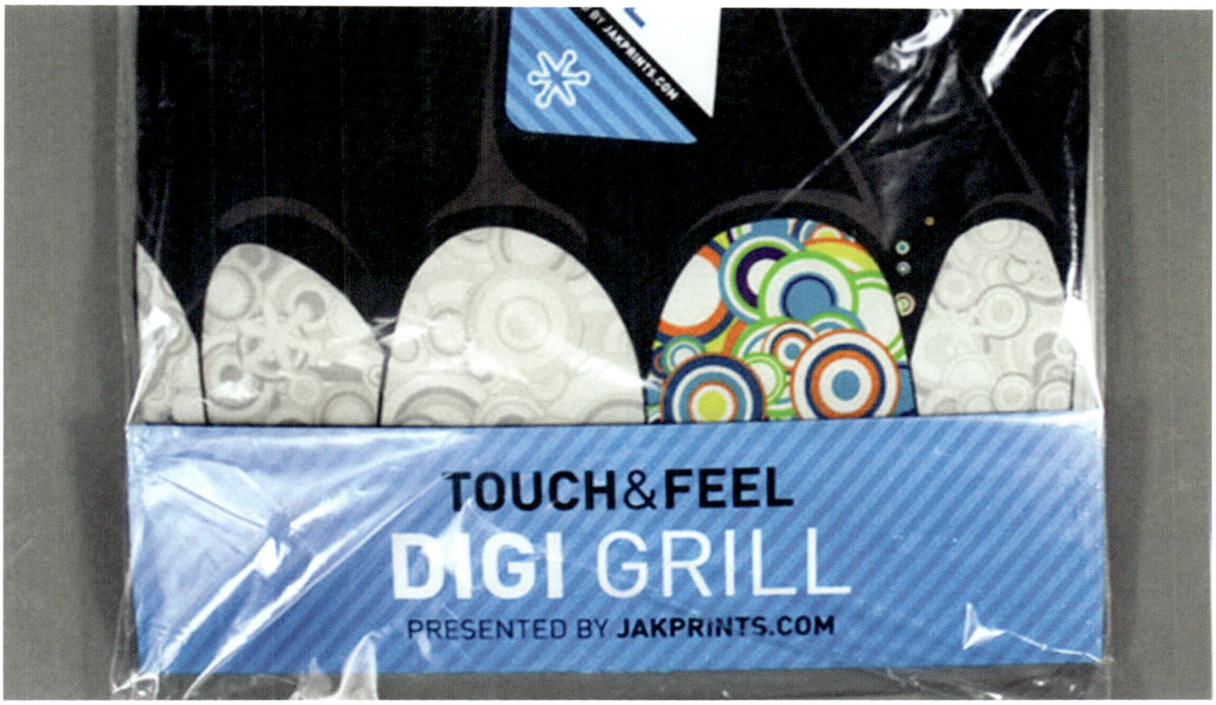

lawyers won't care if it's an ignorant newbie trying to fake it until he makes it. The first thing I would do is to write the offender and ask them to take down the piece. If they're a big company, you could take them to court.

For more info, I wrote a comprehensive article detailing the **various instances of design piracy** and what you can do about it.

Using Stock Images

Stock art, photos, or illustrations are images that designers can use in their work without having to pay royalties. There are many sites where you can find stock images such as **iStockphoto**, **shutterstock**, **Getty Images**, **deviantArt**, **YouWorkForThem**, and of course **Go Media's Arsenal** (shameless plug!). You could find vector art, Photoshop Brushes, fonts, photographs, templates, and other "pre-made" images that you could purchase or download for free/cheap and use it for your own projects. This is totally cool and legal assuming you are within a particular provider's terms of use. Some might not allow you to use a stock image on a commercial project. So check their terms carefully.

Using stock is sometimes a hotly debated issue. While perfectly legal, some circles criticize others who use stock art as unoriginal or lazy. For example, on Emptees, the community values the effort, originality, and attention to detail of hand illustration. So when an artist on Emptees uses obvious stock illustrations, they get negative feedback for their lack of effort and/or originality.

However, artists on Emptees might be using a pre-made website template from **Cargo** and will receive absolutely no complaints from the community. In fact, there could be multiple illustrators using the same website template and the only thing separating them is their colors, logo, and portfolio. This is considered ok in the illustration community, but if you were a web developer, you might look down upon others who use website templates. Same thing with professional photographers taking pride in their own photography and probably won't consider using stock photos.

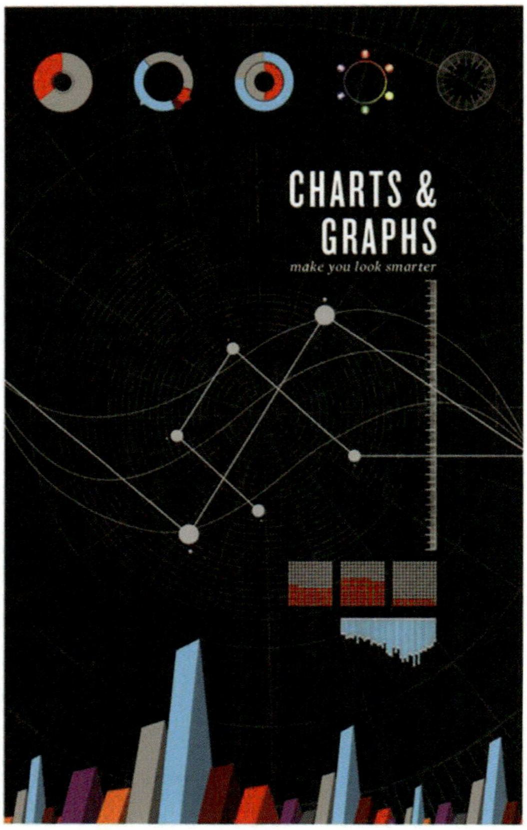

"Charts & Graphs" design by Max Stern, when he interned for Go Media in 2010. The design uses nothing but Royalty Free design elements from Go Media's Arsenal

There is a time and place for using stock. Everyone I've interviewed has used stock in some way or another. It can be extremely helpful. For example, when a client needs a job yesterday and has no budget, stock art is a godsend. You could quickly piece together a design in less than an hour and still keep the client happy. It's also helpful to bridge the gap between what the client wants and what you can realistically complete.

You could also be extremely creative with how you use stock art. **AJ Dimarucot** has produced many outstanding and award winning designs with his creative use of stock. He admits to not being able to draw, so he relies on photo manipulation, textures, and basic shapes. His combination of shapes, colors, textures combined with his unique ideas has earned him the reputation of a great designer.

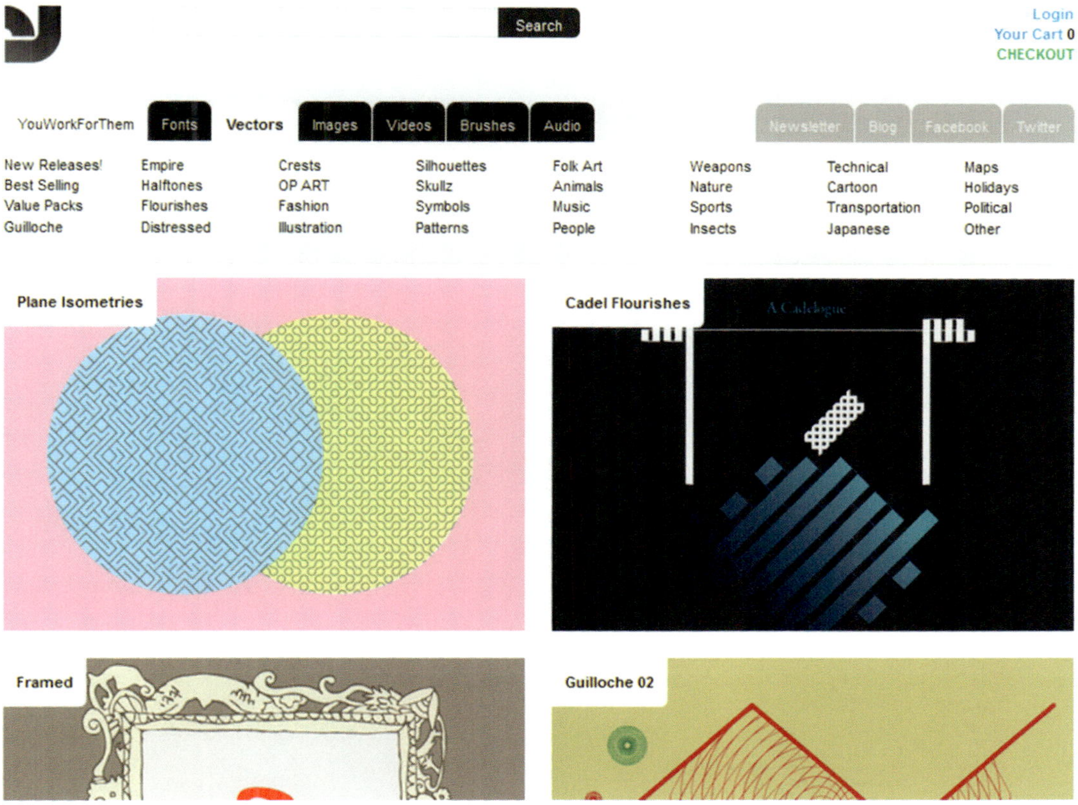

YWFT is one of the best resources for finding stock art and fonts.

In terms of your own clothing line, I recommend being more deliberate in your usage of stock art. As creators and **sellers of our own stock** we see people launching their own line of tees using our graphics as a main focal point. This is perfectly acceptable under our terms of use, but from a branding perspective, these clothing lines aren't differentiating themselves from the competition very much.

If you want to stand out, you need to be unique and worth talking about. You don't want to be the same as everyone else. Personally, I use stock photos all the time because I don't have the resources to shoot my own. But it's important for me to put my own spin on it and mold it into my design.

The Designer/Client Relationship

On your path to mastering the apparel industry, it's time to learn the importance of the designer/client relationship. You've got to keep your clients happy and the relationship needs to be nurtured.

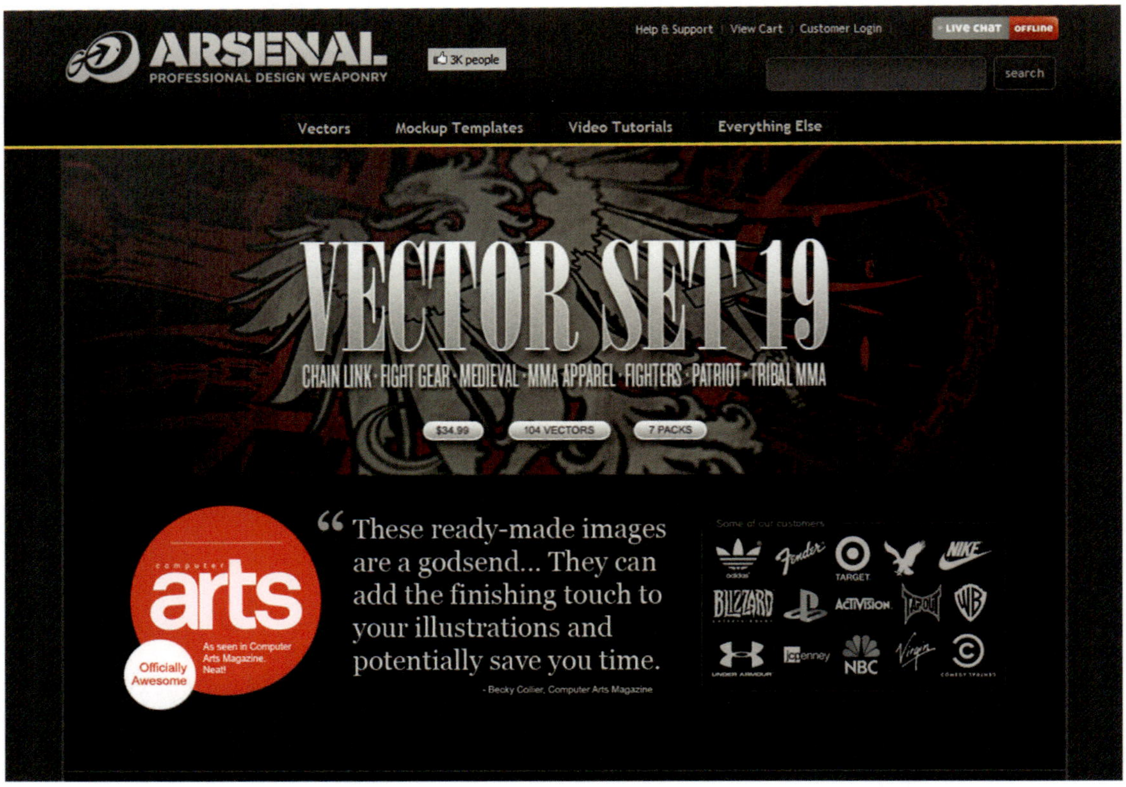

We sell our own stock vectors, textures, and t-shirt templates at **http://arsenal.gomedia.us**

Tricking Your Client into Happiness

From our experience working with clients, there are ways we have found to **trick them into happiness**. We wrote an article about this, but I am going to summarize here.

You're not really "tricking" your client, but you're doing things that make it easier for them to like you and approve your ideas and concepts. For starters, you might consider lowering the client's expectations up front. We like to say, "Under-promise and over-deliver." When you initially set the bar low, as in "Realistically, I'm not sure

I can give you that insane illustration overnight, how about in a couple days?" And then you show them your proofs a day before they expect it. Works like a charm.

When proofing your designs, it's good practice to show no more than three options. This way they can easily understand the differences between each and make a decision quicker. They're also more likely to pick the one you think is best.

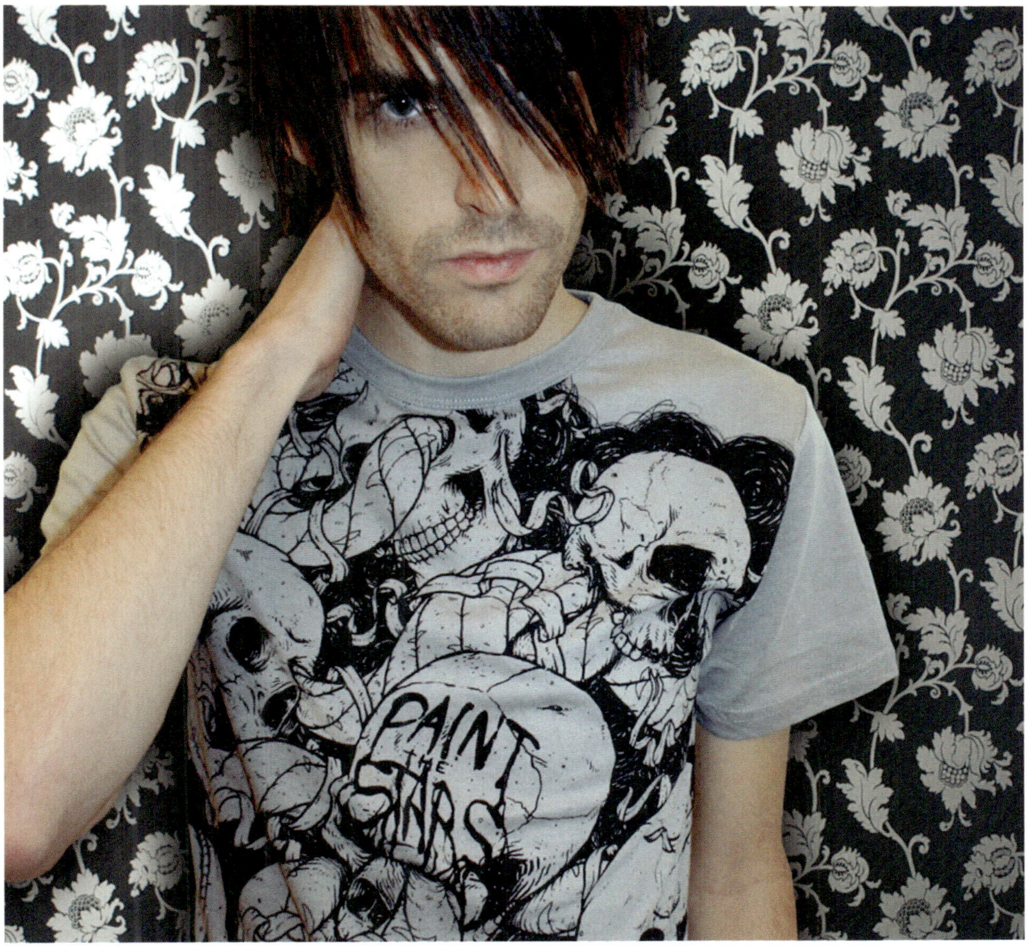

Dave Pearson of Paint the Stars

t-shirt design by Jeff Finley

Another trick is to dress up or simulate real-world usage of the design. We know from experience that using a **photorealistic t-shirt mockup** as opposed to none at all or even worse, a poorly drawn cartoony template, works wonders for getting more approvals.

Tips from Paint the Stars Clothing

I talked with Dave Pearson from **Paint the Stars Clothing** about how designers can improve their relationship with clothing company clients. He strongly recommends showing initial sketches first and foremost. When he hires designers for his line, he remembers some of them showed him a finished design right off the bat. Conceptually it would miss the mark and Dave would feel guilty about telling the designer he didn't like it, or that, if a sketch was shown, some of the mistakes could have been avoided. For example — subject matter, placement, concept, etc. Get that stuff approved in the sketch phase first so your ego isn't bruised when they turn down your final masterpiece! Dave **has a lot more to say** if you want to read the full article.

The most important thing to remember when working with clients is communication. Keep them involved in the design process from the beginning. Pick up the phone and chat with them. Send them flowers or forward them a funny video every once in awhile too. Stay in touch with your clients and they'll keep coming back.

Client and Project Management

When you reach the point of having to keep track of multiple clients and multiple projects, you're going to need a way to manage it all. You could try **Basecamp**, **activeCollab**, or **ProofHQ** for some solid choices. I am fond of Basecamp myself but it wasn't quite what we needed at Go Media. As a growing design firm, we built our own client and project management app and called it Proof Lab. In 2005 we wanted an easy way to post proofs for a client and it would automatically email the client with a link to the proofs. They could type in their feedback directly into a text box under their proof and it worked wonders. Over the years we've continued to customize our app to cater to the our needs as a growing design firm and added features like hour tracking and centralized communication.

We know not everyone has the resources to create their own app, so **we've decided to go public with Proof Lab** and open it up to other designers and studios. For you, Basecamp or other apps might work just fine, but any of these solutions work way better than just email.

Some Books & Articles I Recommend

- Here's an article we wrote on **keeping your integrity with a client**.
- David Allen's ***Getting Things Done***
- ***Making Ideas Happen*** by Scott Belsky.
- ***How to be a Graphic Designer Without Losing Your Soul***

The Truth about Design Contests

One of the easiest ways to get exposure in the t-shirt scene is through design contests. There's **some debate** on whether contests are good or bad for the design community. In my opinion, it's both.

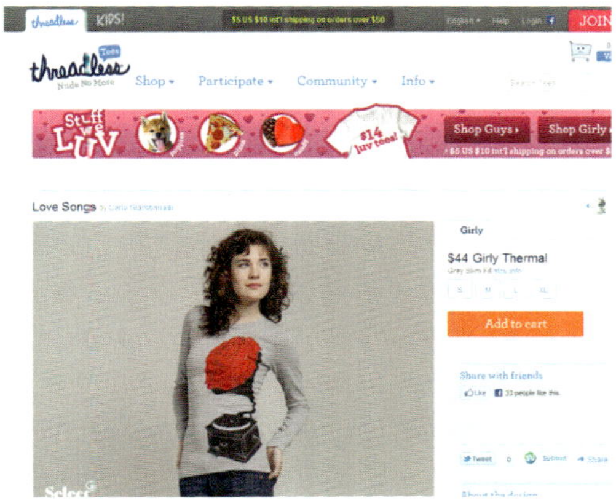

Threadless.com has set the standard for t-shirt contest sites

Sites like Threadless and DesignByHümans are examples of t-shirt design contest sites. But they're more than contest sites — they're communities built around t-shirt art. You upload a tee design, it gets voted on by the community and the ones with the most votes gets printed and sold back to the community. The designer usually gets a cash prize and is promoted to a larger audience, which could lead to bigger and better jobs. Awesome!

Contests can be a good thing, but you must be careful. The sites I listed on the next page are well known and respected in the industry. But beware of companies offering up a job opportunity disguised as a contest. They're just trying to bait designers into giving them free concepts. The contest sponsor then only has to pay for the one that they like best. In rare cases, they might not even choose a design, but steal one of the ideas and have an in-house designer copy it. Kinda scary! Just use your judgment and ask around if you're suspicious.

List of T-Shirt Design Contest Sites

- Threadless
- DesignByHümans
- Shirt.woot
- Uneetee
- Full Metal T-Shirt
- laFraise
- RedisWhite
- Teepay
- Tilteed
- Goodjoe
- Scopial
- bookis.org
- Metal Ink
- ArtyTee

- SwishSwosh
- Badashell
- Camiseteria
- Fair & Bare
- Chimpogo
- Canvas
- Ink-Hound
- Teextile
- Bang Bang T-Shirts
- Edo Label
- teetonic.com
- Allmightys
- Cameesa
- Inkfruit

Crowd Sourcing

This act of soliciting a large audience to design something is called crowd sourcing and is highly debated in the industry. The website **99 Designs** has received mixed reviews as one of the main players in this niche. It's up to you if you want to participate in these types of "contests" but expect lots of work with little to no reward. Your best bet is to get involved in a design community like I mentioned above and participate actively. The more friends you make, the more likely you are to succeed, even if you don't win a contest.

There are a few people who have really made it big doing design contests. **AJ Dimarucot**, **Jimyo** and **RikkiB** are three examples. Jimyo has written about his **experience with lots of contest sites** and RikkiB has offered her case study later in this book.

Five Tips for Design Contest Success

When Mark Hemeon used to be part of DesignByHümans, he gave me five tips to give you the best chance of winning the next Shirt of the Day on DBH.

1. Prepare Artwork at Final Production Size.

On our design submission page we have a footnote which reminds artists to have a high-res print ready version of their artwork ready to go if their artwork is selected as a winner. We get pretty bummed out when we contact a winning artist only to find out he or she does not have a high-res version of their artwork ready for print.

Many artists work exclusively in Illustrator or other vector based programs which allows for the greatest flexibility when it comes to sizing and placement of the artwork without losing quality of the design.

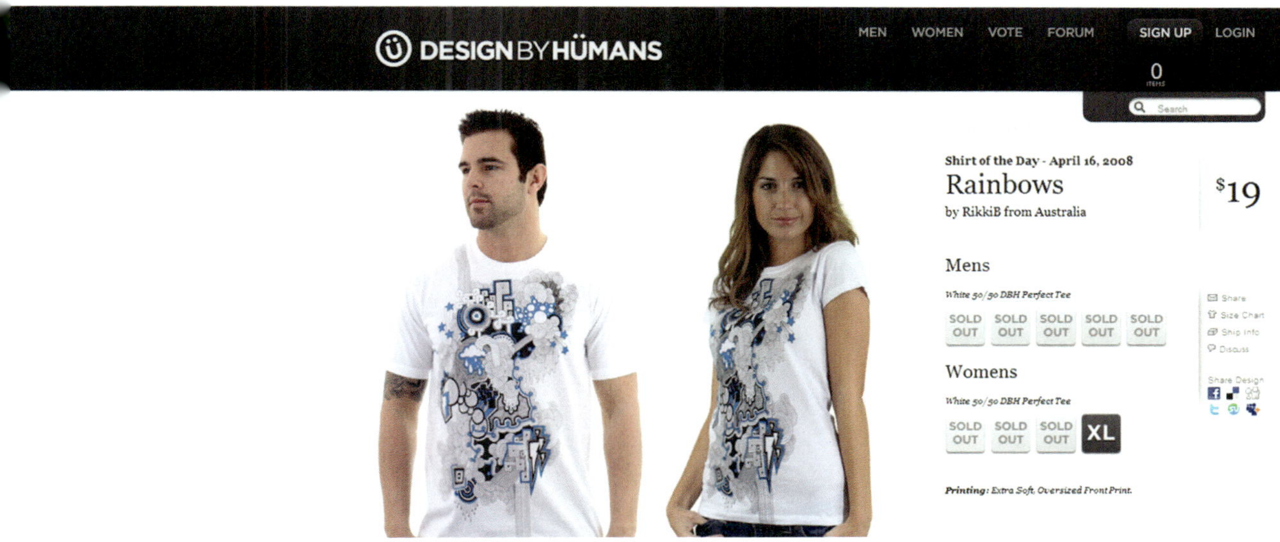

One of RikkiB's winning contest entries on DesignBy Hümans

If you are designing exclusively in a pixel based program like Photoshop then you really need to ensure you are designing your artwork at the correct resolution. For example, if you were to design a center chest graphic and the design was 12 inches wide by 14 inches tall then your Photoshop file should be set to 300 dpi (300 dpi is the minimum resolution we will accept for final artwork) or 3,600 pixels wide and 4,200 pixels tall.

Double check how your artwork will be represented on various t-shirt sizes (view the size chart of the tees you are designing for). The canvas size varies greatly between a small girl's shirt and a XXL men's shirt. Occasionally we will create a separate set of screens for the girl's shirts to shrink the artwork to accommodate the smaller t-shirt size. Producing your artwork for the largest t-shirt size allows us to easily size the design down to create a second set of screens for the girl's version. Sizing up low res artwork creates a big hot pixelated mess.

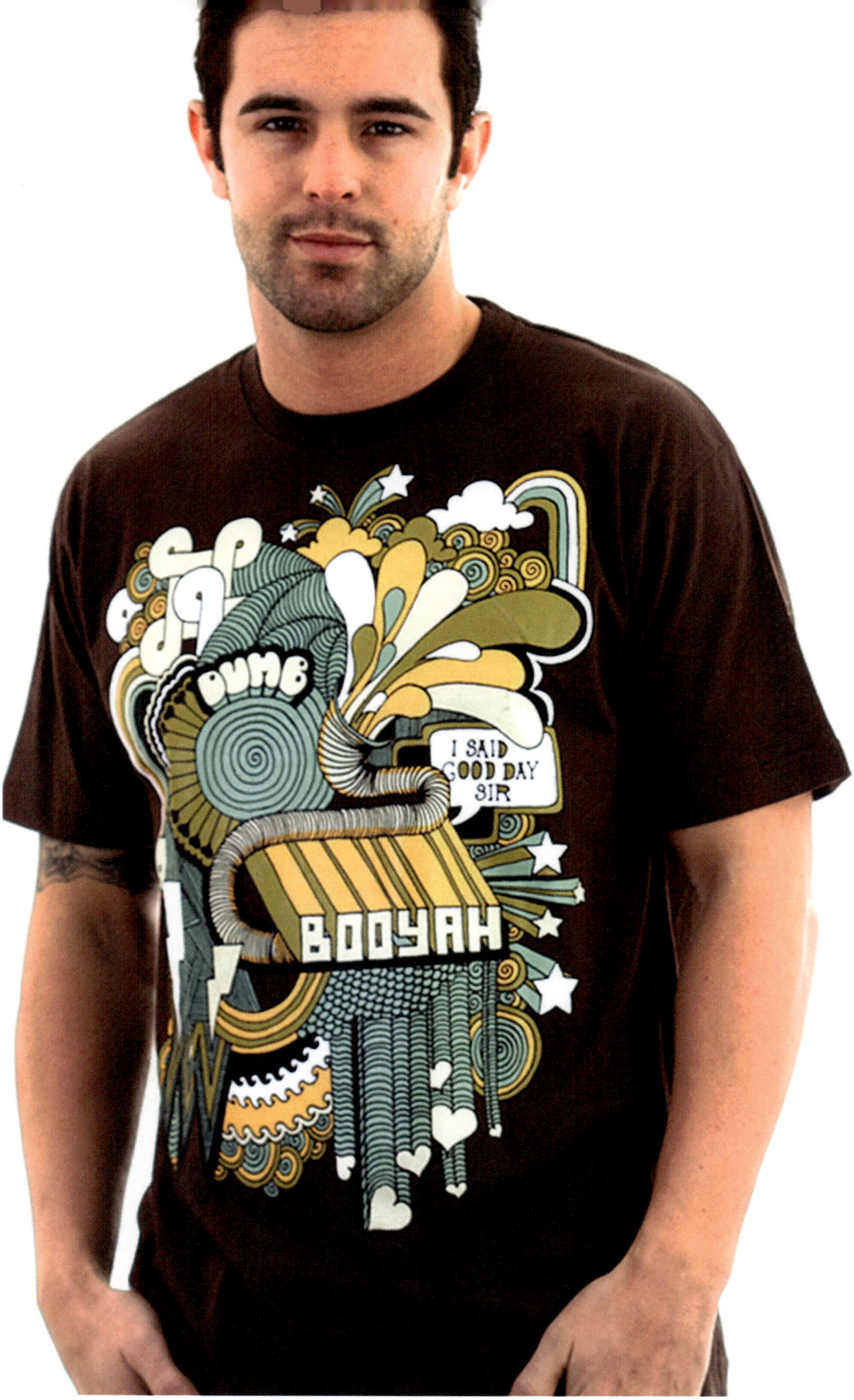

Another winning design by RikkiB at DesignByHümans

2. *Push your design with the reasonable use of mixed media.*

There is a huge trend right now in graphic tees to include various mixed media elements to enhance the underlying illustration. Mixed media is a broad term to include the various bonus techniques currently offered by the more advanced t-shirt printing companies. Some examples include burnout, discharge, embroidery, appliqué, metallic and foil inks (covered later in this book).

One caveat, using mixed media in addition to your illustration is a bit like learning how to make drop shadows with Photoshop — meaning just because you CAN use mixed media does not mean you necessarily *should.*

Mixed media should enhance the artwork and drive home the theme and feeling of the design. One effective way of calling out mixed media is representing the shapes, lines and placement in a separate layer when working with Illustrator or Photoshop. Use one layer for each type of mixed media, labeling your layers by the mixed media type.

For example, your design could call for an appliqué a of a silk-screened heart on top of a silk-screened t-shirt attached with thick embroidery. The embroidery stitching can be displayed to represent brush-like strokes and texture into your designs. So, say you have a cool illustration of Tom Selleck on a tee, you could use embroidery for his hairy chest, giving a nice tactile feel.

3. *Know and call out your colors (Pantone please!)*

Bottom line, if an artist has not called out their specific Pantone colors then we are left to match against the artwork we see on our computer screens. For the most part we are pretty good at getting colors correct when we have to interpret the colors for the artist (our color separator, Dan, is excellent at identifying color).

Not everyone has access to a Pantone book, we get it, but do your best to identify your colors so there is no misunderstanding. Sometimes we have to make a judgment call based on the design submission and what we think the artist would have wanted. If artists can be very specific in their desired colors then our job of producing their vision is a bit easier.

4. Have your own style

Artistic expression is awesome. We read quite a bit in the blogs and forums about where a design "fits" in regards to finding a home for the design. For DBH we are really excited when we see a fresh voice and style and an artist being true to themselves and not catering to what they think will get the votes. Our suggestion is to use the DBH contest as a forum of expression and to explore yourself as an artist and create meaningful artwork for yourself — we find these pieces resonate more with the DBH community rather than something stereotypical of the latest winning designs. And of course, do not under any circumstances copy someone else's design (its okay to be inspired by someone, but make it your own).

5. Be Awe-and-then-Some

This last point isn't regarding art prep per se, but a reminder to spend the time necessary to make your piece as awesome as possible to speak volumes at first impression. T-shirt designs are judged in a split second when they are first seen and for most people there is a bit of a love it or over it mentality when it comes to t-shirt design.

We have seen many great concepts which fall short with the execution of the artwork. Get feedback on your designs in the various online forums and subject yourself to the critiquing process. You and your artwork will only get better.

I also found a cool article on ShirtFight about **10 Tips on Winning t-shirt design contests.**

To view websites cited in this book, please visit www.threadsnotdead.com/links.

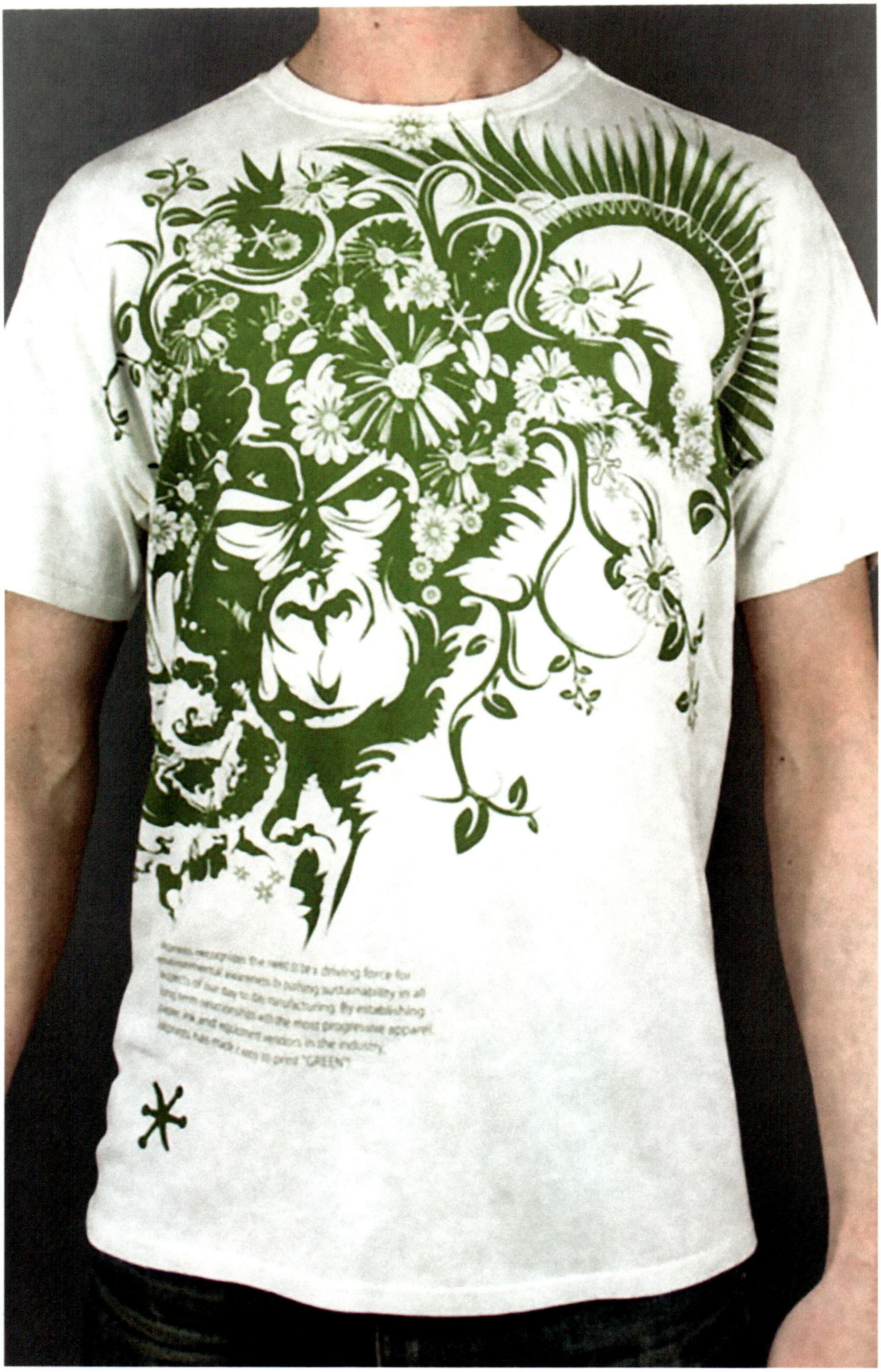

"Eco" t-shirt design by Chris Comella of Go Media for Jakprints

III

DESIGNING FOR TEES

"One should either be a work of art,
or wear a work of art." — OSCAR WILDE

What Do I Need to Know First?

Designing for tees is a unique process. Tees are typically screen printed with limited, specific colors. I don't need to go into detail on the full screen printing process, that's another book in itself. Instead, we're going to focus on design. But to design well, you must have a pretty solid understanding of what happens AFTER you send the design to print. This chapter will show you what makes a great shirt design and how to keep your screen printer happy.

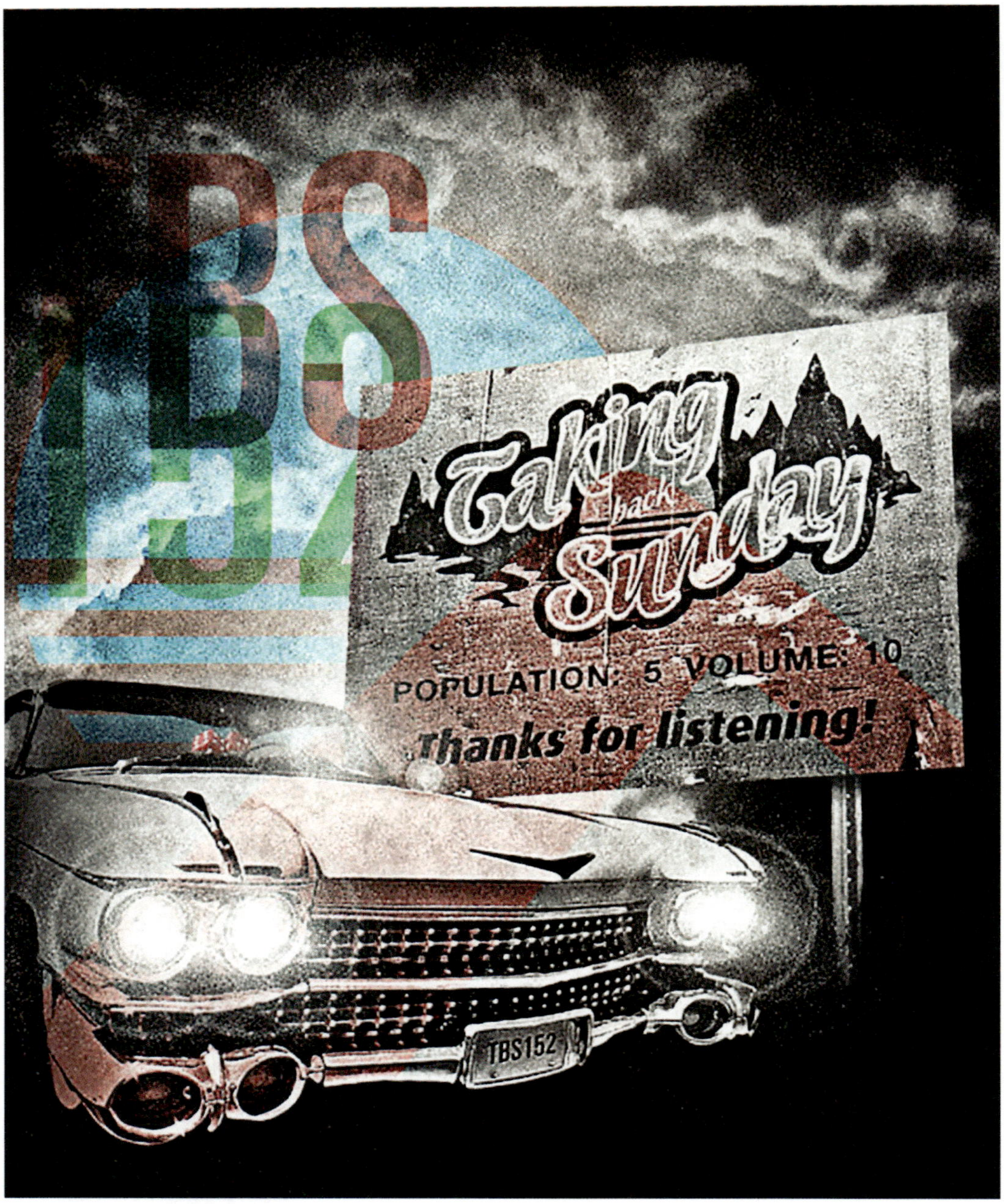

Taking Back Sunday shirt designed by Jeff Finley

Software and Knowledge Required

You're going to need to have a solid understanding of Adobe Photoshop and Illustrator to get the most out of this chapter. Sure, there are other applications that enable you to design for t-shirts but we're going to focus on the two biggest ones.

Furthermore, Munk One reminds us not to use software as a crutch. "Right now it's almost too easy to use computer programs to skip the basic design skills artists should have. Looking at even the simplest design I can tell if someone can actually draw and has the skills to lay something out. To help put you ahead I would recommend learning and perfecting drawing and design skills instead of just using software as a crutch."

To brush up on those design principles like composition, balance, contrast, and spacing, first **learn what constitutes "good design"** and follow it up by reading Bill's **7 Steps to Becoming a Master Designer series.**

The Fundamentals of Good Shirt Design

Despite having a solid knowledge of "design school" basics, people are still asking the question "what makes a good shirt design?" I'm going to talk about some of the not-so-obvious aspects that go into good shirt design.

Would you wear it?

First of all, it helps if you design shirts you actually would want to wear yourself. It's a pretty simple concept and I know it doesn't apply when you're designing tees for a client whose audience might be twice your age and of the opposite sex. But as a rule of thumb, ask yourself "would I wear this?" Put yourself in the wearer's shoes and try to imagine what it'd be like to wear your shirt.

Does it Sell?

Another measuring stick is if a design sells, it's good. Even if the design looks amateur, lazy, or cliché to you, it could still be extremely popular amongst its audience. Sometimes a good design is a sellable design. However, as we know people don't just buy a t-shirt for its design alone. So therefore, the design itself shouldn't be the only indicator for how much a shirt sells. But in general, a shirt that sells a lot is typically well-designed for its audience.

Is it Cost-Effective?

A good design is cost-effective. If you design a shirt that costs a lot to print (a lot of colors), it makes it tougher to recoup the initial expense. Clients and printers are happier if you maximize the impact of your design with as little colors as necessary. It's likely the wearer of your t-shirt design doesn't care if it has two colors or ten colors.

It Pushes the Envelope

Good design will blaze new trails in what people are wearing. Adding foil into your design wasn't something your average designer six or seven years ago

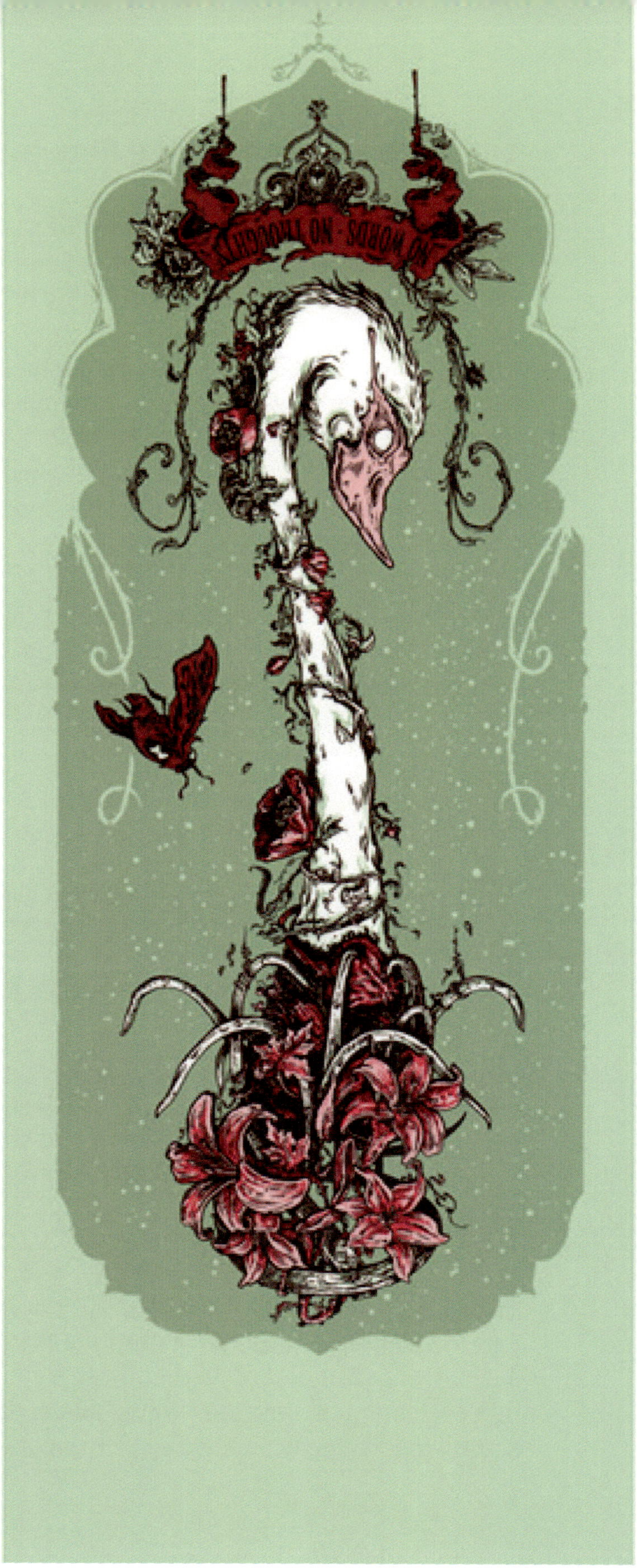

"Swans" by Angryblue

thought of. Foil or printing a full color image isn't really cost-effective but it might be worth it if that's what people are buying. A good design pushes boundaries and does things differently. It starts new trends, forges new printing solutions, and advances the industry. A good example of this is the Bold is Beautiful shirt that I designed that **people said could never be printed**. The design featured a full spectrum of colors and took up a large area on a black shirt. I imagine it was costly to print, but the team at DesignByHümans pulled it off with flying colors, pun intended.

It's Popular

In today's social web, the **"like" button** is everywhere. It allows us to earn social proof on our designs and decide what the community surrounding us likes or dislikes. Community sites like **Mintees** or **Threadless** have a voting feature like this built in and you can see what the most popular shirt designs are in the community. **Behance** has an "appreciate it" button and promotes projects that have a lot of clicks. If you click around and sort by "most loved" or "most commented" — you'll see what that particular community thinks are good designs.

Is the Client Happy?

If your clients are loving your designs, then you're doing something right. Another factor in "what's good" is whether your clients are happy with you. If you're not getting approvals from your clients, there's something missing. Personally speaking, we at Go Media don't always get approvals from clients. In fact we DO get our share of rejections! We feel our designs are good, but the client doesn't always agree. They don't think anyone will buy it when THEY start selling it. Or maybe the design was too expensive to print. Or maybe the design we spent so long perfecting wasn't the client's personal taste?

Although an unhappy client doesn't necessarily mean your designs are bad — you could have great designs that other designers are raving about but a client isn't digging it. You could even have a design that other CLIENTS are raving about, just not the one you did it for. This just goes to show the complexities of dealing with clients. However, as another rule of thumb, if you're making your clients happy, keep doing what you're doing.

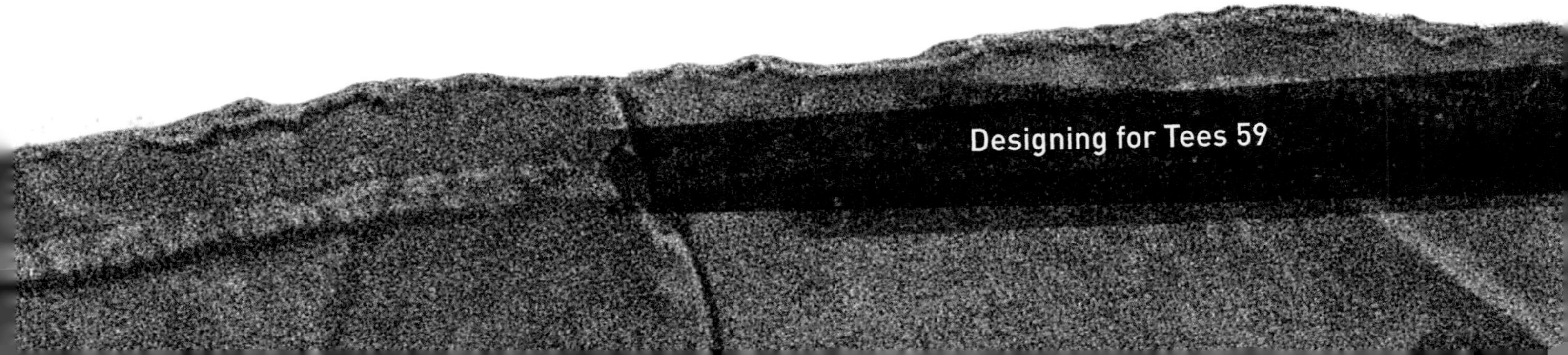

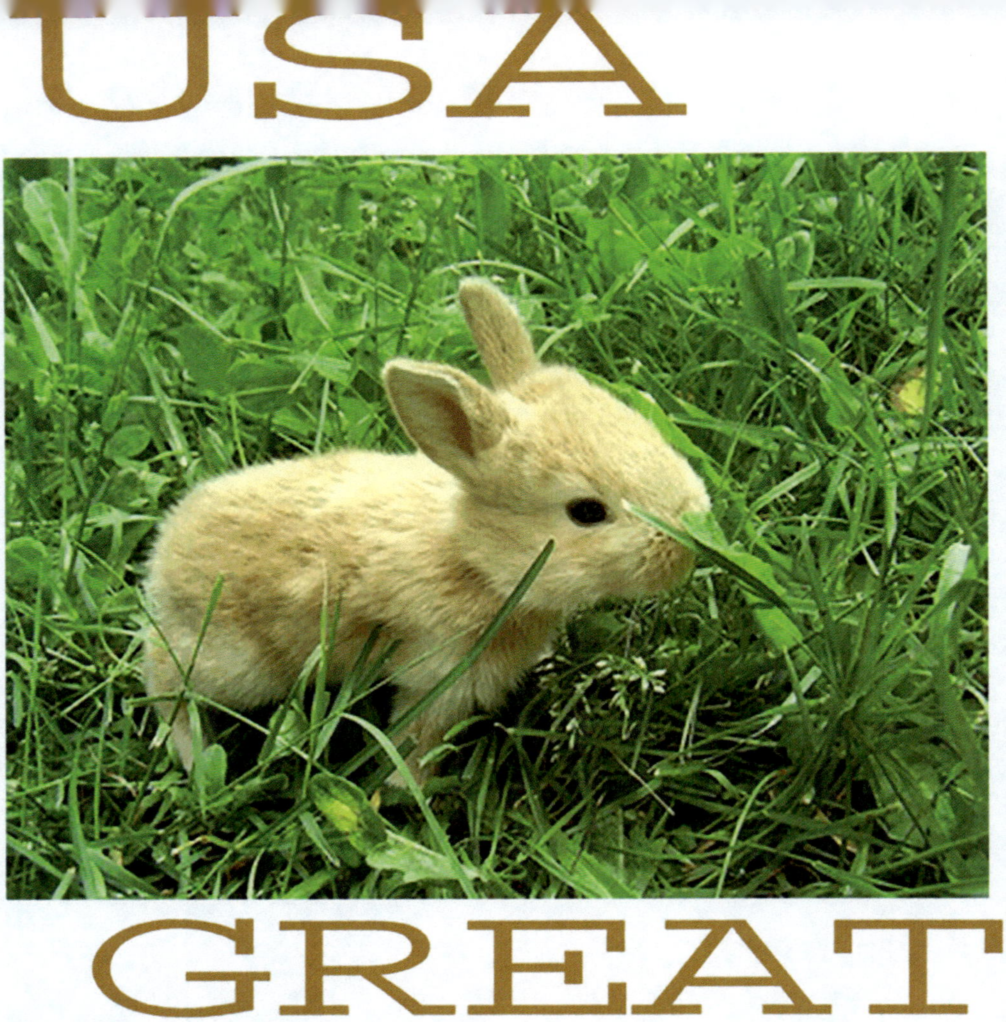

This shirt design by "Gunter" ironically was very popular in the Emptees community

It Pleases the Audience

This sums up all the points above. In every scenario, the factor for determining a good t-shirt design is whether your audience likes it and is buying it. If you feel you have a great design on your hands but it's not popular or selling, you might not have discovered the right audience for it yet. There are "bad designs" that defy logic and are ignorant to clichés and typography but they seem to sell well. Why? Because the owners understand their audience. That is key!

Sometimes a design you might not expect to do well becomes a hit, like this **"USA Great" t-shirt** that struck the right chord with the Emptees community.

If your design is good and you have the right audience, but it's still not doing well, then what? It's likely that your audience doesn't even know about your design, or, if they do, there's something else holding them back from liking it or purchasing it. This gets into marketing, branding, and selling your tees, which is something we'll get into later.

Is the Idea Solid?

Is the design backed by a good idea? What's the meaning of the design? Do the elements in the design have significance or is it just a collage of meaningless junk?

A good design has a solid idea and purpose behind it. Sure there are top selling t-shirts that exploit the popularity of stylistic trends like ornate flourishes or **SFSS** (skulls for skulls sake). But the point is, designs with a solid idea that mean something to your client or customer favor better.

It could be argued that there are plenty of generic "idea-less" t-shirts out there that we use to decorate our bodies with graphics or thematic images. People are walking into a department store right now to buy a "graphic tee" with some wings and scrolls on it. On the surface, the meaning behind such a common design is unclear. But somewhere, a customer is buying that because those images, and the way they are arranged, mean something to that person. Maybe the shirt makes them feel kinda cool or helps them fit into a certain crowd. Or maybe the person associates those images with a particular idea that does have meaning to them.

In a rut? Remind yourself why you got into this in the first place.

Again, we go back to your audience. Does your t-shirt design have meaning to your client and customer? What moves them and makes them feel good? How do you come up with these good ideas?

Additional Reading:

- **What makes a design good? (DesignByHümans)**
- **What is "good" t-shirt design? (t-shirt forums)**
- **Art Doesn't Sell: How to Design for the Apparel Market**

How to Come up With Good Ideas?

Every idea has been done before, right? There's nothing new and original out there so why bother trying? I'm sure you've said that to yourself before. I know I have.

But don't let that stop you. You don't have to think of something completely original, just something that resonates well with your audience and most importantly yourself. If you don't love your ideas, then why would anyone else?

Finding Inspiration

Sometimes when I'm stuck in an idealess funk I surf the web for inspiration. I find that **www.ffffound.com** is a great stimulus for visual ideas. I also like **www.booooooom.com**. Those are pretty non-tee related inspiration pools, which is my point. Sometimes the best inspiration comes from looking outside of your niche for unique angles that you can take to a project. Looking at packaging design, photography, typography, or fine art can sometimes stimulate an idea cooking in the back of my brain.

Here's an inspiration trick that is so simple it's easy to forget: Remind yourself why you got into this in the first place. Look up the other artists that you admire and drool over their work for a bit. Then, have a cup of coffee and start sketching out your concepts.

Once you're inspired, try to think of a clever way to solve your "problem." What kind of design do you want to make? What's an approach that's fresh in the eyes of your audience? Rob Dobi always has great, clever ideas and idioms behind his tees at **Fullbleed**, like a person diving into a **pool that's shaped like a coffin**. What does that mean? A simple visual design but it has an underlying feeling of dread behind it. It says something. So what are you trying to say with your designs?

Just keep sketching and do it more and more. Try to get out all the clichés in your mind and put them in your sketchbook. Nobody's going to see them.

How can you be unique?

Well, you could try to draw something in a new style or experiment with an unconventional layout. You could go Googling for metaphors, idioms, myths, fables, or

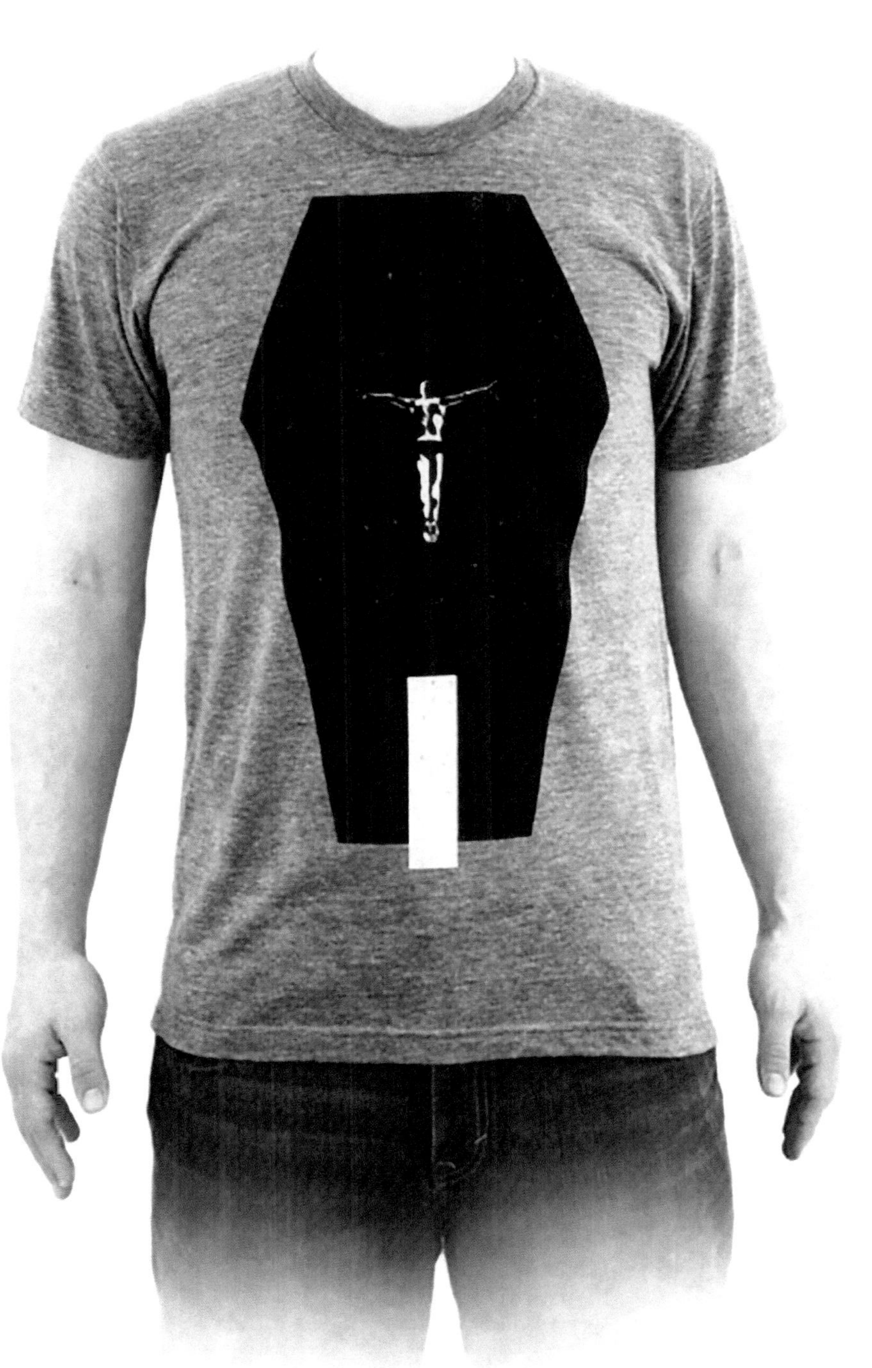

"Shallow Grave" designed by Rob Dobi for his clothing line Fullbleed

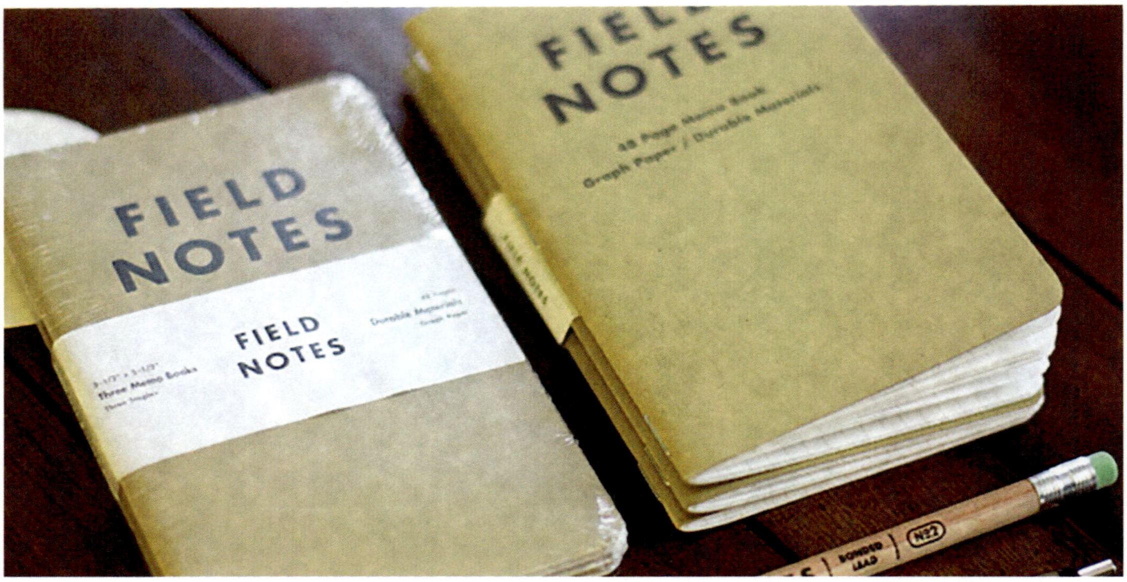

I use a small notebook like these to jot down notes while I'm out. If I can remember that is!

paradoxes and illustrate one of the concepts. Search the Wikipedia for subject matter that means a lot to you and pick out lines that have cool phrasing together. For example, I remember reading about the Dogme 95 film movement and they had a line that said it was "drafted by friends." I just thought that idea was a cool concept that could be a seed for a new design.

When I ask people where they get their ideas from, they often answer with the cliché "oh you know, life in general." Or "I don't know, they just come to me." I think they just don't know how to articulate where they get their ideas. That could be the case with you. You don't know where an idea comes from, it just pops in your head. This happens to me all the time.

Don't Lose Your Good Ideas

I got tired of forgetting those ideas so now I bring a **small notebook** with me everywhere and write them down so I don't forget. So here's a tip, start by being more aware that ideas will come to you when you're shopping for groceries, getting gas, taking a shower, etc. If you understand that, you'll take notice when a new idea sprouts up that's worth remembering. Jot it down and then look for a way to execute it next time you sit down to design.

What if I Can't Draw?

Big deal. Not everyone has the gift of drawing. Some of my favorite t-shirt designers these days do absolutely NO drawing in their designs.

A few years ago, there was a huge trend emerging of hand-drawn illustration. This was sort of an evolution of the "grunge era" of splattery t-shirt designs that were filling people's portfolios at that time. It continued the "back-to-basics" movement and chances were good that if it was hand-drawn or "natural" it was going to be popular. Drawing skills were not as important as the **handmade look** and they still sell this style today.

Even today as I write this, illustration is huge in t-shirt design. There are some amazing artists that are **rendering full scenes of zombified terror** on a t-shirt and they're getting lots of love from the community. They're getting hired too — as most of these insane illustrations are for bands or other clothing lines.

When you see their success and the sheer amount of love they're getting, don't feel bad. In fact, give them props for being so amazing and then go do your own thing. You don't need to have an uncanny sense of anatomy, lighting, linework, and attention to detail. That stuff is important but there is still a market, a big one, for simpler and more graphic-based tees.

Graphic Based Tees VS Illustration

So what's better? Graphic-based tees or illustrated ones? It depends on who you ask! Visit various t-shirt communities and you'll see they're made up of users who appreciate different styles. As trends come and go, you'll see these communities evolving with them. As one gets tired of a trend, another site will pick it up and put its own spin on it.

There's no "better" answer. People still look at t-shirts as a medium for art and for a message. There is no question that the t-shirt itself is here to stay. When you wear a t-shirt with an image or text on it, you're saying something about yourself. You're sending a message to all those who see it. The message may be simple like "I like this band." Or "I love New York." You might also just think that the style or the imagery represents your interests and makes you feel part of something bigger than yourself.

So the message is important. Does a hand-drawn illustration get your message across better? Or does your icon enclosed in a circle say what you want to say? Remember, what does your audience like? What do they respond to? What do YOU like? There's room for both and those who can't draw should never be discouraged, even if illustration and zombies are the tee du jour.

Let's Talk Trends Shall We?

Some say trends are bad, some say trends are good. But both sides agree that trends come and go and are an integral part of the apparel industry. Styles come out fresh and inspiring, get popular and go mainstream, then turn into clichés that nobody wants anything to do with.

I had a chat with Justin Kamerer, aka **Angryblue** about trends. He's an expert on the history of rock music art and a veteran designer in the apparel industry. He has created art for everyone from Slayer to Paul McCartney. Together we listed out what we thought were some of the most prevalent trends the past five to ten years.

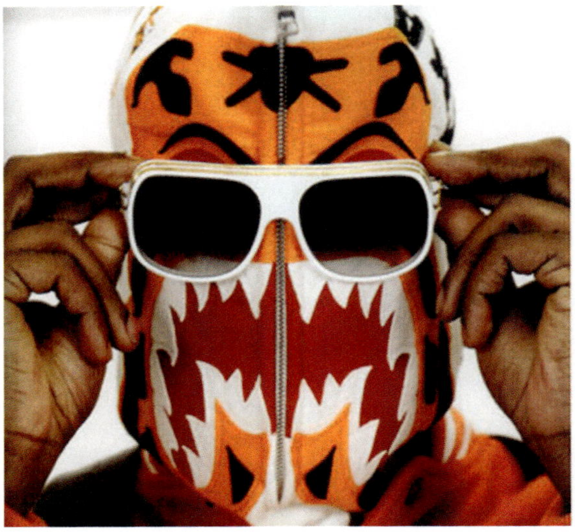

Hoodie by BAPE

Affliction/Ed Hardy/MMA

Obviously, in the past few years, we've seen the rise and decline of the **Affliction** style and the explosion of knock-off companies **rising up** with the popularity of Mixed Martial Arts. **Tapout** and **Ed Hardy** are other popular examples. With that came the return of belt printing to execute oversized prints of tattoo-inspired "skull & wings" ephemera and the introduction of discharge inks for an awesome **soft-hand**. Along with that came foil and other embellishments that were "safe" for dudes to wear. Bodybuilders rocking rhinestones on their t-shirts became a common sighting. It seems nearly every brand had once tried to ride on the coattails of the popular Affliction style.

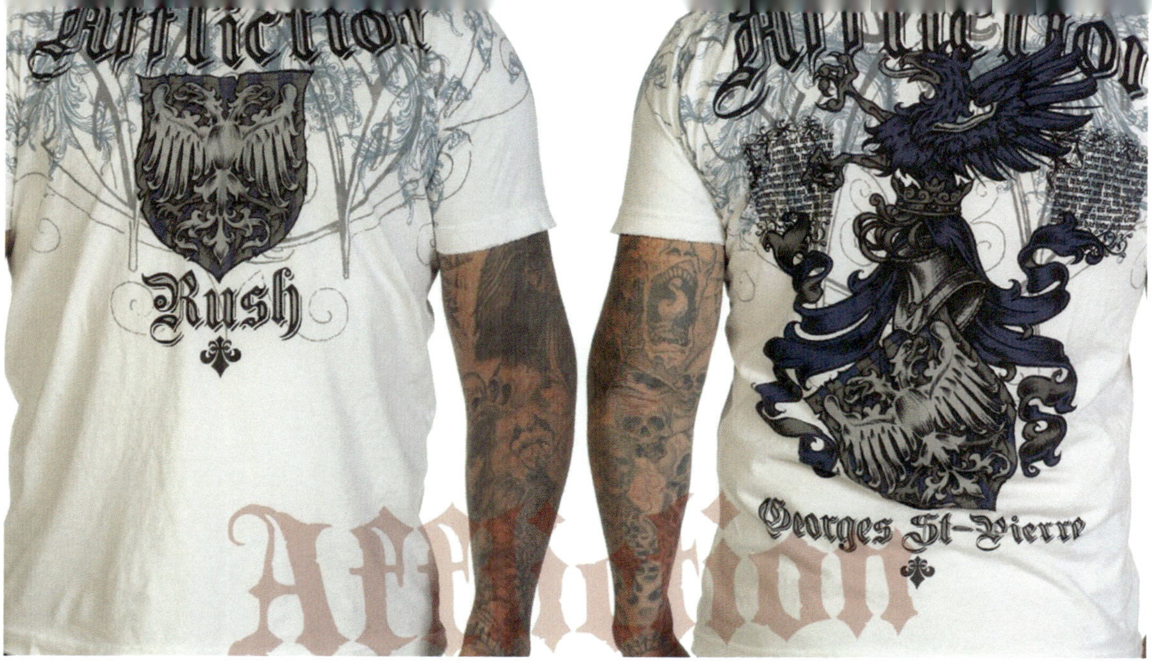

Affliction and MMA have heavily influenced the apparel industry the past five years

At Go Media, we get requests for new brands that want to look like Affliction. I wrote an **article about this** a few years ago and we still get requests from those who like to show up fashionably late to the trend party.

Affliction also made garment distressing and dying popular. It's like tie-dye but more monochromatic. Brands everywhere started fraying the edges of their tees and staining their ultra-lightweight soft shirts. They weren't the first to do it, but I credit Affliction with making it mainstream and forcing apparel printers to reinvent their printing processes. There are also companies like **Bare Apparel** that sell premade blank tees with this type of treatment.

Streetwear and Subculture

Streetwear is used to describe fashion that draws influence from the culture and surroundings of the creators. For example, urban art, graffiti, pop culture, consumerism, social and political messages, etc. The trend started taking off with a convergence of punk rock surf/skate culture and hip hop. Both cultures rooted themselves in an anti-mainstream DIY approach with a focus on individuality. In the 1980s the underground trend caught on in Japan which introduced themes around anime, toys, or other gadgets.

Angryblue says, "The boutique approach to apparel design has been engaging as well. Just like sneaker pimps are to shoes, there are people obsessively into the

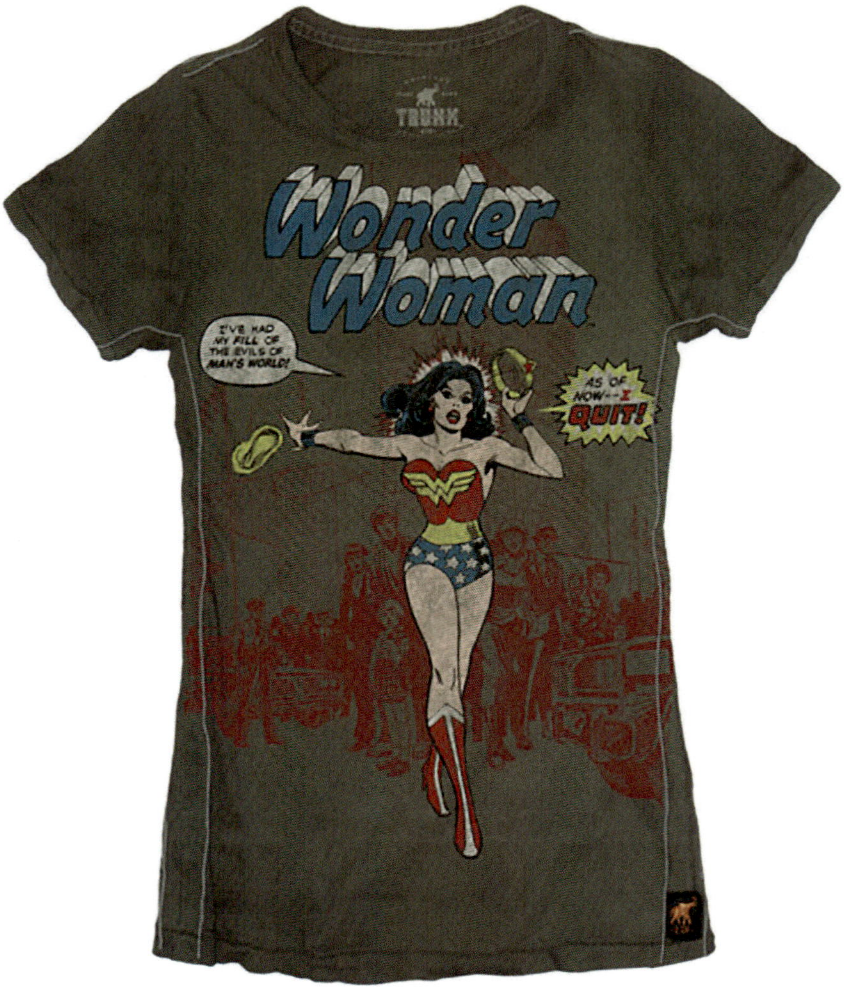

Wonder Woman t-shirt from Trunk LTD

subculture of apparel design. There are lots of sub-categories to this that are style based whether it's punk (**Obey**), tattoo culture (**ToDieFor**), or hip-hop (**Bape**)." For some inspiration check out: **Karmaloop.com**

Retro, Vintage, Nostalgic

Retro, vintage, worn — whatever you want to call it — has been big the past few years. There are new garments being made intended to look like they were pulled out of an attic 30 years ago. They feel and look like they've been washed a million times. The designs often recycle bands from decades past like AC/DC or other nostalgic ephemera like TV shows, games, and logos from the childhood of young adults currently their 20s. See **Trunk LTD** .

However, "grunge" has been a pretty sustainable trend that has evolved and matured the past 10–15 years. It's an effort to "humanize" the typical clean look that digital software gives us. There are different variations such as destroyed designs, grungy fonts, ink splatters, noise and dust, and effects that simulate offset or screen

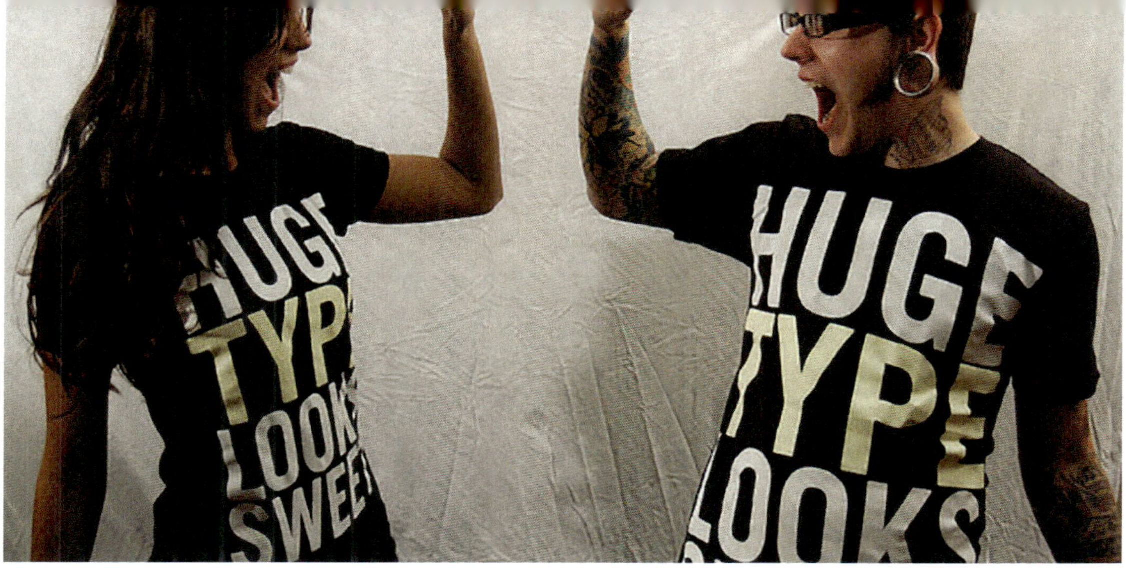

This shirt by Matt McInerney was a clever play on the big type trend.

printing techniques. I think we're starting to see more controlled and subtle usage of grunge, but it's not going away. With **Machine Wash Filters**, **Textures**, and **Grunge Vectors/Brushes**, it's become incredibly easy to make something look dirty or worn.

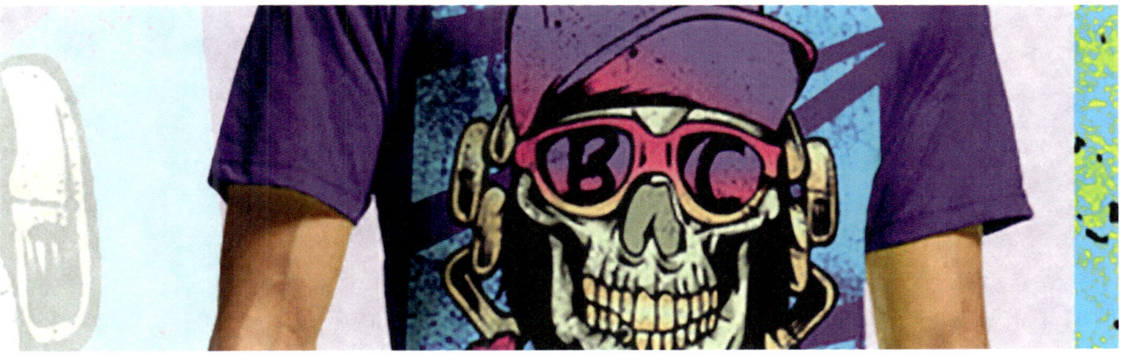

BrokeN-CYDE shirt designed by Kyle Crawford

Typography Tees

There was a **sudden rise** of minimalist t-shirts with a focus on type. The tees would often convey a straightforward message like "**Huge Type Looks Sweet**" or something equally profound. However, **Ugmonk** has risen to popularity with his single-letter tees.

Neon Colors

The use of neon and bright colors like "Jim Phillips on methamphetamines" as Angryblue put it, has been an overwhelming trend. With the popularity of dancy-screamo-rap bands like BrokeNCYDE, we saw a sea of splattery shutter shade zombies colored in all sorts of bright, glow-in-the-dark inks.

Dan Mumford has inspired many with his intricately drawn illustrations.

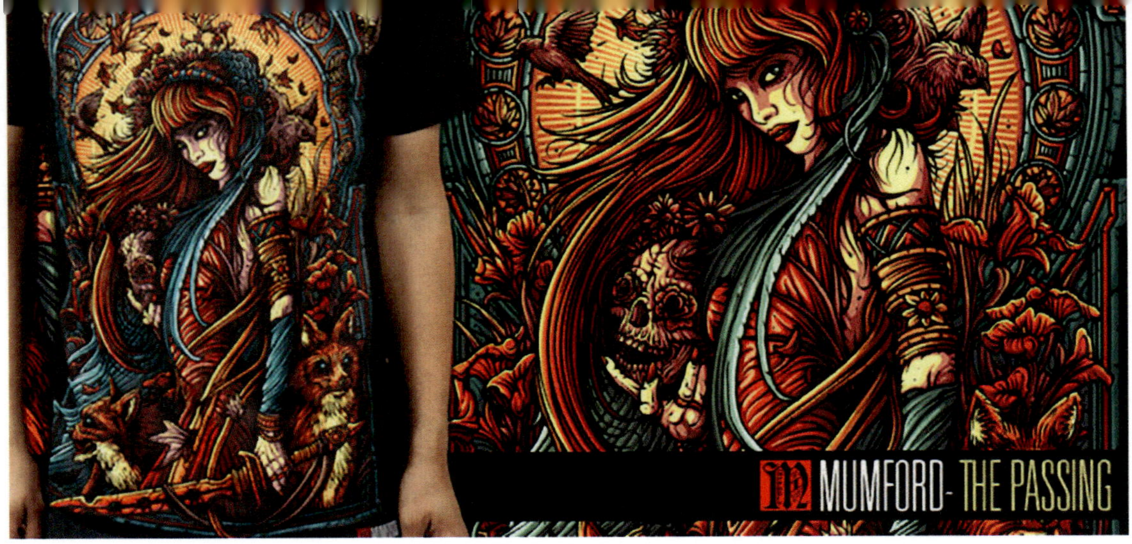

Heavy Illustration

The past few years saw a rise in extremely heavy illustrated t-shirts. Just about every popular shirt on Emptees was an elaborate drawing. Artists were one-upping each other seeing who could get even more detailed. The designs featured lots of figure drawing, advanced lighting, texturing, shading, etc. It was as if artists were creating full page comic book covers and putting them on a shirt. This trend saw a lot of talented artists like **Dan Mumford** and **Godmachine** take off. They were using the t-shirt as a platform to showcase their artwork and were getting lots of love and exposure for it.

The Hand-Drawn Look

This trend seemed to come and go rather quickly. A combination of "anti-digital" efforts and the popularity of **Napoleon Dynamite**, the cute hand-drawn look took off. The "bad-on-purpose" look was exploding. We also called this trend the "3rd grader art" trend.

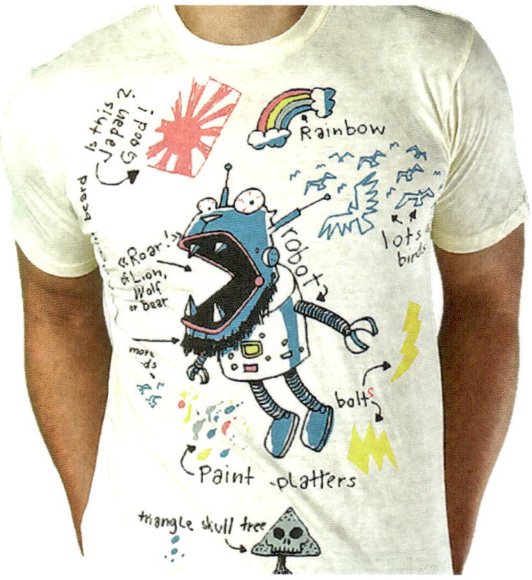

"Perfect Tee" by Sven Palmowski which won at DesignByHümans. It features a collage of overused hand-drawn elements in a cute and clever way.

Zombies, Horror, Gore

As far as subject matter is concerned, we saw LOTS of bands and indie clothing companies hiring artists to make zombies or other horror and bloody imagery. Whether it was **zombifying celeb-**

rities, or trying to **gross-out** their friends, this trend **took over**. I cannot say why blood and guts were showing up in a large percentage of designs. Perhaps some of the more talented artists grew up on horror films, and, due to their own popularity, the rest of the community followed suit.

To view websites cited in this book, please visit www.threadsnotdead.com/links.

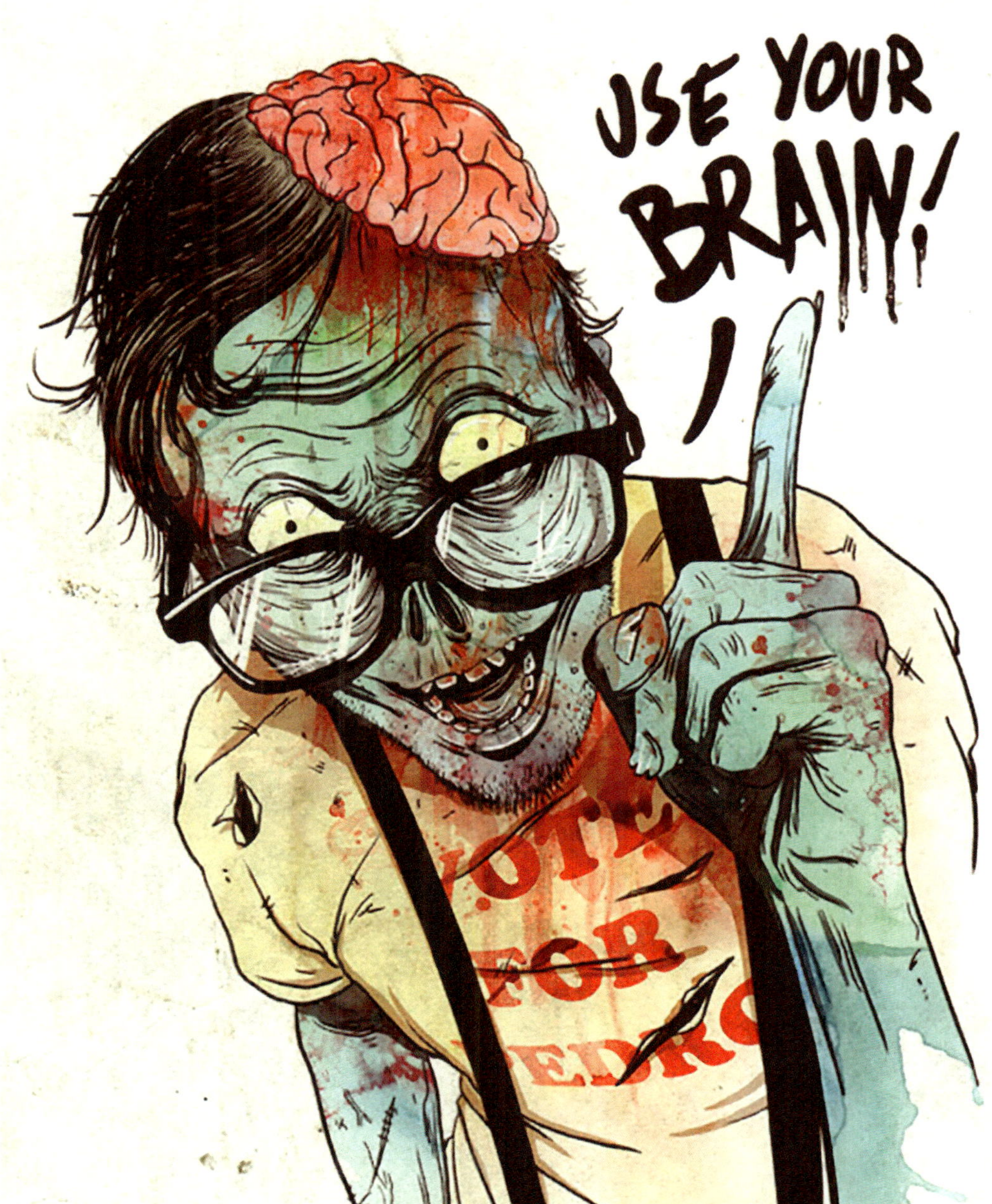

This design by Matheus Lopes won Tee of the Year on Emptees in 2010

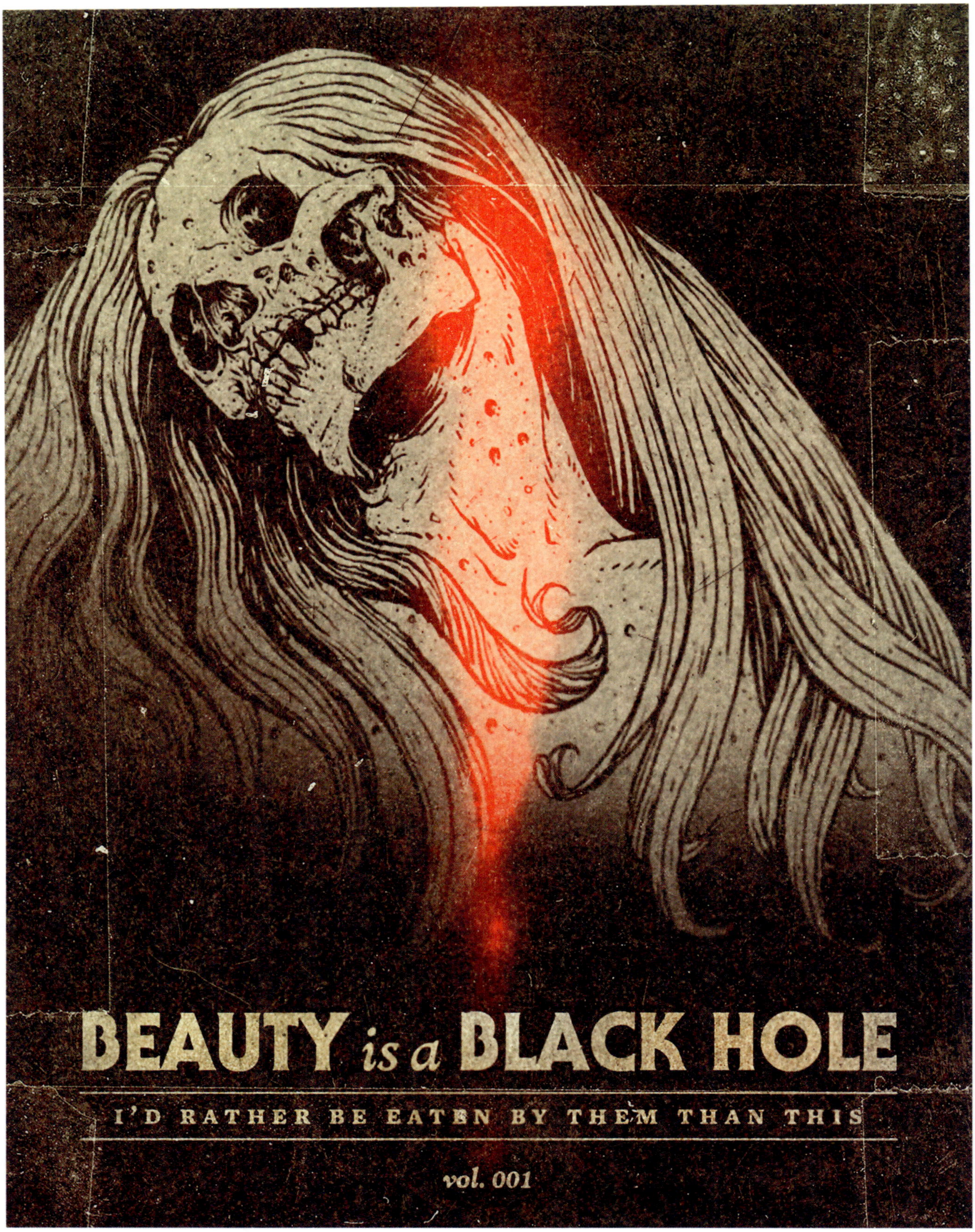

"Beauty is a Black Hole" by Jeff Finley. You can learn how to create this design in a two-hour video tutorial on Wacom Illustration Techniques available at *http://arsenal.gomedia.us*

IV

DESIGN TECHNIQUES & TUTORIALS

"Wisdom is not a product of schooling but of the lifelong attempt to acquire it" — ALBERT EINSTEIN

A Typical Shirt Design Process

People have asked what happens when I get a design project. What is my workflow like? I'm going to discuss a hypothetical project and how I would tackle it.

The Project Brief

Let's say I'm hired to create a "sick" t-shirt design for a major label metal band. Their fans also listen to Metallica, Slayer, Slipknot, and Mushroomhead. I should make something that would appeal to those fans and sell at stores like Hot Topic or

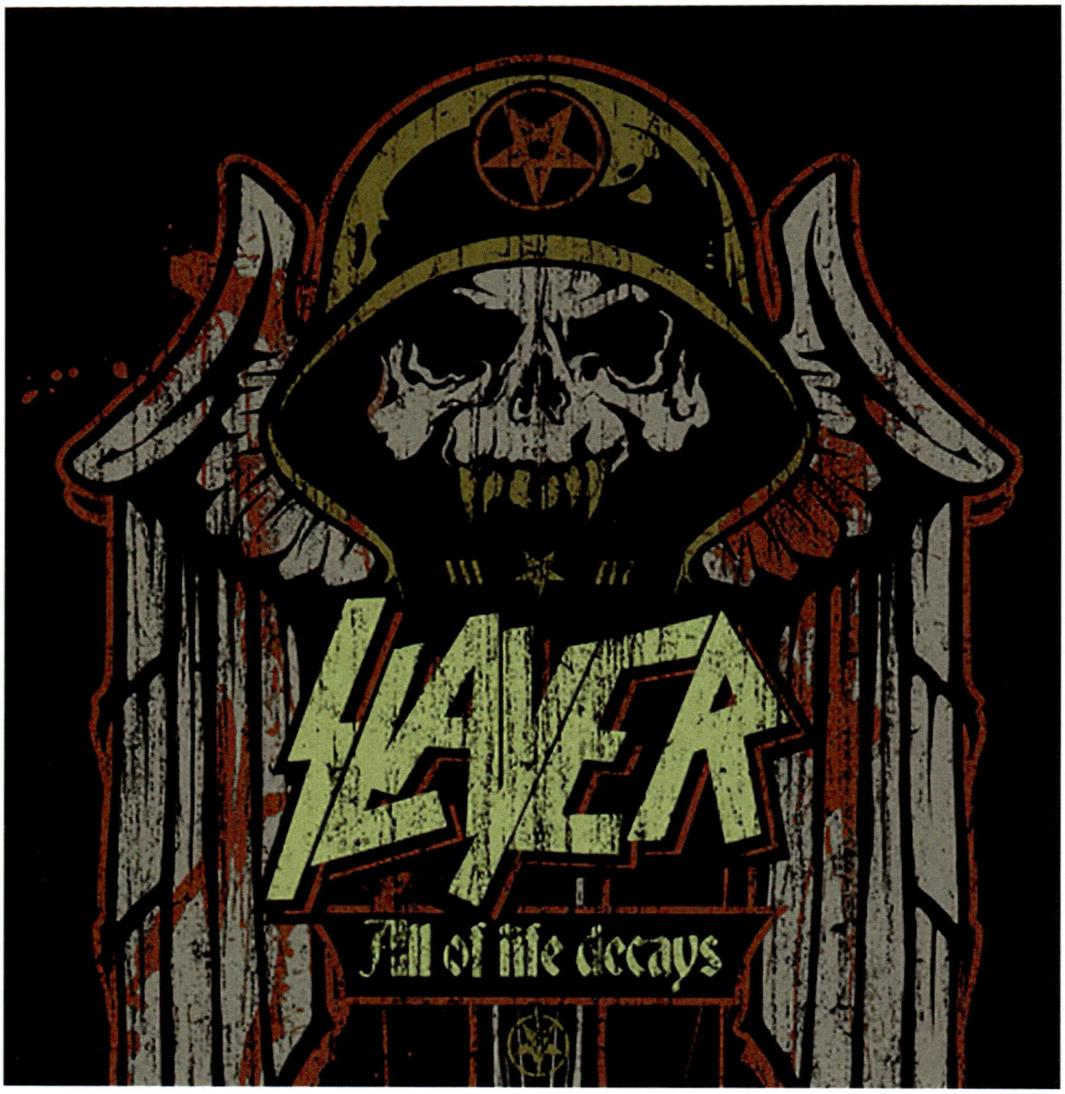

T-shirt design for Slayer by Angryblue

Spencer Gifts. I'd keep in mind the look of those bands' existing merchandise and try to stay consistent.

A Ten Step Process

1. **Get Familiar.** The first step is to get acquainted with the project and familiarize myself with the bands, fans, and the merch referenced in the brief. I don't need to be a fan of the band I'm designing for, nor do I really have to be a fan of any of the others. But I like to at least listen to the band, maybe check out some lyrics, and their previous merch to see what has been done before.
2. **Determine the Design Style.** My main responsibility is to understand the vibe and aesthetic. In this case, I'll hand draw something. What am I going to draw? My instinct tells me it's going to be dark, demonic, and scary on a black t-shirt. But I shouldn't be so quick to assume that, maybe the band wants something different. I better go back and reread their brief. Brb...
3. **Read the Brief.** OK, just read the brief and it turns out they want nothing new. OK, just like I thought. The brief says "We're not trying to reinvent the wheel here. We just want something sick that will appeal to people are into metal. You know, skulls, roses, blood, blades, etc."
4. **Assess the Budget.** At this point, I would normally talk to the client about what subject matter they want in the tee and propose some ideas. Once I have a good idea of what they want and how much they can afford, I'll get to the sketch phase. I suggest that maybe we use some of their lyrics about collecting dead birds and how it relates to a broken heart. I don't need to REALLY understand it, but I can use some of those images in my sketch. Client likes the idea, I move on.
5. **Concept Sketches.** I'll flesh out my approved idea on paper and I'll show the client. This way they can give me feedback on overall composition, the meaning, the subject matter, etc. Just for sake of this article, my sketch might be a dead bird lying on its back autopsy style with a beating heart inside. Around the design I might add embellishments like graphical spikes, flourishes, grunge, etc.
6. **Go Digital.** I like to move to the computer after the client has approved my sketch. In this stage, I will likely use my **Wacom tablet** to digitally ink my sketches. I'll gather reference material for the subject matter I am creating (in this case birds and hearts). My linework usually is black and I limit my color palette to about 3–4 colors. I might use some stock vector elements from the **Arsenal** if I'm adding in decorative vector ornaments, flourishes, tribals, etc.
7. **Post proofs and mockups.** Once I have a design finished how I like it under the budget they have given me, I'll mock up the shirts on our **photo-realistic t-shirt templates** so the client can better see how the design will look on a shirt. I've found the more realistic you can present their idea in the real world, the more approvals you'll win.

8. Revisions. Turns out the client liked the design, but they just want some color changes. So I'll go back and make those changes, log my time spent on them and show the client new revised proofs. If they hate the design (unlikely, because they already approved the sketch and concept) then we reassess the budget and how much they can afford to start over. This rarely happens.

9. Final design. They give me a final approval on the design, and then I send the invoice for the remaining hours. Once they're all paid up, I prepare the final files for print. Usually that just means organizing the PSD or AI files, saving out flattened high-res versions, etc. I don't typically do color separations for tees, we save that job for the printer.

10. Send the files. At Go Media we like to burn everything on a disc and mail the final files to the client. We also send them online via **YouSendIt**. Both ways to make sure they get the file.

That's typically how I personally work. But in reality at Go Media, we have a project manager in place who usually takes the incoming project and deals with budgets and briefs. Once that's ironed out, it's handed off to the designer who finishes the project. We have this in place so that the designer isn't worrying about closing sales on new leads and can focus on what they do best, the art.

To view websites cited in this book, please visit www.threadsnotdead.com/links.

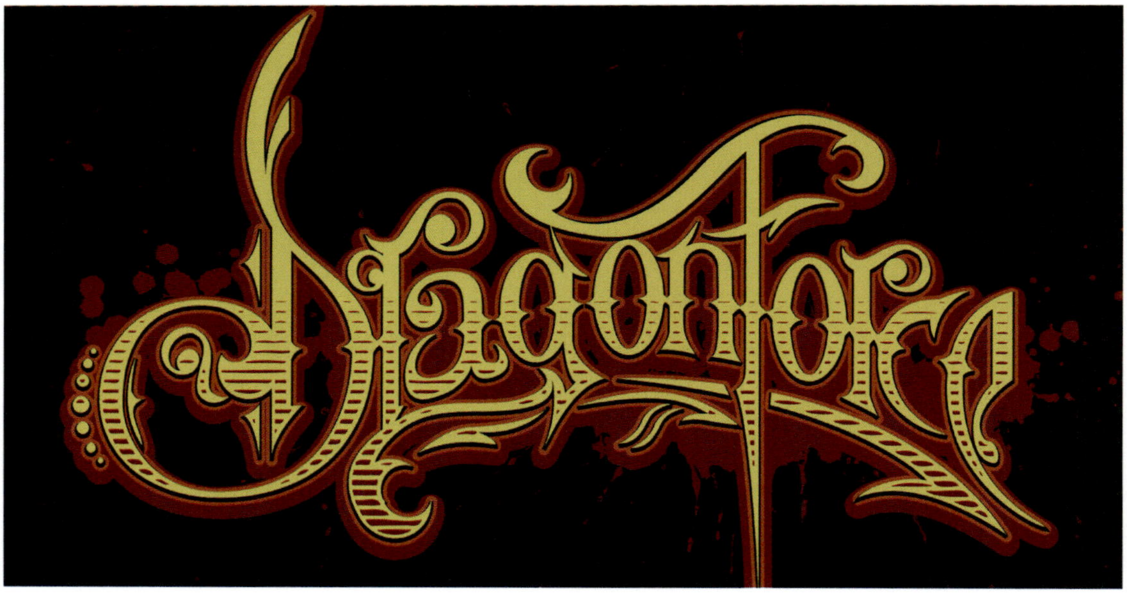

Dragonforce type treatment by Jeff Finley.Read about this technique at http://www.gomediazine.com/tutorials/old-school-type-line-gradients/

List of Design & Illustration Tutorials

Do you want to learn exactly HOW to create these designs? I want to show you! Since there's not enough room in this book to provide detailed lessons in design, here are some links to help you learn some techniques used by some of the industry's most talented artists. Most of these are FREE tutorials and some are video tutorials that you can purchase to learn more advanced illustration and texturing techniques.

Photoshop Tutorials

- Jeff Finley's Wacom Techniques
- Ray Frenden Illustration Techniques
- Designing Your Own Hoodie
- 3-color Design for Screen Printing

Vector Illustration Tutorials

- Rapid Fire Illustration Technique
- DIY Vintage T-shirts
- Vector Pinup Girl tutorial
- Create a Balanced T-Shirt Graphic
- From Sketch to Vector Illustration
- Designing SceneXcore Apparel

Lettering Techniques

- BJ Betts Custom Lettering Guides
- Ornate Lettering Process Video
- Calligraphy and Penmanship
- Ornate Lettering in AI and PS

Coloring Techniques

- Quick Tips: Coloring by Sol Amstutz
- Watercolor Effects by HeavyPrints

Distressing Techniques

- Machine Wash Filters
- Creating Screen-printing effects

Organizing Layers in Photoshop

Layer organization is important when other people (like printers) are handling your files. You don't want them to have to sort through "layer 55" or get frustrated when certain parts of your image are merged with other parts. It can get confusing.

Try to keep things separated in layers and don't flatten your layers unless you have to. However, sometimes your Photoshop files can have hundreds of layers and can be over 1 GB in file size! If that's the case, try merging common layers like overlaid textures, line art, etc. Or merge layers that have the same color if file size or complexity is an issue.

Organizing your layers in Photoshop is like tidying up your house before Mom comes to visit.

Best Practices

- **Name your layers.** Even if you only plan on having 2–5 layers in your design. Get in the habit of naming as you go.
- **Groups are your friend!** Groups are great to categorize multiple layers that make up a specific element in your design. Have a bunch of stuff making up your background? You could group your layers in Photoshop and name it "bg stuff"
- **Color coding** is useful to distinguish layers and groups from one another. Just right click on it and choose "layer properties" and select a color.

Layer Organization Tutorials:

These three links are geared toward web design, but they can still help you understand some tips and strategies for layer organization.

- **How to Effectively Organize your Photoshop Layers**
- **Helpful Photoshop Layer Organization**
- **The Photoshop Etiquette Manifesto**

Color Separation and File Prep

One of the most frustrating parts of t-shirt design is prepping your files for print. It's confusing because everyone seems to do it differently and some people don't even do it at all. When I say file prep, I mean color separation.

Most tees are screen printed one color at a time. It's important that your digital files be properly set up for this process.

However, if you're looking for the tried and true method to color separation, you cannot find it here. *(why did I buy this book?)* Truth is, I am not an expert on color separation because I happen to work with a printer that has one on staff that does it for me. But the good news is you don't have to be an expert on color separation either! But you still need to know a little bit about it. Read on.

Leaving it to the Experts

The truth is you don't HAVE to worry about color separation as much as you think. Look for a good printer who does their own color separation and file prep. We use **Jakprints** and have heard good things about **Storenvy**. Just like designers, printers do things differently too. You may find yourself giving your printer MORE work if you try to prep a file yourself and they don't like the way you do it.

For those who ARE interested in color separation and prepping files for screen print, here are some good free tutorials:

Color Separation Tutorials

- **Video: Spot Color Separations in Photoshop**
- **Full Color Simulation: 4-Color Process Separations in Photoshop**
- **How to Prepare Artwork for Screen Printing**
- **Color Separation in Illustrator**
- **Color Separation in Photoshop**

To view websites cited in this book, please visit www.threadsnotdead.com/links.

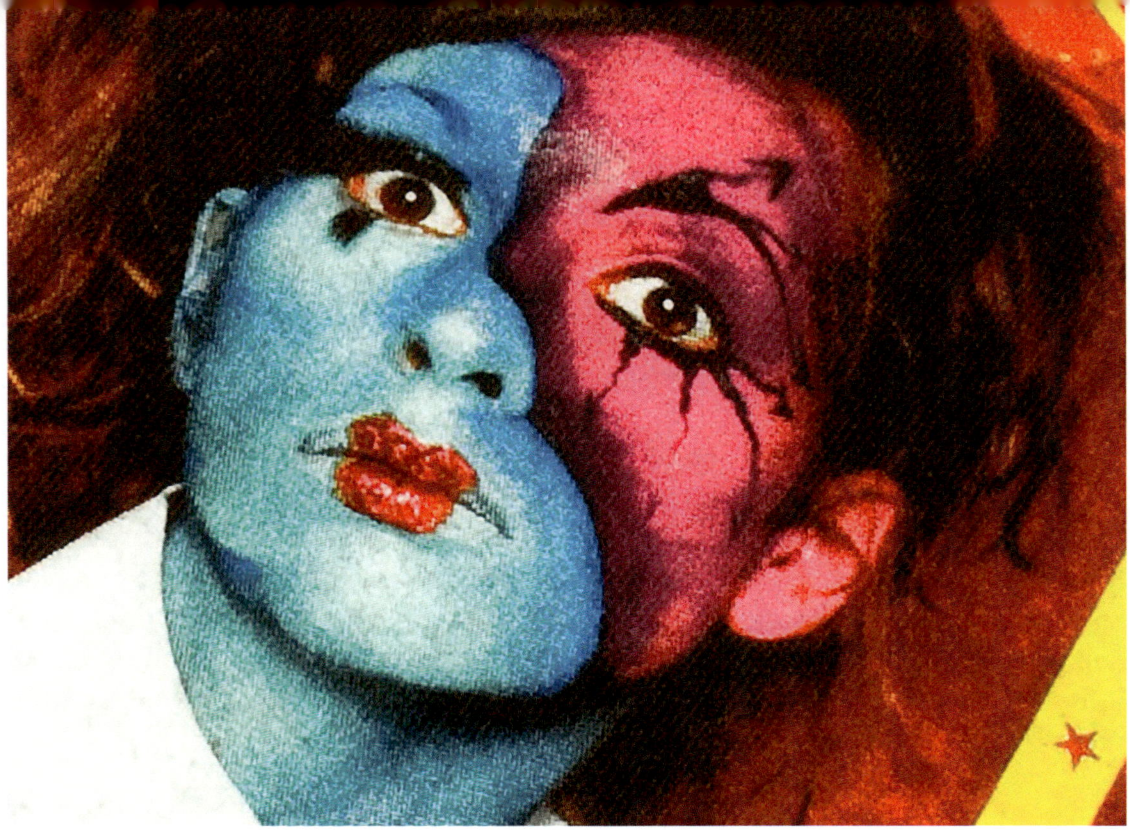

This image would be very challenging to separate and print. But it was done amazingly by Jakprints' in-house color separator LT Magnotto.

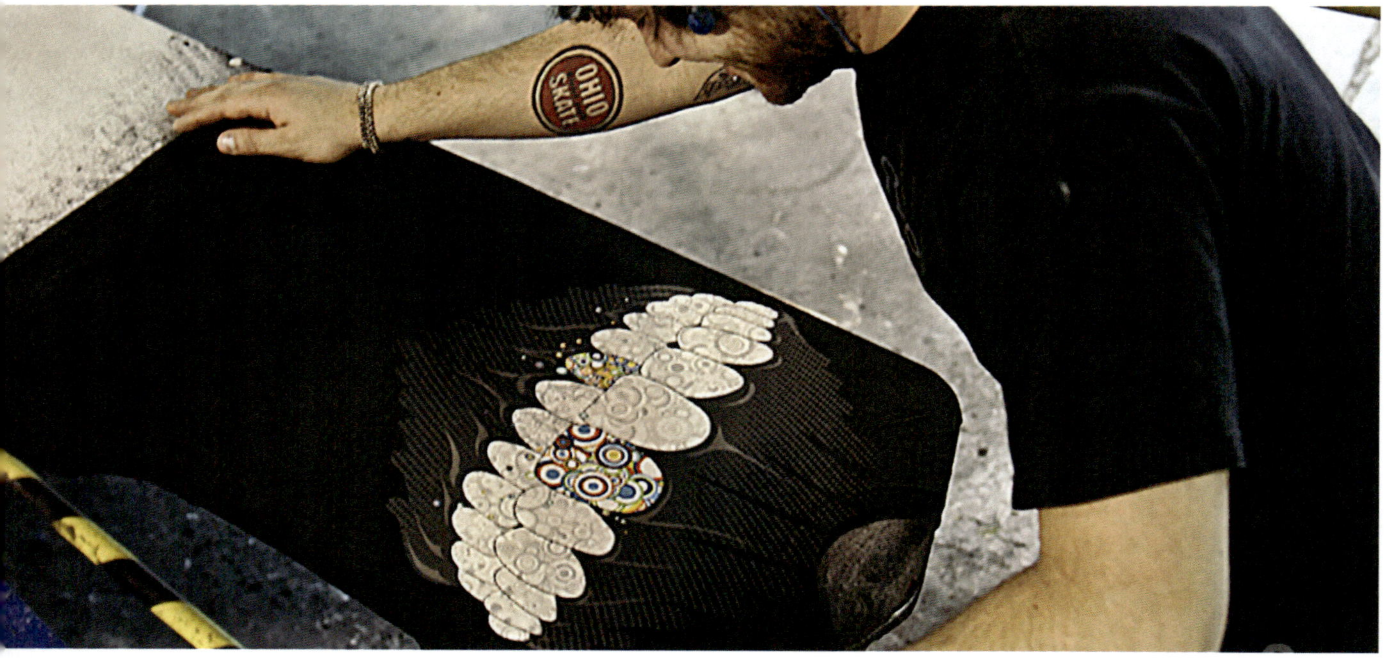

Behind the scenes at Jakprints.

The Truth about Halftones and Bitmaps

I talked with LT, the color separation ninja at **Jakprints.com**. Whenever I send over a flat JPG of my design, he's the guy that sets it up for print, and it comes out perfect. Other print shops I've worked with won't accept a flat file. If my designs are complex, he asks for the PSD or AI file and works his magic. All I know is that the prints come out amazing, even with gradients and full color. He has seen it all in his 6 years as a color separator and he will share some advice with you. This gets a little technical.

> *"My biggest pet peeve with designers who take a stab at [file prep for] printing is bitmapping! STOP IT! Bitmapped areas of designs seem to be a popular design trend. Let the professionals handle your halftoning and angles! Most designers when they bitmap an image have no clue what their printer's capabilities are. The size of your halftone dot is determining the mesh that your image can be burned on and sometimes the dots can't even be held! Your standard shop is going to be able to print in the range of 35 LPI–65 LPI. Please keep that in mind when designing with halftone dots. Any dot smaller than 65 will, more than likely, not be held on press."*
>
> *— LT Magnotto, Jakprints*

To view websites cited in this book, please visit www.threadsnotdead.com/links.

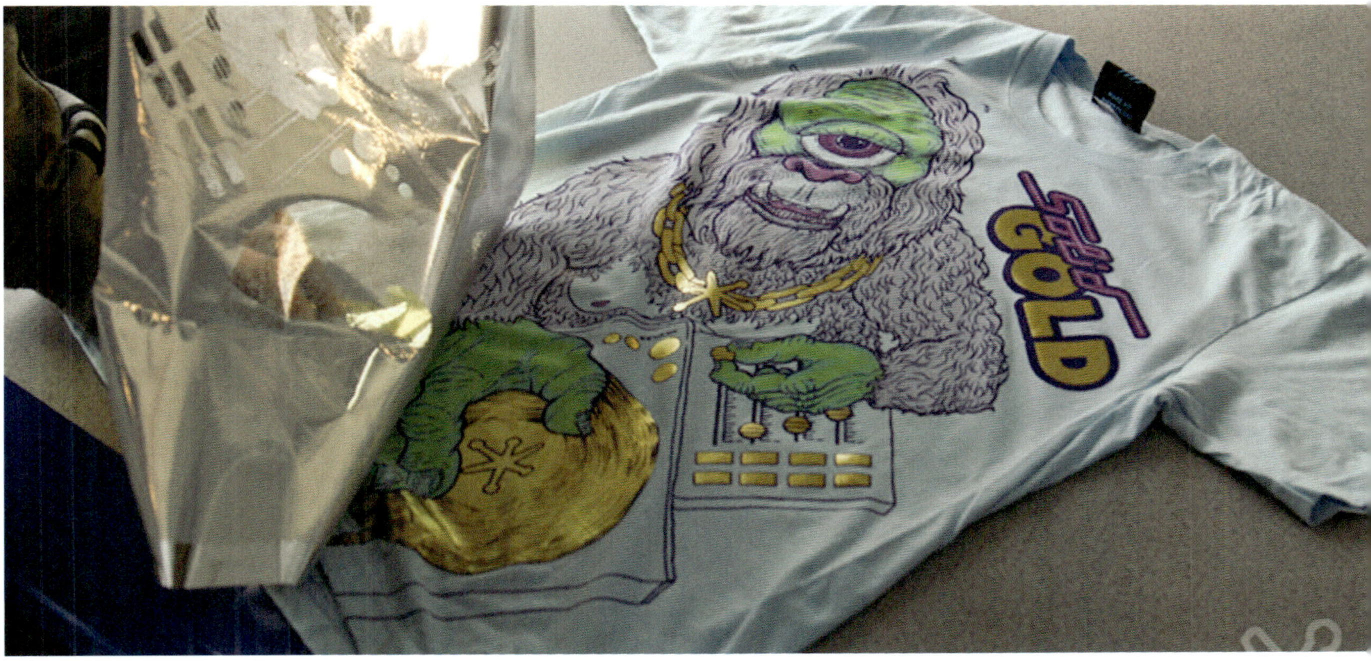

Designs by Go Media

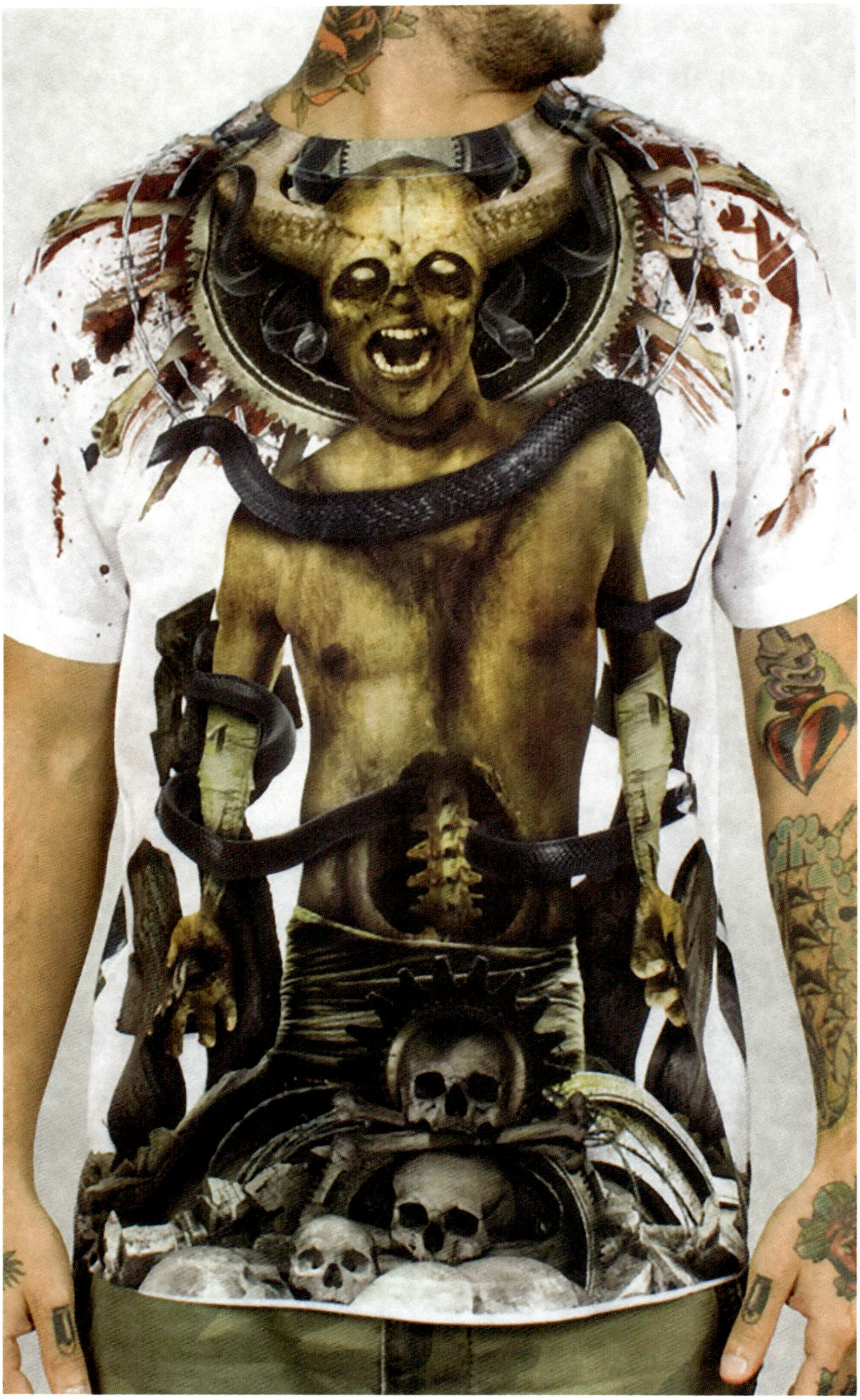

This Despised Icon t-shirt is a great example of all-over printing using Dye Sublimation.

Printed by Jakprints

V

PRINTING & PRODUCTION

Nowadays, if you can dream it, you can print it. From full color all-over prints to glittery foil jumbo prints with rhinestones and embroidery, the sky is the limit.

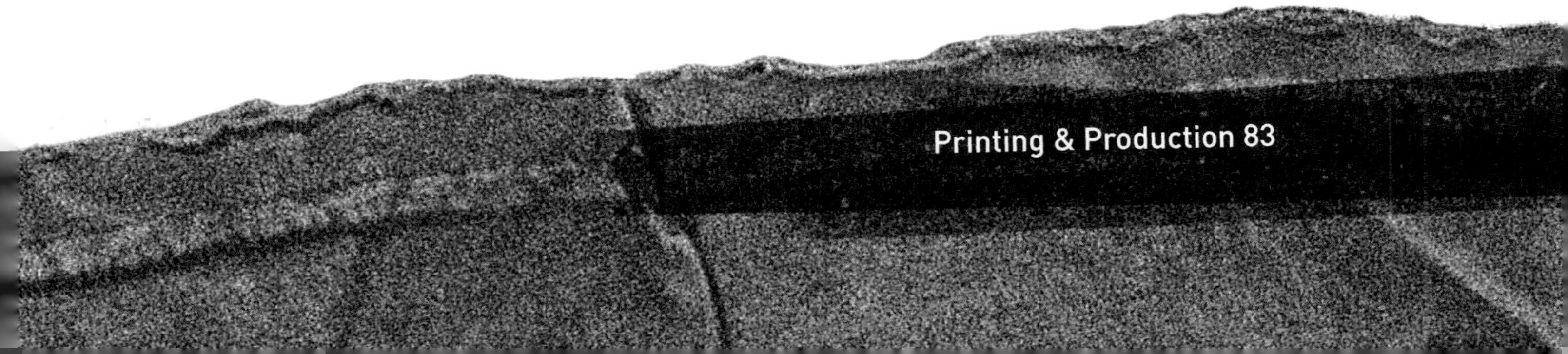

How Does My Art Get onto Shirts?

What happens to your awesome design once you send it to the printer? Do you send it off into "thin air" and a box of shirts shows up at your door a week later? Have you ever received something back from the printer and got pissed because the colors were off or the design was too small or in the wrong location? I have! And I wonder, what goes on over there?!

That feeling of sending your design off into "thin air" is a common one. To alleviate that feeling, you need to get comfortable with your printer and make friends so you can ensure your shirts come back just like you designed them. Talk to the sales reps at your print shop. Try to talk with the actual human being that is looking at your design and setting it up on the press. The idea is to understand what's happening behind the scenes so you can be more efficient and confident in your designs. And make sure to get a press proof!

So how exactly DOES your design get onto a shirt? It totally depends on the printing method. Are they **screen printing** or using some sort of **direct to garment** process? You can find a ton of information about this stuff at **t-shirtforums.com** but I'm going to outline the most common t-shirt printing methods:

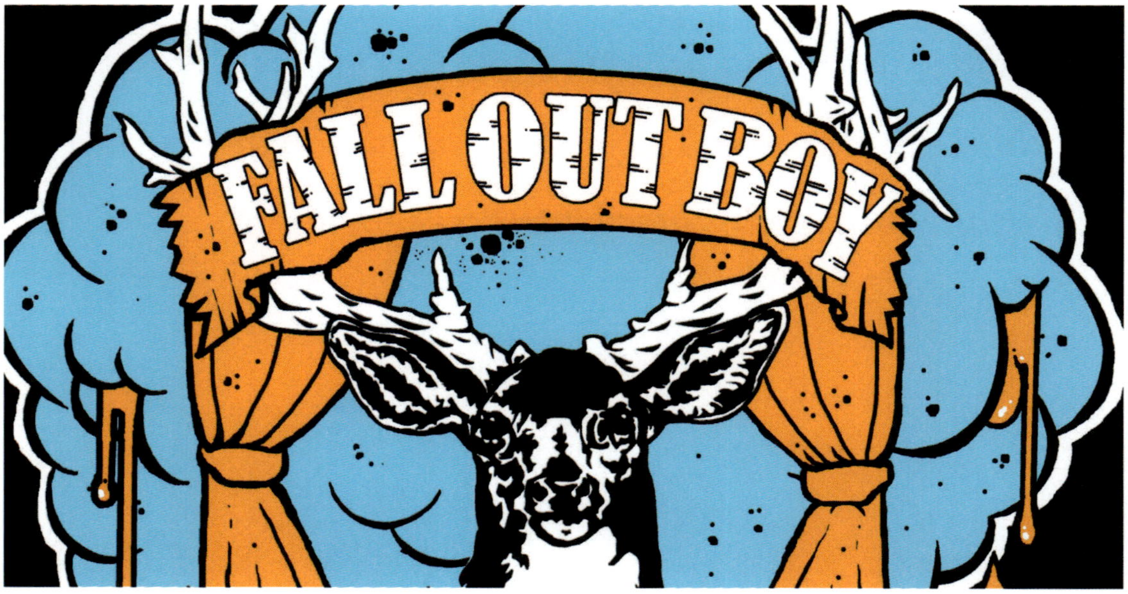

Fall Out Boy design by HorseBites

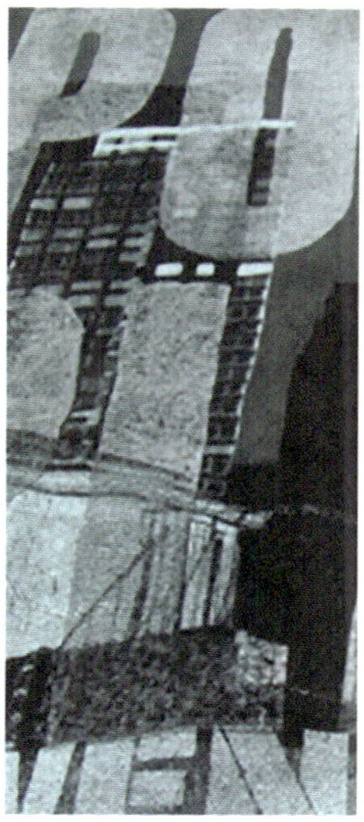

Screen Printing

This is by far the most common way your art gets onto a t-shirt. Most graphic t-shirts in retail stores use this method. The print is achieved by forcing ink through a mesh "stencil" one color at a time. There are typically limitations on how many colors you can print as well as the print size. Today, screen printing shops are working to reduce these limitations by offering full color process printing (where they print a blend of Cyan, Magenta, Yellow, and Black to simulate a full color print). They're also creating larger screen sizes to accompany the popularity of jumbo prints. Links: **Jakprints.com** and **Storenvy.com**

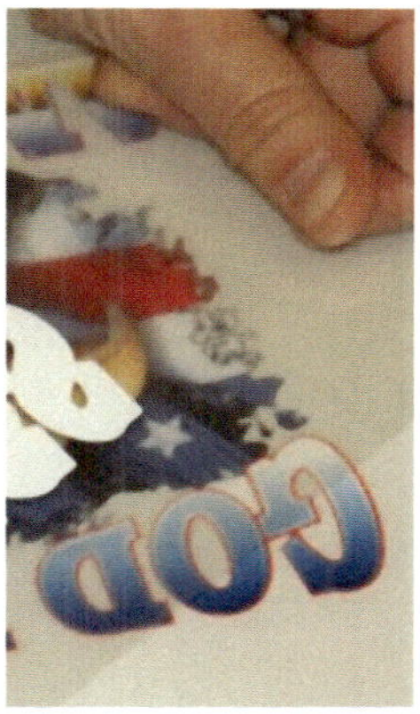

Heat Transfer

This is the classic iron-on method. Anyone can buy special paper and print designs onto it. Then an iron is used to apply heat and sort of melts the design into the t-shirt. Heat transfers can achieve full color, photo-like prints. These are ideal for one-off or small run orders. However, the prints crackle and come off the t-shirt after about 20 washes. I would reserve this method for the hobbyist. Check out these **common question**s for more info.

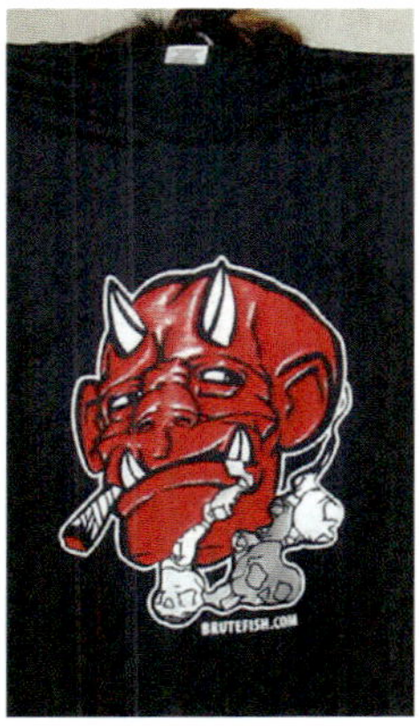

Vinyl

Another, more obscure printing method is with vinyl. A machine is used to cut out designs on vinyl one color at a time. Similar to heat transfer, heat is used to apply the cut vinyl to the t-shirt. I've never used this method myself, but from what I have heard, designs printed in this method generally do not last and are very heavy to wear. This method wouldn't be ideal for complex designs. Here's a **video tutorial** to demonstrate the process of using heat transfer vinyl.

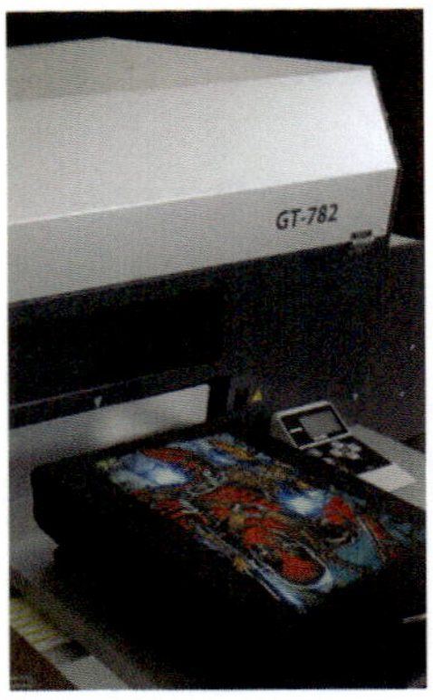

Direct to Garment (DTG)

This method of printing directly onto the t-shirt is really taking off. With the popularity of one-off printing sites like CaféPress, Zazzle, and Spreadshirt, designers are looking at this method to quickly get their designs onto shirts without a large initial investment. In fact, shirts can be printed "to-order" when a customer orders them. DTG printing methods are also being used to print onto hats and shoes and other garments.

Some are saying this is the most exciting thing to happen to the garment industry since automatic screen printing machines and dye sub (below). But for more info on DTG Printing check out **what you need to know first.**

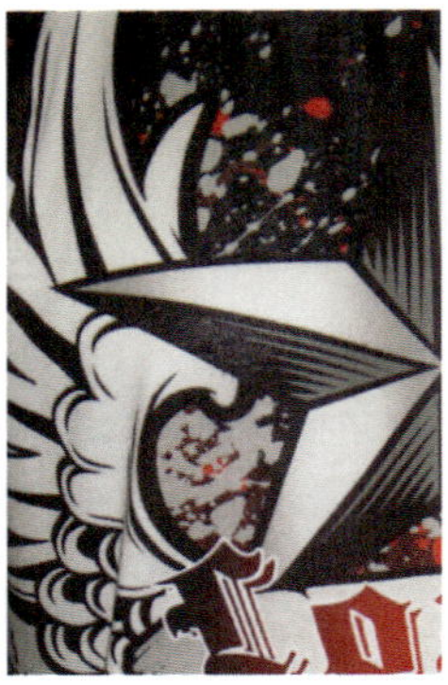

Dye Sublimation

This method is great for full-color designs and all-over prints that have "no-feel." Meaning the design feels like it's actually one with the shirt. Dye sub prints are usually on light colored garments and cannot be printed on 100% cotton t-shirts. 50–100% polyester shirts like **Vapor** brand tees yield the best results. Here are some frequently **asked questions** about dye sub.

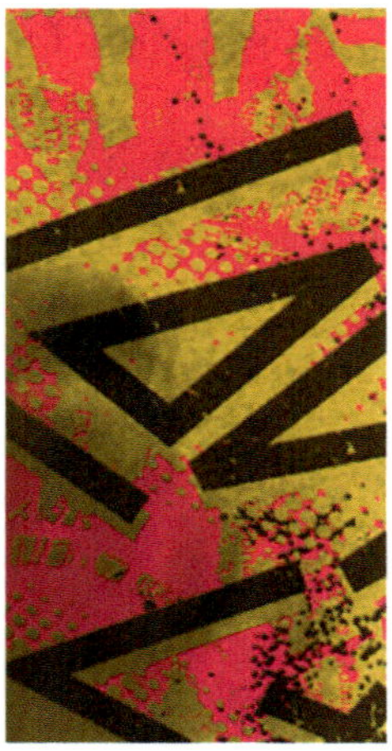

Belt Printing

This is how you get huge designs and all-over prints onto shirts. This was popular in the 70s and 80s and has seen resurgence thanks to the popularity of Affliction. Essentially, a t-shirt is laid flat on a belt and huge screens are used to print all over the front and/or back of the shirt. However, this method is less precise and each print tends to come out differently. It's great for one-color designs where registration (lining things up perfectly) is not an issue. Here's a link to a thread with **more info on belt printing** and how to get it done.

Cut & Sew

This is a pretty advanced method of getting your designs onto shirts. Your design is actually printed onto fabric first, and then cut and sewn into a t-shirt. This way you can get all-over patterns and a really custom, high-end look. Brands often send these jobs overseas. See **what people are saying** about cut and sew techniques.

To view websites cited in this book, please visit www.threadsnotdead.com/links.

Choosing the Proper Printing Method

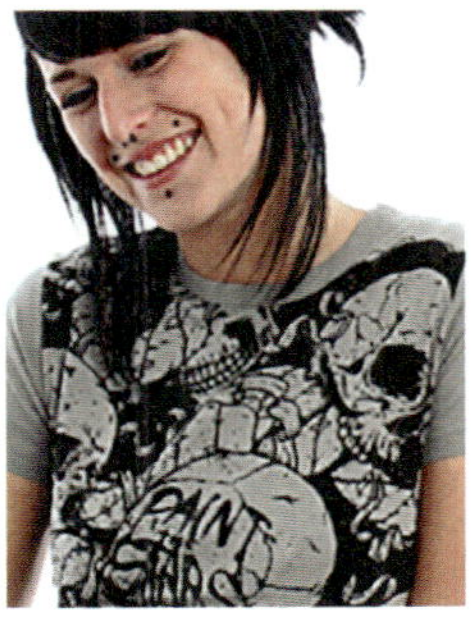

If you're confused on this, just go with screen printing. It's the default. But think about your needs — how big of designs do you need to print? What's your budget for printing? How custom or unique do you want your prints? Do you need a large run or small run? Talk with your printer and they should help you decide what's best for you.

From my experience, most people start out with screen printing and then move into more advanced techniques like Belt Printing or Cut & Sew. Today, people are often starting with DTG sites to "test" designs without having to spend money to order their initial inventory.

Definitely check out **t-shirtforums.com** to read about other people's experience with these methods and you can make your own informed decision.

The Right Blank for the Job

When you send off your design to print, you typically have to specify WHAT brand of t-shirt you want it printed on. This is as much a part of your brand as your designs. Customers are paying more attention to the fit of their tees these days. The more fashionable blank garments will be more expensive and the budget blanks are typically for audiences that are not concerned about fit or fashion. To them, a t-shirt is a t-shirt.

If you go to a printer like Jakprints, they offer a lot of different brands to choose from. If you don't specify, you might get their cheapest brand and this could result in not-so-great shirts. So pay attention!

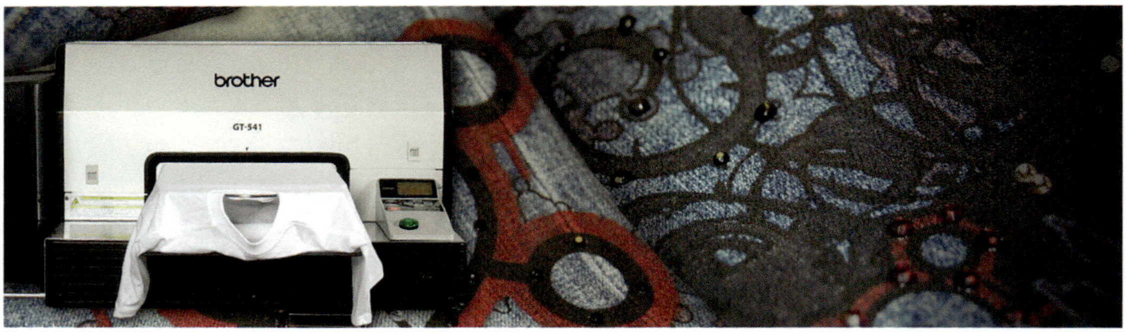

Direct to Garment printers make t-shirt printing accessible to almost anyone these days. Check out www.garmentprinter.com

Fashion Blanks

American Apparel is by far the most talked-about brand of blank garments used in the industry. They're also quite expensive. Same goes for **Alternative Apparel**. Both brands carry exceptional quality garments in a variety of colors and styles. If you're looking to be ahead of the curve, use these brands.

Bare Apparel and **JS Apparel** are also excellent, high-quality blanks. If you want something distressed or tea stained, Bare Apparel offers some great blanks to start from.

Budget Blanks:

Tultex and **Anvil** brands have a fine jersey tee that is comparable to American Apparel at a much lesser cost. I've used these when cost was a concern but I still wanted a fashionable and soft feel. Some would say they're better than AA, but that is subjective.

Hanes, Fruit of the Loom, Gildan, Jerzees, or Allstyle brands are the budget blanks. They tend to have a boxier fit and most reputable apparel brands these days do not print on these blanks. However, you'll find plenty of band t-shirts still printing on these shirts because they're so cheap.

How Many Shirts Should I Print? What Sizes?

When you're just starting out, keep it small. It's better to order less and sell out than to order more "just in case." Most newbie clothing lines print 50–100 shirts per design, which is a good start. They typically start out with 3–5 designs for their initial launch.

Something you must pay attention to when ordering your first run of shirts is sizing. If you don't say anything about sizes when you order shirts, the printer might assume you want 100 mediums or an even distribution amongst all available sizes. This won't do you any good. So what sizes should you get? Do you need sizes XS all the way to XXL? What about women's or kid's sizes?

When in doubt, order less. If you sell out, it makes you look popular.

I'll tell you what most new lines do. They go with the 1/2/2/1 ratio or the 2/3/3/2/2/1 size ratio. This breaks down to s/m/l/xl and xs/s/m/l/xl/xxl.

Let's say you order 144 shirts for your initial line. That would be 24s, 48m, 48lg, and 24xl. Or the other option would be 24xs, 36s, 36m, 24l, 24xl, 12xxl.

Generally you want to order more S, M, and L sizes but it also depends on your audience. Are they young teens who are typically fit or slim and like their shirts tight? Get a larger amount of smaller sizes. If they like their clothes baggy, get a larger proportion of bigger sizes. Your first run is an experiment; you might not really know what sizes people are buying until they start buying. You could also try doing a pre-order first to see what sizes people select and then adjust your print quantities that way.

Extras: Foil, Flocking, and Other Embellishments

There's a lot more to tees than just ink and a t-shirt. Dave from Paint the Stars explored these extras as a way to stand out from the crowd. "We figured that if we put more emphasis on custom garments and pushing the boundaries of the production process, then it would give us an edge and would make us harder to imitate."

There are lots of specialty applications and printing methods you can experiment with for your line. I had a chat with Dave Woodall of **Amb3r** and he gave me a rundown of some of the most popular techniques.

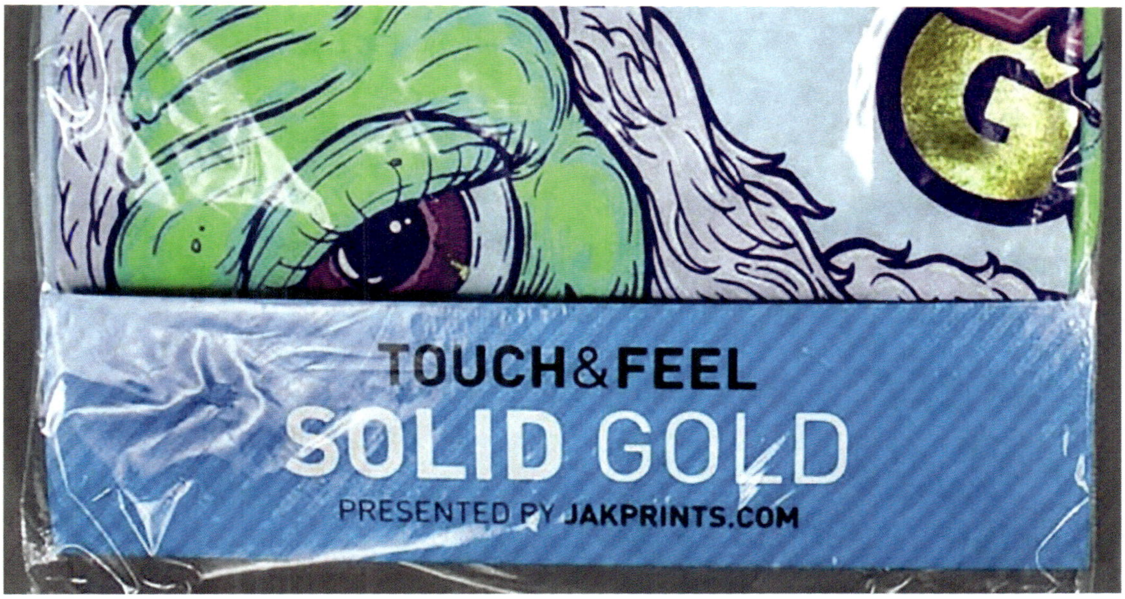

"Solid Gold" designed by Adam Law of Go Media for Jakprints features gold foil

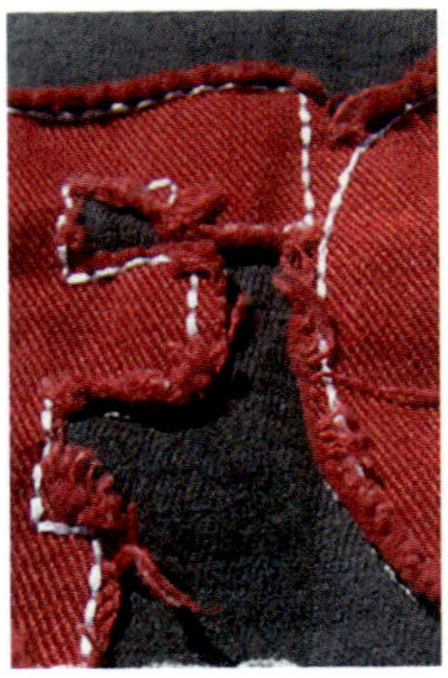

Appliqué

This is a generic term for sewing fabric on a shirt. Attached with embroidery and also helps cost by lowering the number of stitches. Fabrics have different characteristics to the style you're trying to achieve should influence which fabric you choose. For example, cotton twill fabric will fray when washed, giving it a vintage look. While felt fabric remains intact, it can have a more athletic or sturdy look.

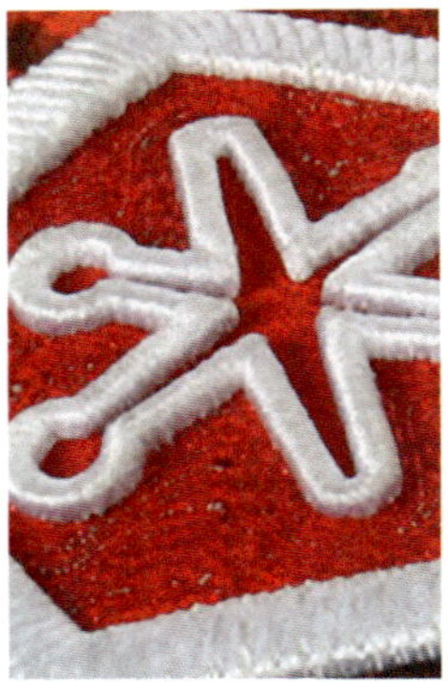

Thread

More commonly called embroidery. However embroidery has a more traditional style associated to it. When we say thread, it gets the vendor to listen to the effect and style we are trying to achieve. Threads can be used in tight and loose stitches. The most important person is the digitizer who will make your design come to life or kill the essence and move onto the next job...

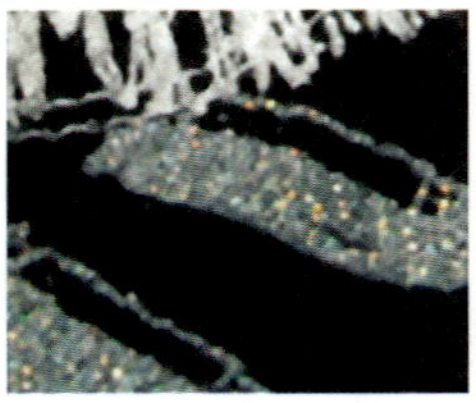

Crystalina Ink

This is a glitter-like application that gives some sparkle to the design. This is not a part of the ink but applied on top. Some flaking will happen when washed.

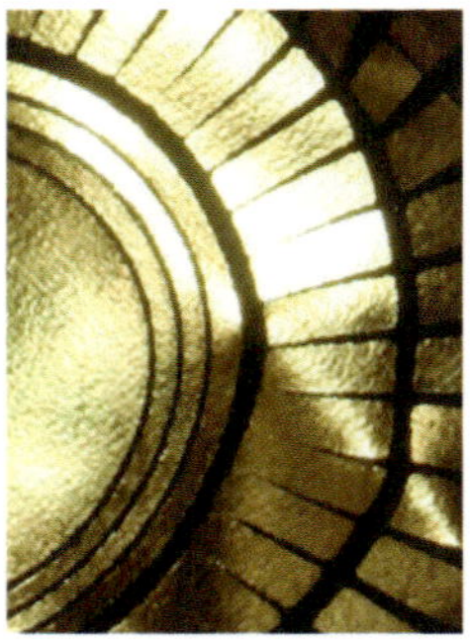

Foil Transfer

This process uses a shiny paper-like transfer available in many colors and variations such as black, blue, copper, holographic, and many more. It uses a heat press to add foil paper to a screen printed design. Works best with one color prints or water-based inks unless a "foil resist" is added to the other plastisol inks.

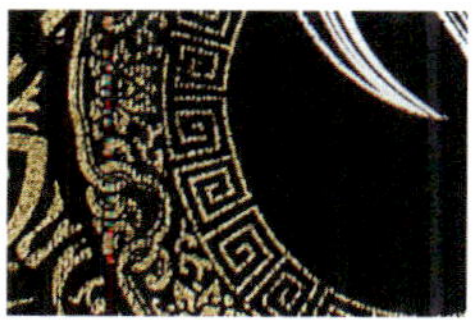

Metallic Ink

Similar to foil ink but a little more matted. An economical alternative to foil.

High-Density Ink

High-Density printing gives a three-dimensional effect and allows you to add texture and depth to a print. This ink has a raised feel with crisp edges. Specialty screens and production skills are needed for this process.

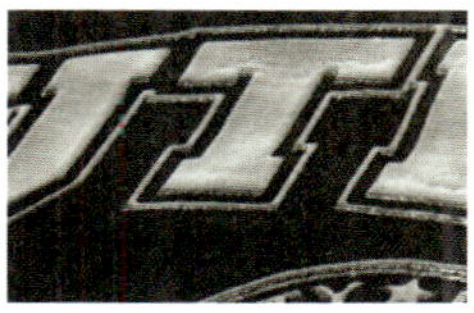

Gel Ink

Gel prints are high gloss or “wet looking” prints that have a raised feel to them. Gel ink is clear plastisol and printed.

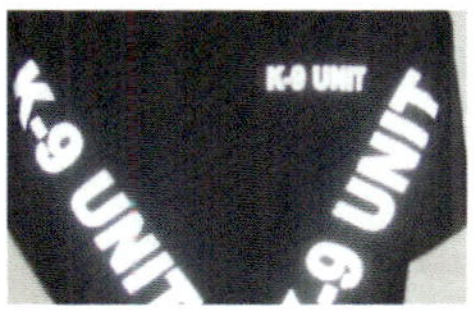

Reflective Ink

Reflective ink is a plastisol-based ink which has a reflection once a light source is shined on it.

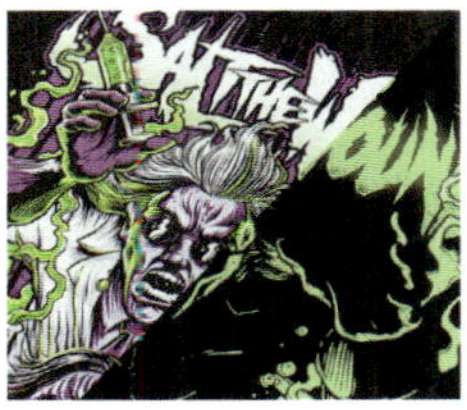

Glow-in-the-Dark Ink

Translucent Ink that glows in the dark or under black light. It has a soft green hue in the light, but goes undetected until the lights go out.

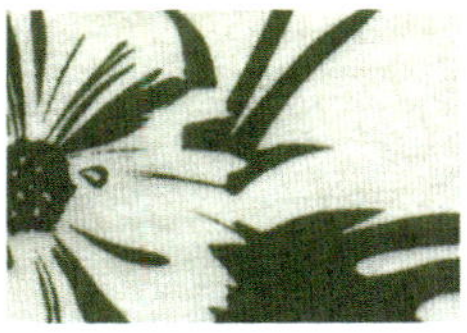

Eco-Friendly Inks

Water-based, PVC-free, and formaldehyde-free inks that have a low impact on the environment.

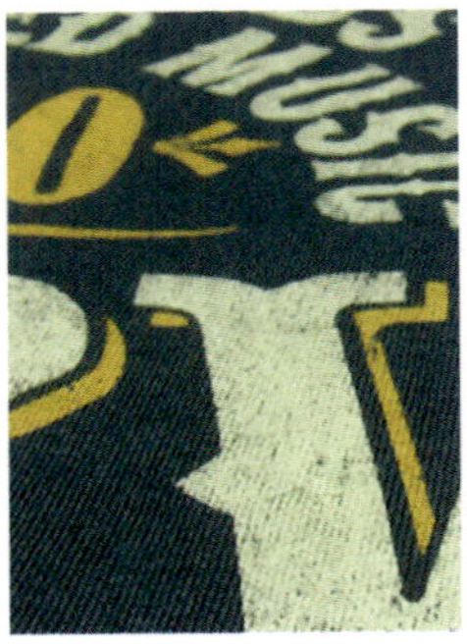

Soft Hand Additive

Soft hand plastisol inks are made through a process of mixing an additive to plastisol inks to reduce the coverage area. This is the closest option to a softer print other than water-based inks. (Note: With the ink being plastisol base, there is variation in touch depending on how crisp and detailed the artwork is as well as garment color).

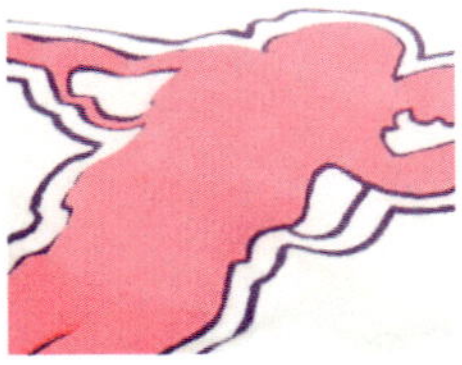

Puff Additive

This is the least expensive way to generate a print that gives you the 3D raised feel and look. An additive is combined with plastisol inks to give it a soft puffy feel.

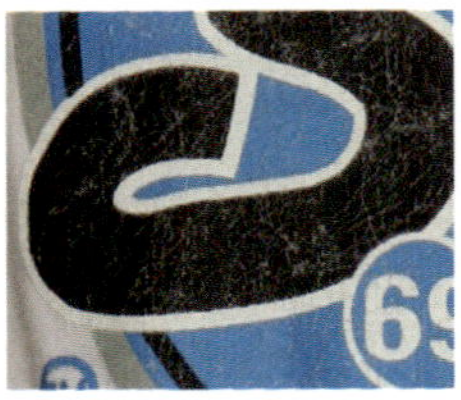

Crackle Additive

A special additive to inks that creates a washed aged look after drying. Slight tugging of the garment assists in the cracking process.

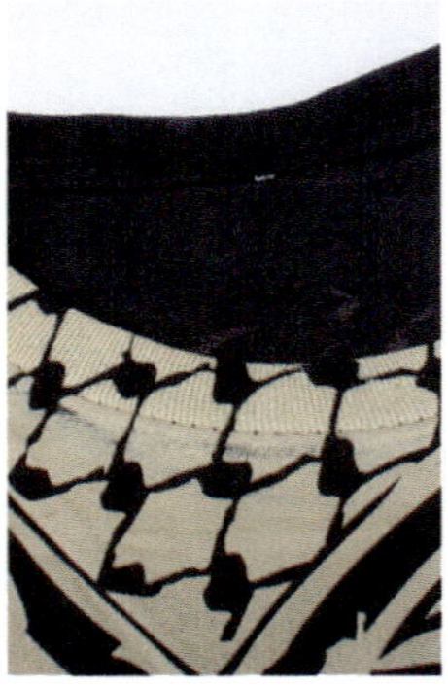

Discharge

Discharge printing is a technique of printing that removes the pigment of the garment to its natural color (off white). Discharge is a water-based ink that it blends with the fabric fibers giving a no-hand feel after washing. It's also "not eco-friendly" as LT from Jakprints reminds us. He says, "Some brands of discharge ink have formaldehyde in it to keep if from exploding."

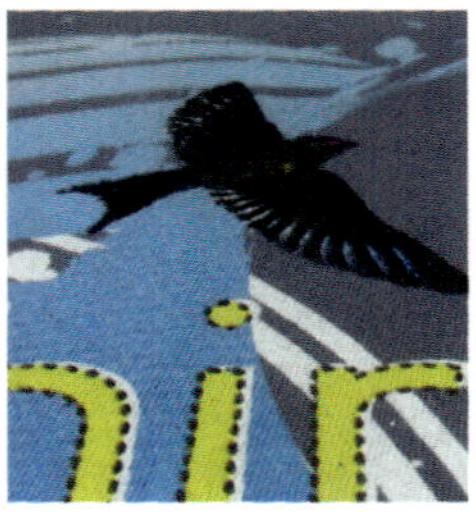

Flock Transfer (or Direct Flock)

A soft fuzzy surface application, similar to velvet or felt, available in a variety of colors. Goes on in two different processes (Direct & Transfer) Direct is a more labor and equipment intensive custom approach.

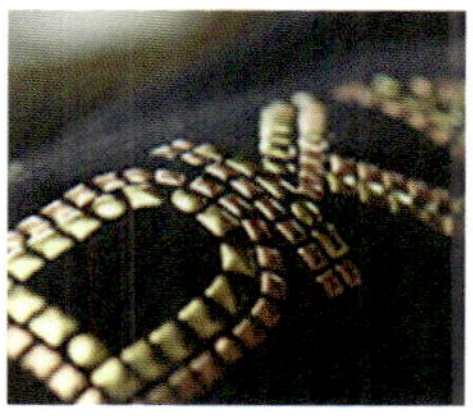

Rhinestones & Nailheads

Stones or studs that are heat-fixed to a garment in a specific pattern or for accenting a design giving it a higher quality look.

If you're looking for these specialty printing processes, a good place to start is ***www.jakprints.com, www.amb3r.com,*** *or* ***www.variantart.com***

Common Screen Size options

- Regular — Varies but average is 14" wide by 16" tall
- Oversize — Varies but average is 21" wide by 30" tall
- Jumbo Winged — 25" wide (shoulder) x 21" wide (body) x 31" (tall)
- Belt — 42" x 44" Few printers have these.

To view websites cited in this book, please visit www.threadsnotdead.com/links.

What's it Gonna Cost Me?

If you're starting your line, you can't really avoid some of the typical startup costs involved. But try not to let these get in your way. You can do a lot for free these days or for no up-front cost. I am going to outline the approximate costs of what you might expect when starting a line.

But first, ask yourself how serious you intend to get with your line? Most designers start a line on a whim or as another way to promote their own work. Some of those designers find they enjoy the business of building a brand and growing the t-shirt line beyond just a kickin' side project. And a small number of those end up taking it to the next level — like getting into retail or setting up their own brick and mortar storefront.

You could call those three stages the side project, indie brand, and professional brand. The thought process is much different behind starting a side project with little to no up-front costs vs. starting a professional brand with retail expectations right off the bat.

No matter which way you think, you have to start somewhere. And most people have no money and no resources to do so. But thankfully, it is pretty easy to start a line these days. Here are some of the most common expenses you'll incur as you start out.

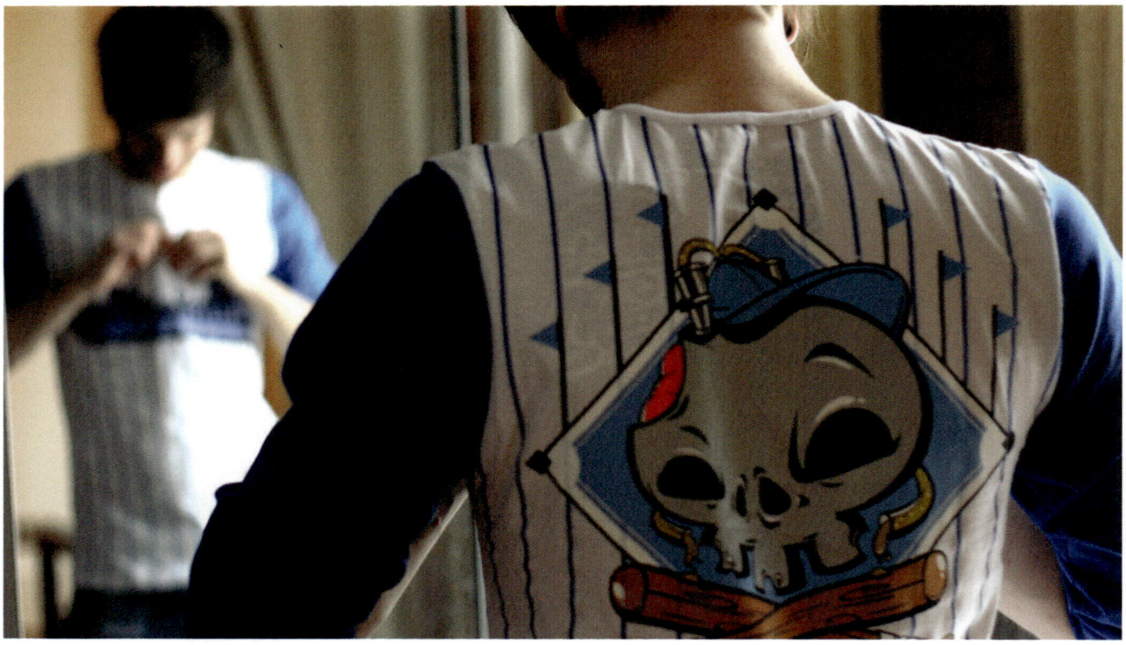

Beerhat Skull Placket tee by Paint the Stars

Side Project Startup Costs: $0–$300

You could potentially start a clothing line for free. You design a few tees yourself and mockup product shots using **shirtmockup.com**, upload them to **Spreadshirt, Zazzle, CaféPress**, or other **on-demand sites**, and tell your friends on Facebook. Bam, you've done it, you now have a line of tees! Perhaps you know a friend who screen prints or you want to spray paint your own tees with stencils and other DIY methods. If you just want to please your friends and family, this is totally cool!

Indie Brand Startup Costs: $500–$10,000

You are in this realm if you're looking at ordering at least 50 t-shirts of a single design from a printer like Jakprints or Storenvy. You could probably get some good quality shirts on American Apparel for about $6–10 per tee.

Serious brand owners know that they get what they pay for. Free or cheap isn't always the best option so research and choose wisely.

You care about good designs and good branding and will either spend lots of time doing it yourself (because you're already a great designer right?) or will collaborate or hire other talented designers to do it for you. Successful indie brands are comfortable paying $500+ per design to make sure their line is legit.

Indie brand owners generally have their own websites and that is at least $100/year for domain and hosting. They can also expect to budget about $3,000–$10,000 for a custom website. These brands are typically selling and shipping their own tees with e-commerce solutions like Big Cartel, Storenvy, IndieMerchstore, Magento, Zen Cart, etc.

There are also some minor fees with accepting payments with PayPal or credit cards, sales tax, shipping rates, etc. Those fees are typically a small percentage of the money you make on each transaction.

Selling offline gets a little pricey. You could haul your inventory to shows and events but you will likely have to pay for travel expenses, exhibitor fees for setting up a booth, etc. If you're traveling and selling offline, you'll also need more printed swag like flyers, buttons, stickers, and other freebies.

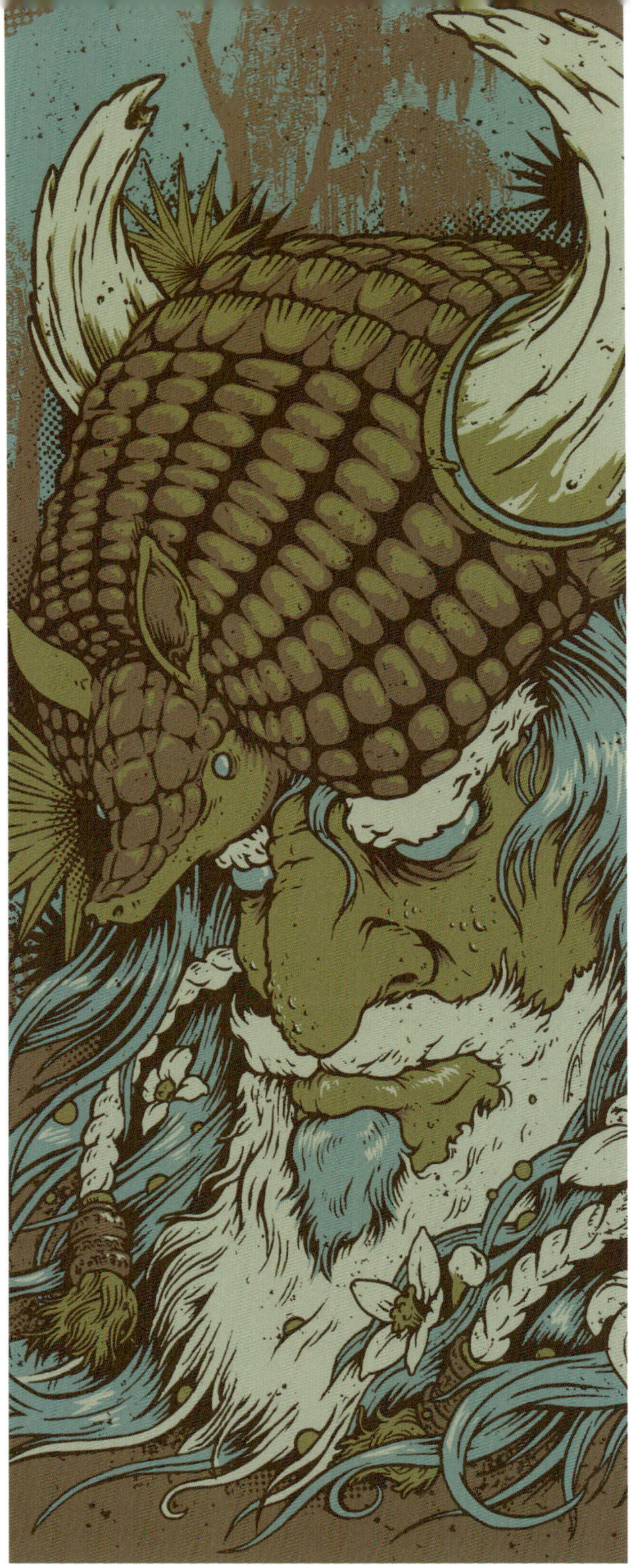

"Swamp Viking" Design by HorseBites for Saulvation

Serious indie brands also need to consider advertising costs. While a lot of advertising is done free via word of mouth and hustling, you might want to look at shelling out $3,000+ for a full-page ad in your customer's favorite magazine. Printing flyers, business cards, and other advertising collateral can be costly but it helps build even more awareness for your brand.

Professional Brand Startup Costs: $25,000+

This is where the big boys and girls play. Most of you reading this probably aren't at this level and might not even want to be. These days, it's incredibly rewarding to build an indie clothing brand, but to take to the pro level requires lots of business savvy, not to mention time, money, and commitment. Three things a lot of designers don't have much of. We're often busy as hell, broke, and distracted by so many creative ideas it's hard to commit to anything for a long time.

But if your indie brand is really taking off and money is flowing, there are many ways to spend it. You could start looking at renting space in a downtown shopping district to give yourself that street presence of a "real" brand. You could look into spending more money on advertising for longer periods of time, sponsoring celebrities or big events, or hiring famous designers to develop products for you.

Any professional brand likely has employees that need a good salary and benefits. Taxes are a bigger issue and you'll need good lawyers and accountants. If you're big, you might even need to hire PR firms or Ad Agencies to handle these aspects of your brand so you can focus on the bigger picture. What about franchising your brand and opening multiple stores across the country? What about globally? What about sub-brands to target different markets?

Don't Be Overwhelmed

As you can see, this stuff can get costly! Most of us aren't there yet, so don't worry. Every one of the brands you see at the mall had to start somewhere. **Mark Ecko** has an **inspiring story** about how he started out small by airbrushing tees for his friends in high school and how he was able to turn that into a big-time brand.

To view websites cited in this book, please visit www.threadsnotdead.com/links.

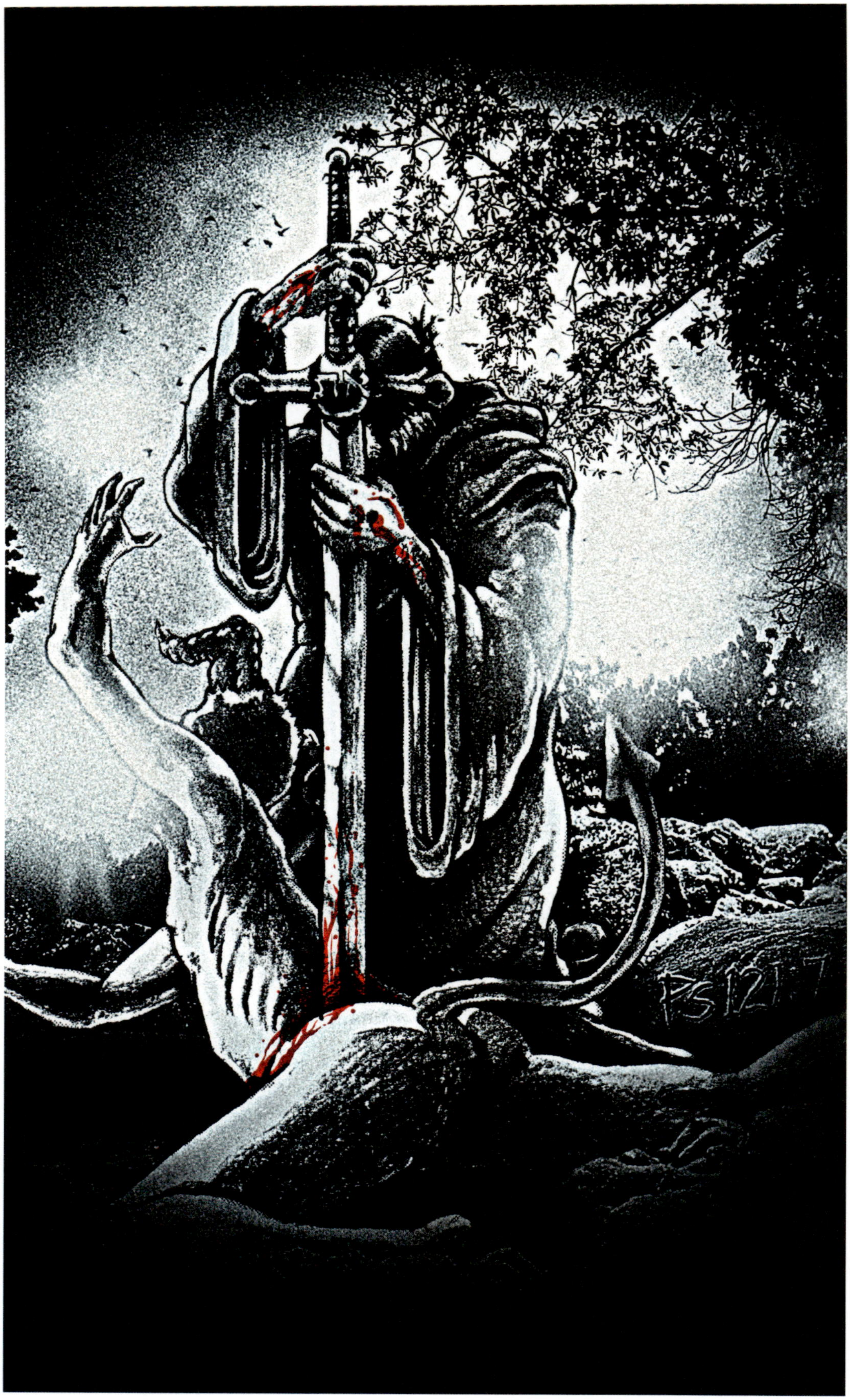

Design by Jeff Finley for Disciple Clothing

VI

BRANDING & MARKETING

"Right now, everything is changing too fast due to digital culture. The fashion experience needs to once again become exclusive and personal."

— DAVID GENSLER, PRESIDENT, THE KDU

Branding Fundamentals

It's a common misconception that a brand is a company's logo. That's just part of it. Some experts say that a company's brand is the "gut feeling" in their audience. The brand is actually a combination of all experiences that a person has with a company. When you think of every interaction as "branding" you can begin to shape the way people feel about your company in a natural way. I'm going to give you some advice to make sure your brand is on point.

Consistency is Key

The most important thing in branding is consistency. You need consistency in your designs, website, packaging, and social media presence. You need consistency in the way you talk to customers, how you answer the phone, what your email signa-

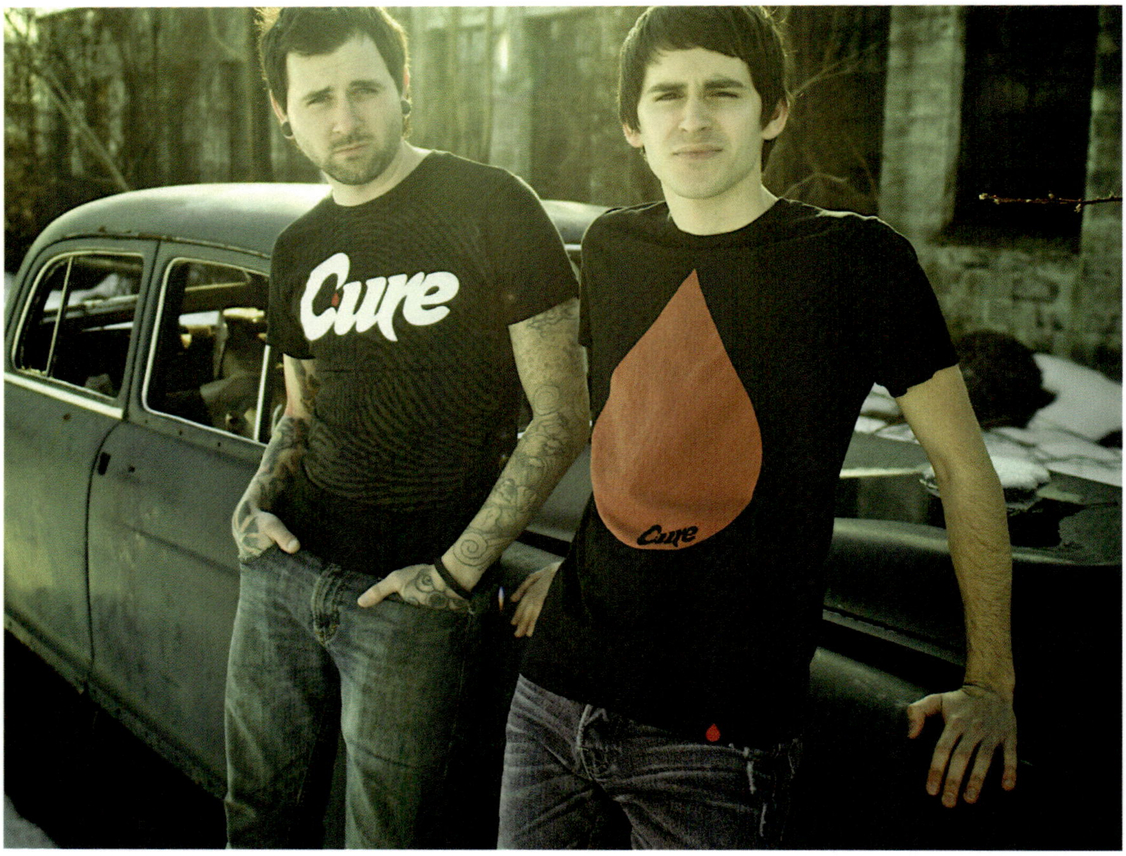

Cure Apparel started from scratch in 2008 and is a great example of a t-shirt startup

ture says, and the verbiage on your website, etc. The number one thing to remember is you are setting and meeting customer expectations.

Cure Apparel Does it Right

For instance, Kelly Kiernan at **Cure Apparel** has type 1 diabetes. He started a line because he wanted to help "find the cure" and raise awareness. As an appreciator of music and fashion, this was his avenue.

Now Kelly realized that there many "find the cure" type t-shirts for diabetes but they all seem to have that "free giveaway" look you might see at a fundraiser event. He wanted to make supporting the cure for diabetes a "cool thing to do."

With that in mind, Kelly came to Go Media and asked me to design their logo, website, and first line of t-shirts. This basically ensured consistency across the board. Everything had a very cohesive look to things — the colors, symbols, textures, etc. So when they launched, they immediately set the expectations that they were a legit clothing brand and it DID feel cool to support the cure!

When people ordered t-shirts from Cure, they were shipped in a custom package (with help from **Derisory Designs** who do great packaging) with the cure logo and included stickers and a handwritten note thanking them. This leaves the customer with a wholesome feeling of being cared for. The customer's experience through the whole process was consistently good and this leaves a lasting impression in their gut.

So for you, work hard to make the entire customer experience a great one that consistently pleases and exceeds their expectations. Make sure all your designs look like they belong together and aren't a smorgasbord of various design styles and themes.

Be Human

I keep reading how important it is to be human in your branding and marketing. As if this thought was new! But we saw how automated bots destroyed Myspace and now major brands are pulling back the curtain to reveal real people behind their Twitter and Facebook profiles. Because you have a brand name, you don't have to act like a faceless company.

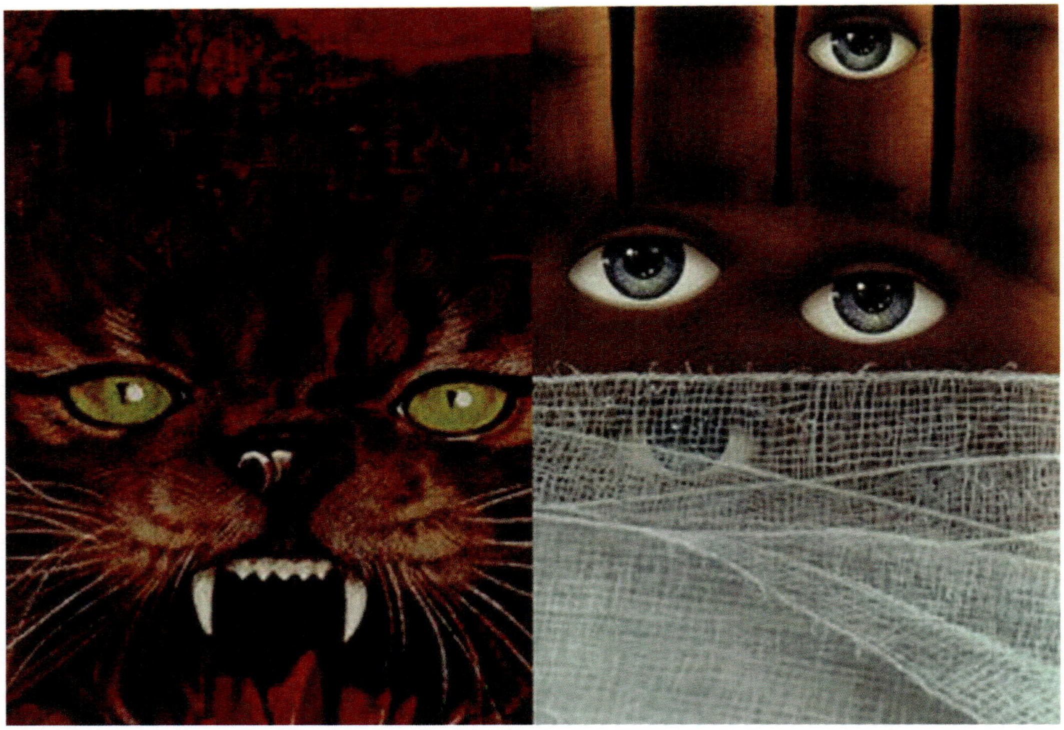

Designs from Fright-Rags "King" Collection

Ben Scrivens from Fright-Rags says,

"It's all too common for people just starting out to tout themselves as bigger than they are. They use terms like 'we' when it's just one guy in his basement. I did the same exact thing... Ironically, as I really did become a 'we' I gravitated to using my own name and identity with my brand. I personalized emails to my customers, and even shot videos of myself talking about how I got into horror and why it means so much to me.

With social media, you have the tools to create a real culture around your brand.

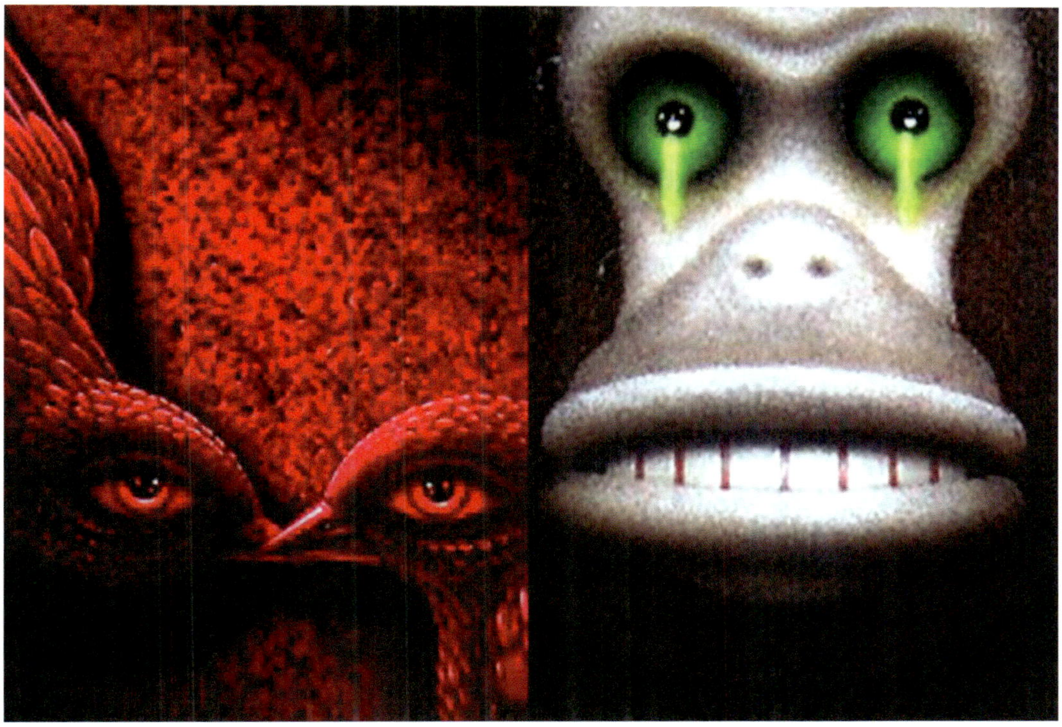

Little did I know, I was crafting my story behind our brand and putting a face and voice to the company that customers could relate to. Now I spend a lot of my time cultivating those relationships by doing things like sending surveys, allowing customers to vote on designs, showing them the process of taking a design from sketch to shirt, and even showing them how a shirt is printed."

Five Tips to Improve Your Brand

1. **What makes you different or unique? Why is your brand worth talking about?**
2. **Rarity factor. Everyone wants what nobody has.**
3. **Consistency. Consistency. Consistency.**
4. **Polarize your audience. They should love or loath you.**
5. **What else can you do to make your customer's experience more enjoyable?**

Some Branding Inspiration:

- Take a close look at how Johnny Cupcakes has honed branding for his clothing company. If you haven't already, go **read his story**.
- Another good read is about the **Linty Fresh branding experience**.
- See why Adam from IATT **gives an A+** to Declaration Clothing's initial launch.
- I also liked this article about **making your t-shirt company stand out**.

Pricing Your Tees

The simple answer on how much to charge for your shirts is whatever price makes you the most money. We creative people love what we do, so we would do this for free (for a while at least). Remember though, you are in business to make money. If you can make more money in the long run selling your shirts at $25 compared to $15, do it. You'll make more of a profit selling your shirts for $25 but you can probably sell more at $15. You'll need to do some testing of various price points to find that magic number that makes you the most money.

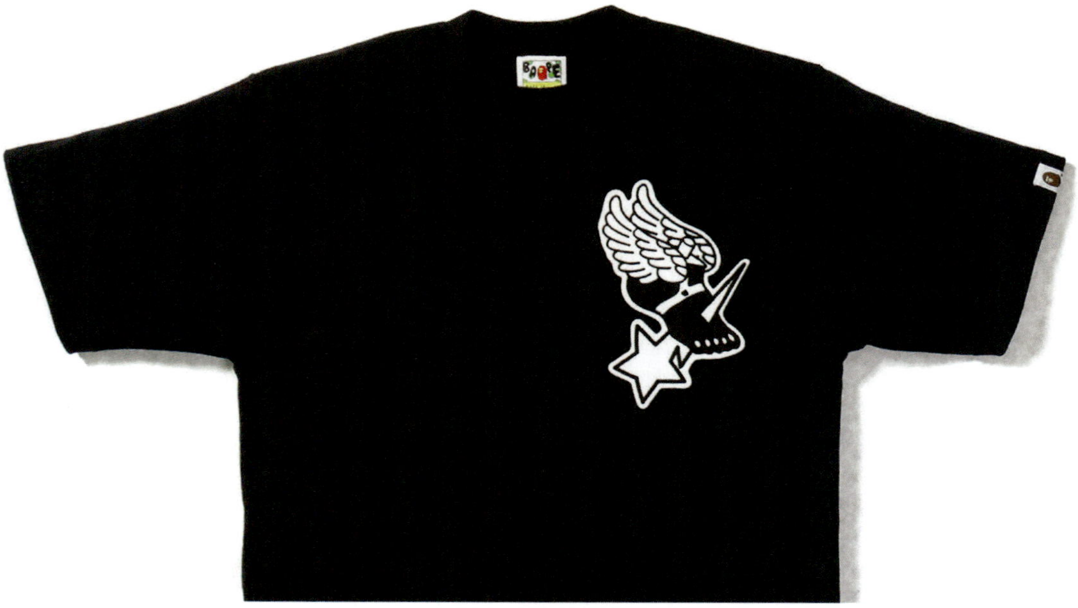

This simple shirt by BAPE is priced at $75

How Much are Your Customers Willing to Pay?

Lots of the pricing is going to be dictated by your market. How much are they willing to pay for your products? Look at other similar clothing companies as examples or ask your target market what they would pay. The best information will come from you actually selling your product and seeing how well products do at different prices.

Typically, if you spend a lot of money to create a very high quality garment that people describe as "boutique" then you're looking at the $20–$40 range. If you're just printing a simple graphic onto a tee, people generally expect to pay in the $10–$20 range. Of course, this is just a rough idea because some brands like BAPE can get away with selling one-color tees for over $70. Why? Because people are buying into the culture surrounding the brand, not the quality or cost of the garment. Will your audience pay that much for a t-shirt? Have they done so in the past with other brands?

Product Shots and Mockups

When selling anything online, you need high-quality photos of your products. In the t-shirt world, this is just as important. Photos add character and context to your products. However, not everyone has access to pro photography so that's where mockups come in.

Professional Photos are the Secret Sauce

"When showing off your products online or in print, be sure to use beautiful and consistent photos," says Matt Wigham of Big Cartel. "Even if you need to hire someone, it's worth it. You can have the best designs in the world, but they can only look as good as the photos they're in. Use a solid photographer, great models, consistent cropping, maybe some subtle branding, and your designs will look like a million bucks."

If you cannot afford a photographer, chances are you know someone who wants to be. Let them shoot your photos or shoot them yourself with an everyday consumer level camera. Shoot photos of your friends wearing your tees. Make sure the background isn't super busy and distracting and that your design is visible. Shoot them from the waist up to show off your designs and make sure things are in focus.

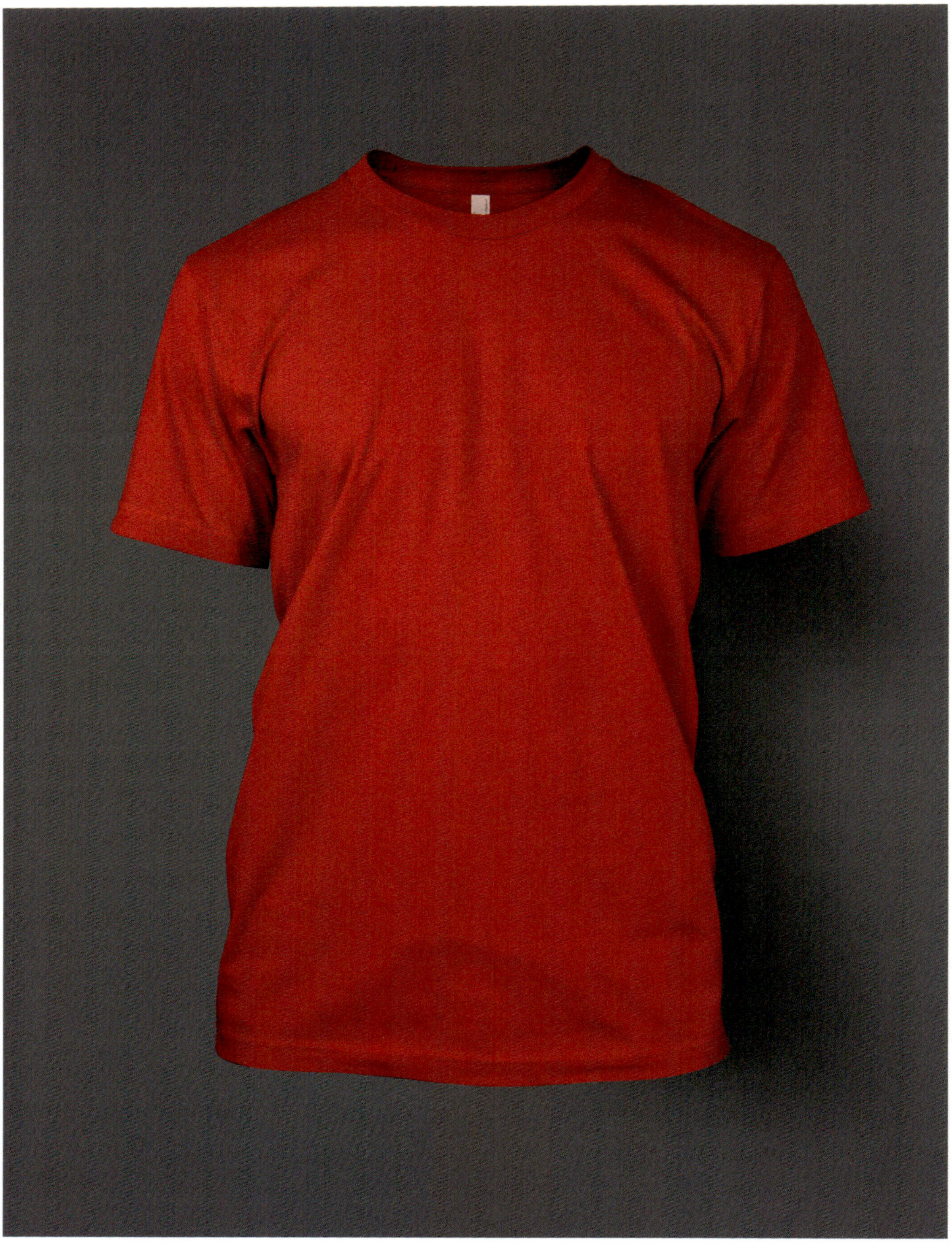

One of the new ghosted shirt mockup templates available on the Arsenal

Mockups Can Save the Day

If you don't have access to a camera or semi-attractive models, that's where the mockups come in. A mockup is a "faked" simulation of your tee. You literally mock up your design onto a t-shirt and show that as your product. Some people do it on a simple vector template and some do it on a realistic photograph of a blank tee.

At Go Media, we have created **photorealistic t-shirt mockup templates** for Photoshop users to easily cut and paste their artwork onto a shirt. The layers are set up in a way that gives the illusion that the design is actually printed on the tee. The goal is to create the most lifelike product photo without actually shooting the real product. For people who want to skip the Photoshop part, we made a web-based version called **ShirtMockup.com**.

This has been a huge help to designers who want to show off their designs in their portfolios or make a consistent array of product photos in their store. As long as the mockups look like the real thing, there's absolutely nothing wrong with doing this. It looks great.

Custom Packaging & The Customer Experience

As I mentioned in the section about branding, some of the best brands out there keep a consistent look throughout the entire customer experience.

The Customer Experience

Imagine this scenario: You dig a particular clothing company and think their designs are rad. You decide you must own one of their tees so you browse their site and make a purchase. A few days later, amidst all the bills and junk mail, you notice a wonderful eye-catching package. It's the t-shirt you ordered!

The package isn't just a tan bubble envelope, it's a sturdy box that tries its hardest not to look like mail. It's well-designed and feels substantial. You almost don't want to open it out of fear of ruining it!

But of course you bust it open immediately and inside you see a carefully arranged blanket of tissue paper decorated with the brand's logo. It's even secured with a wax seal or a custom sticker! You gently release the seal and unfold the tissue paper to find your new shirt precisely folded with the most exciting part of the design facing outward. It even has a custom hang tag popping out like a little hand waving "Hello! Nice to meet you!"

You reach in and cradle the new t-shirt like a newborn baby. As you lift it out, you see a collection of surprises underneath! A sticker, button, a baseball card, and a hand written note from the owner of the company. She thanks you by name and tells you that she digs what you're doing and to keep up the good work. Wow, how did she know?

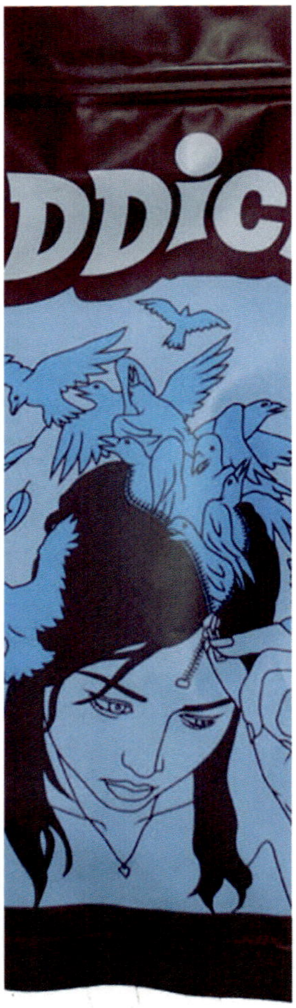

At this point, you're probably gushing over the t-shirt and it feels like Christmas morning. As a brand owner you want to instill this feeling in each and every one of your customers.

Custom packaging is one of the ways to make sure your customer has a great experience from start to finish.

I saw this **cool video where you see the care and dedication** Glen Infante takes in preparing his t-shirt packaging for his brand **ILTHY**. Really cool!

Criticisms of Custom Packaging

But like most things, custom packaging has a down side. Some customers will argue that they don't even want the packaging, they just want the t-shirt. They complain that it's wasteful, bad for the environment, and they'll just throw it away anyway. There's a **movement toward less packaging** nowadays and people are taking responsibility to **live without waste**.

If you're on the fence and not sure what you should do about your packaging, try asking your fans! Try a quick quiz or poll on your site or ask your Facebook and Twitter followers. Do they think custom packaging is wasteful and just another reason to jack up the price? Or do they think of it as a collector's item and part of the experience?

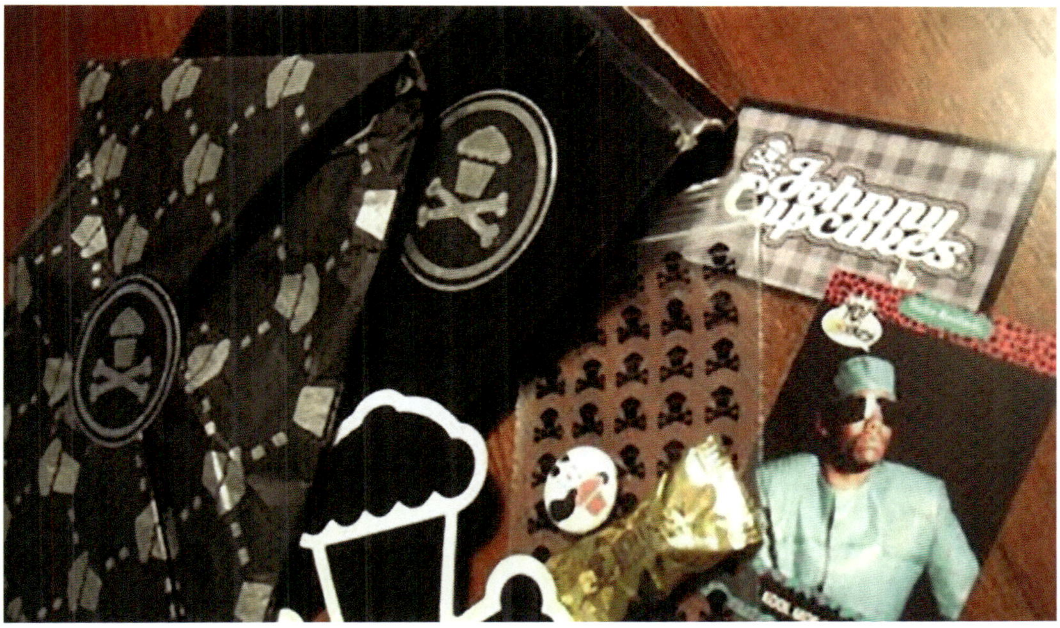

The "extras" are aplenty when you order from Johnny Cupcakes

More reading

- How to make your t-shirt package more memorable
- Product Presentation and Packaging Tutorial
- T-shirt packaging tips

Stickers, Swag, and Extras

Brands like Johnny Cupcakes really take pride in their "extras" they send along with their order. You aren't just getting a t-shirt, you get stickers, bubble gum, or other novelties. As a brand owner, you could think about what your customers might like and toss in some freebies to show you care.

Stickers are cheap as ever and you can get them any way you want them. I've used **StandOutStickers** many times for this and they do a great job. They **also make buttons too**, which are also great throw-ins to boost customers' loyalty to your brand.

Swag is good to hand out at events. Paint the Stars says, "One of the things we do is hand out a bunch of custom shaped stickers, drink mats, or cool little knick-knacks that people could keep with our website and discount codes on them." It's always a good idea to attend events and leave stacks of freebies out or hand them to fans one by one.

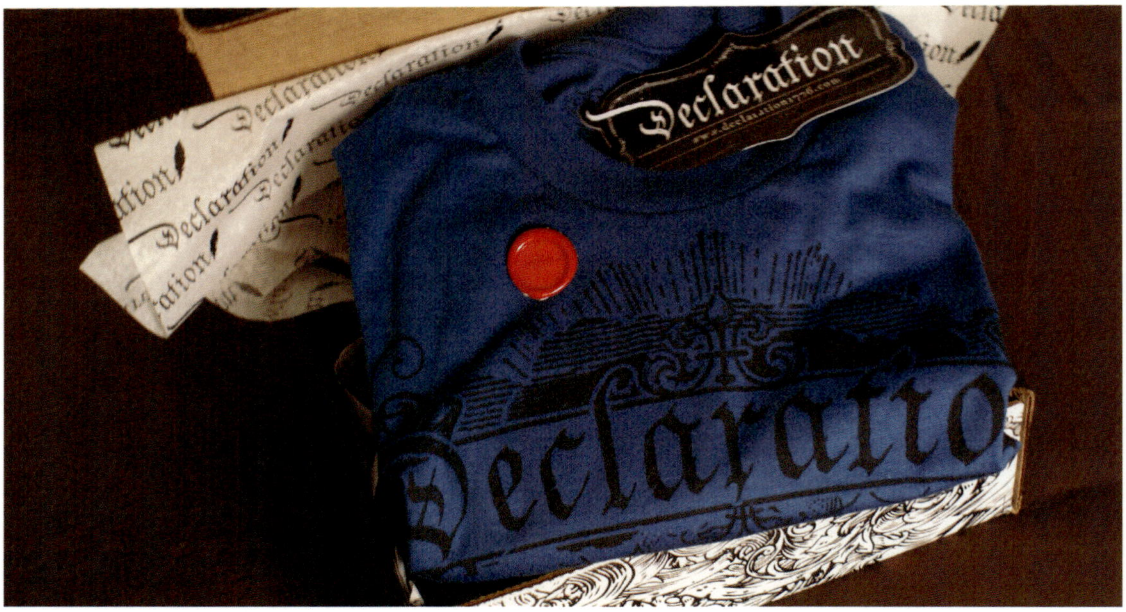

Declaration Apparel made a huge impact with its debut line by going all out with the custom packaging, tissue paper, stickers, and even a wax seal to round out its brand identity.

Personalize Your Orders

But aside from brand-centric swag like stickers and buttons, think about how you can personalize your order. Make it about your customer, not about you! Personalized and handwritten notes go a long way. You can win their heart by showing you really care about them. If you can, take time to learn about your customer's individual uniqueness and mention that in their order. This is easier said than done — because if you have a ton of orders it's not likely you have time. But it's something to think about. At the very least, do this for your best customers and they'll turn into brand evangelists without you ever having to spend a dime.

The Smartest Ways to Advertise

From my personal experience, the most effective ways to advertise are often free or cheap. You don't need to have a huge advertising budget to get the word out about your tees. Let's talk about the essentials that brand owners often overlook while they drop a few grand on a full-page magazine ad.

SEO: Four Things NOT to Overlook

It all starts here really. SEO stands for Search Engine Optimization. This is how you show up #1 on Google when someone types in keywords related to your site. There are probably thousands of books on this topic alone, so there's way too much information to cover here. If you're ready to dive into SEO, here are three appetizers to get you started:

1. Have great content on your site on a regular basis (blogging helps).
2. Get popular and reputable sites to link to yours.
3. Have easily searchable text and images with alt tags.
4. Check out this **video on SEO for t-shirt companies** and some **SEO Secrets.**

Social Media: Seven Simple Rules

As I write this, every business is jumping on the Twitter and Facebook bandwagon as a way to connect with their customers. There are good and bad ways to do this, as you know. I'm sure you've mentioned some brand on Twitter and noticed shortly thereafter that the brand has started following you! Is this cool or kinda creepy?

Here are Seven Simple Rules you must follow to see more success on social media.

1. **Act like a human being, not a faceless company.**
2. **Actually care about your followers. Brands often forget this after a while.**
3. **Promote others 5–10 times (ok maybe 2–3 times) more than yourself**
4. **Don't focus on the number of followers. Focus on the personal relationships.**
5. **Reward your most passionate followers with exclusive content and products.**
6. **Inspire your most dedicated followers to become leaders.**
7. **Ask your fans for opinions on new designs or promos. Get them involved!**

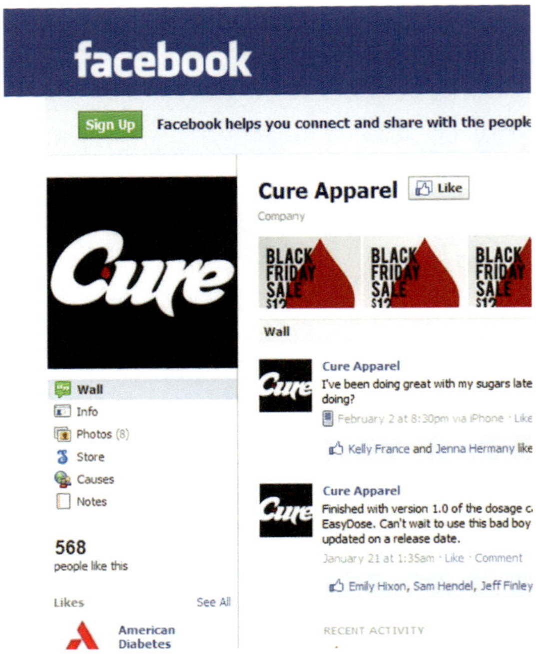

Cure Apparel does a good job of personally interacting with its fans on Facebook

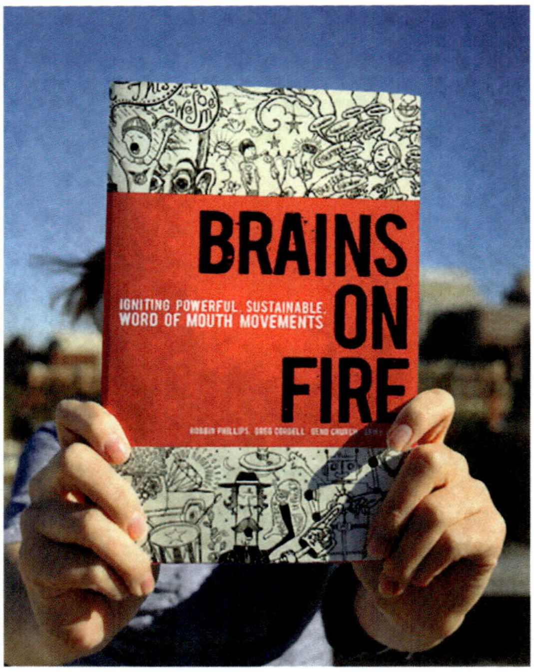

Brains on Fire discusses Word of Mouth movements for your brand.

Facebook Tips

Also, did you know that you can tag photos with your website on Facebook? I didn't realize that you didn't actually have to tag a real person in a photo. You could tag the photo and enter ***www.yourbrand.com***. If you happen to find photos of people wearing your tees, it couldn't hurt to tag their photo or at the very least add a comment saying, "Thanks for rocking [your brand here]!" Now other people can see where they are getting that awesome shirt from! Jon Kruse goes into some ***finer detail on Facebook marketing***.

Speaking of Facebook, do you have a ***fan page*** yet? If not, get on it. Every business is jumping on the bandwagon so it's getting kind of tired already. But as I write this, it's essential. Most books I read reiterate the fact that you shouldn't just get on Facebook because everyone is doing it. You do it to get involved with your customer's lives and add real value to them. This is social media 101 and a reminder that it's not always about you.

Don't use a fan page as a self promotional shout box. But use it to empower your fans and promote them. Offer exclusive deals they can't get anywhere else. Give them sneak peeks of new products and ask for their insight into what designs you should print next. I see Kelly from **Cure Apparel** do this often. He'll give the fans a choice and they have a say in what gets released. He also posts links to content relevant to his audience that's NOT about him. By doing so, he's creating a loyal following. Pretty cool huh?

If what I said wasn't enough, there are lots of articles and books on social media. Anthony at TeeBiz posted some tips on ***selling tees through social media.*** For books, I recommend Trust Agents and Brains on Fire. ***Trust Agents*** is like the bible for anyone who is trying to build influence on the web. ***Brains on Fire*** is about igniting authentic word of mouth movements. Two must-reads for any social media nerd. (like me)

Blog Your Way to Success

The hands down best way to advertise for free is blogging. Keep putting out great content and people will keep coming back. It sounds so easy and in fact it IS really easy to start blogging. But people tend to run out of things to say and their blog dries up like a shriveled hamburger patty left out in the sun.

If you think of blogging as a way to promote your brand, it makes it easier to find that motivation to post. Come up with interesting posts that engage the user but also help drive traffic and sales to your site. That's the reward you get for writing good content!

We've been able to build a solid fan base and other sources of income through our blog* GoMediaZine.com*. It's a platform for us to write about our expertise.

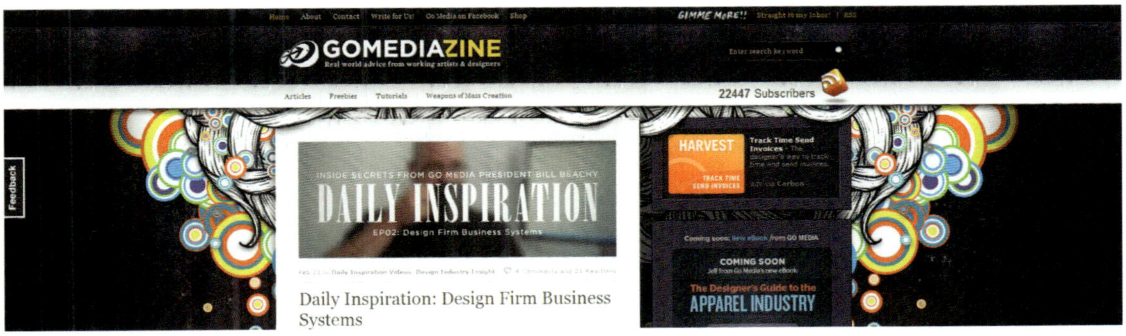

We've been able to build a solid fan base and other sources of income through our blog GoMediaZine.com. It's a platform for us to write about our expertise.

The Power of Other Bloggers

I must mention how important it is to network with other bloggers. As a clothing company, you have products that you can offer in exchange for write-ups and reviews. There are currently lots of blogs dedicated to the t-shirt world like ***IAMTHETREND***, ***Assault***, ***Pop Culture Tees***, ***Hide Your Arms***, ***OMG Tees***, and more.

Jon Kruse of Mediocore Clothing was smart about this from the beginning. He says, "I make friends with blog owners and have them get the word out for me. Each of these people gets thousands of visitors to their t-shirt blogs every month and by just sending them an email about a new shirt or sale I can spread the word quickly."

When you contact these blogs to review your tees, there are some ***dos and don'ts*** from Pop Culture Tees. They talk about t-shirt brands and get lots of requests from brands hoping to be featured. I imagine they've seen it all from the automated canned emails to the desperate and pleading newcomers.

Getting Reviewed: Dos and Don'ts

- Don't CC lots of other blogs simultaneously. It's obvious that you're trying to blast everyone and do as little work as possible. It's spammy and this will likely give your brand a black mark and make people frown when they hear about you.

FAIL! Don't Do What I Did

I once copied LOTS of bloggers on an email announcing the launch of our Arsenal store back in 2006. Little did I know I cc'd the blog of one of our competitors at the time and he was taken aback. It was obviously a boilerplate "hey check us out!" email and had I known what company he worked for I wouldn't have worded it that way. He got pissed at me and actually criticized us for even launching in the first place. Whoops!

Lesson learned: Pay attention. Take time to write personal emails, don't just copy the same email to everyone else and blast away. You'll get a better response when you craft a personal email. Also, don't make your first email too long. Generally ask a simple question to gauge their interest, then follow up with more details. It's a great way to start.

If you still don't get a response, don't sweat it. I've written **Booooooom.com** twice over the past two years asking them to feature some of my design work. Both emails were simple emails to the author from my heart. I love that website and would be honored to be included. I referenced other great content and my relationship with some of the subjects they write about. But I never got a reply. Oh well, as the Mail Chimp says "maybe they just weren't that into me!"

- Don't annoy the blogger with constant requests to be featured. Follow up once if you haven't heard back, but after that, forget it. The last thing you want to do is beg someone to talk about your brand.
- Don't email someone and simply ask for a repost or retweet. Bad taste.
- Do actually READ the blogs you submit to. If you aren't a regular reader, that's ok, but take the time to brush up. It helps if you can reference some of their content and how it affected you.
- Do write each one a personal email that shows you care and are legit. Don't send a canned message. I've done this before and it backfired on me.

More Resources for Getting Blog Press

- Check out ***Shirt Launch*** to get your brand more exposure.
- Be friends with this ***giant list of popular t-shirt sites***.

Communities and Forums

I can't stress enough how important it is to make friends and connections online. Websites where lots of users gather to chat about a common interest are "gold mines" for brand owners. Just don't treat it like a gold mine and you'll be ok. Users are people, not gold.

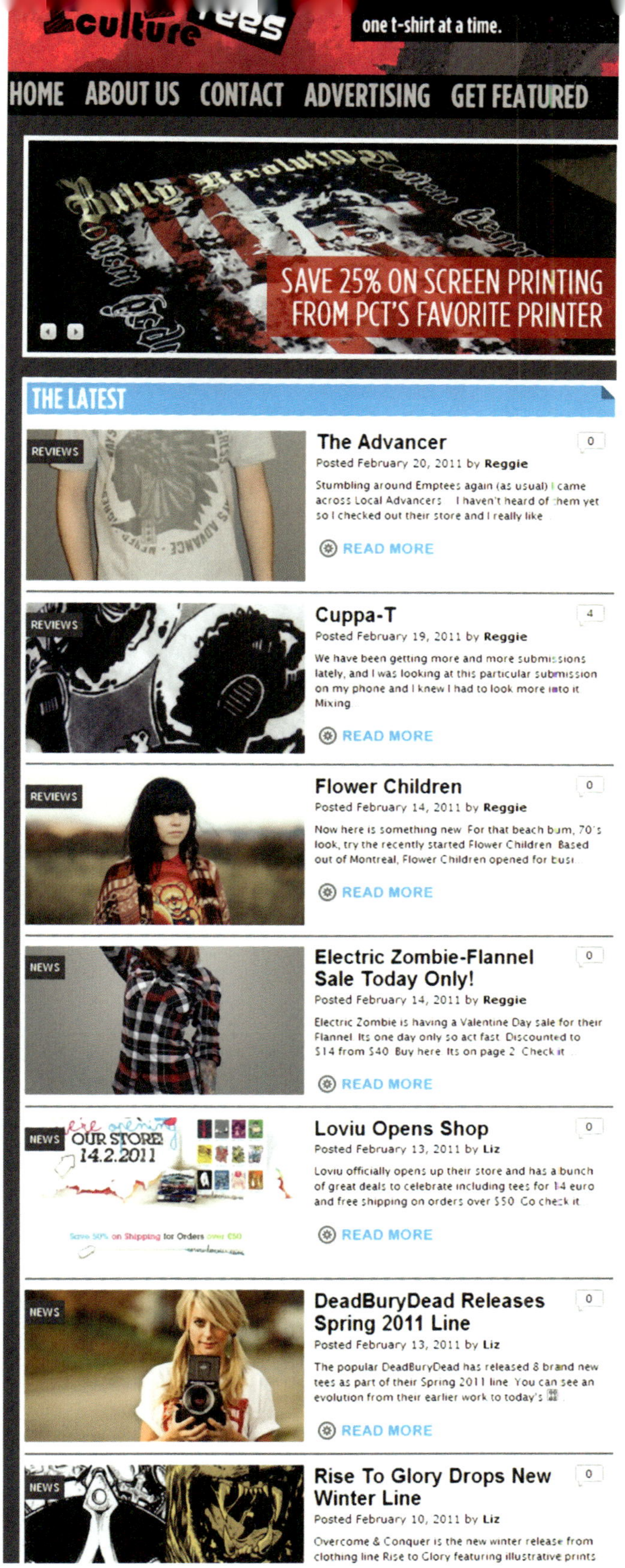

Pop Culture Tees is an example of a blog that features and highlights indie apparel brands.

It's tempting to jump into a forum and drop links to your brand and expect sales to boom. What usually happens is the community members jump on the brand for intruding on their turf and spamming them. Even if the brand is legit, it's just not cool!

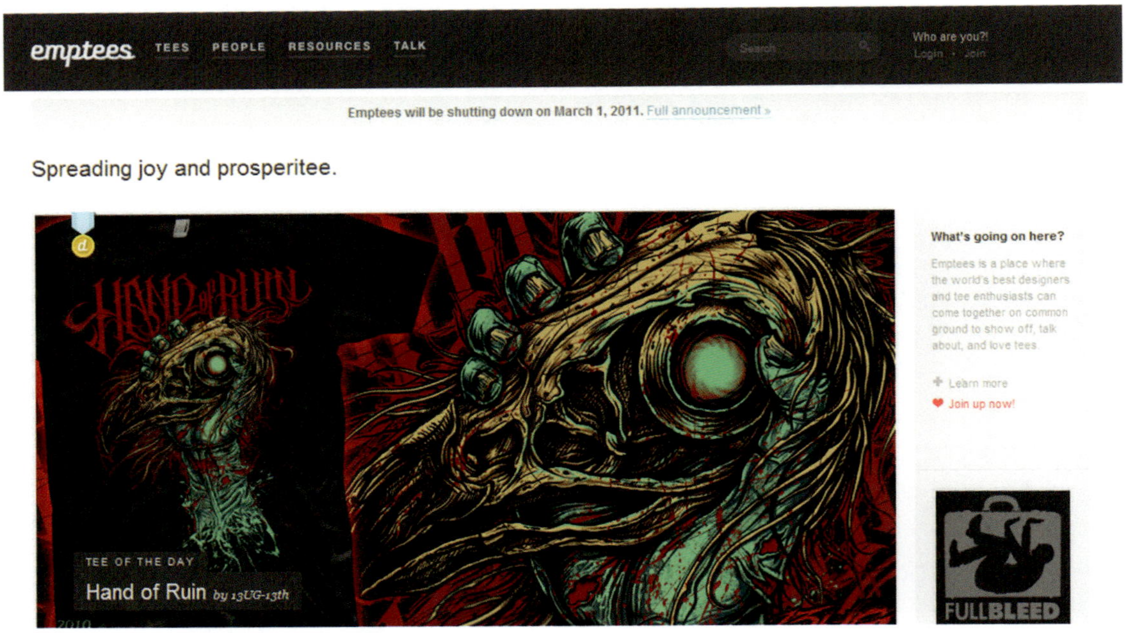

Emptees.com was a great site that brought together t-shirt designers from around the world. The site shut down on March 1st, 2011 and was replaced by **Mintees.com**

Self Promotion on Forums

Sigh, yes I've done this before too. Bad Jeff. But this was when I was first getting started and didn't know how the world worked yet. I was trying to promote my friend Brent Simon's viral ***videos of him playing and singing songs*** on his keyboard. One of his songs was called The Bittorrent Song so I went on sites like Mininova and Ebaum's World, signed up, and dropped the link to his videos with a comment like "Lol, look at this dork."

Some members of the community called me out on it and realized I was one of the people behind it. While some actually liked the videos, others bashed me for self promoting it. People can be mean, let me tell you! Somehow the video caught on anyway (the videos were actually pretty good) and it did go viral and, as luck would have it, Brent landed on the Jimmy Kimmel show.

Signing up and self-promoting right away is bad taste. People call it spam, but it's not quite. Spamming would be flooding their site with your links and messaging. So let's just call this tacky self-promo "Spam Lite." It's the ugly cousin. Either way, there are more effective ways to promote.

Forums are sensitive communities with their own house rules. Respect them.

As if you haven't learned this by now, it's best to be real and human. Participate in a community for quite some time and get to know everyone. Let your personality shine through and then when it feels right show off your goods! Chances are people will support you if you're a good member of their community. If you are supportive of others, they will likely support you. The more positive vibes you generate around your brand the more you can watch your sales go up.

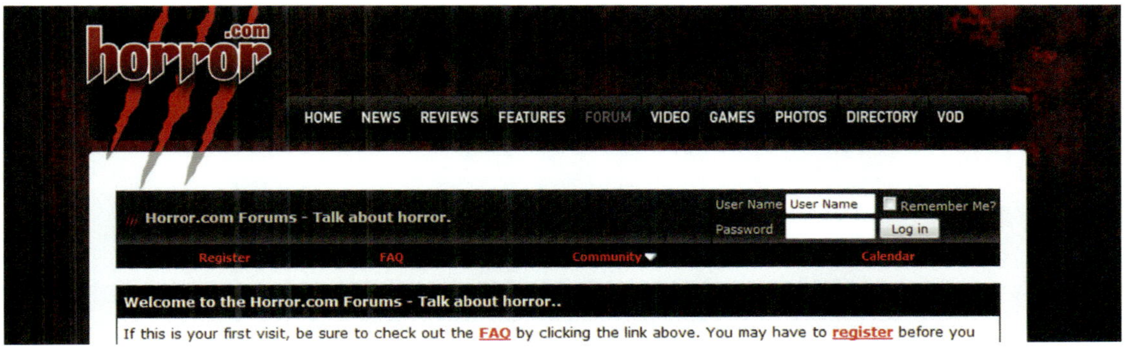

Horror.com is an example of a community of horror lovers. If you love horror and sell products that other fans like, you should fit right in and might get some new customers!

Find a website with a community of people who are interested in the same stuff that your brand is about. Is your brand about horror films like ***Fright-Rags***? Then go where fans of horror films hang out. Pretty simple really!

Mailing Lists

Another great way to keep in touch with customers is through a mailing list. We use ***MailChimp*** and it works great. When we launch new products we can tell all our customers and we always see a spike in sales when we send out an email. Side note: MailChimp isn't a clothing brand, but it's one of the best examples of a brand with personality that I know of.

Tips for better email "blasting"

- Be as "unspammy" as possible
- Be personal and real
- Always include an unsubscribe link
- Once or twice a month is plenty
- Offer exclusive content (products or articles)

I've had good luck sending plain text emails over fancy HTML "newsletter" types. If you can, include the recipient's first name in the email using what are called Merge Tags. Mailchimp has them, look into it.

Watch out though, I sent a plain text "personalized" email to over 60,000 customers to our Arsenal store asking for feedback on a new product. Chances are some of you reading this remember that email. I really DID want to hear legit feedback from our customers and I sure got it! I must have received over 1,000 replies and spent nearly a month writing people back. Although I still think some fell through the cracks and I never was able to reply.

As a brand owner, you can use plain text emails to come across more personal and conversational. However, sometimes you might want to announce a new product and show it off in the email. Some customers like to see the "newsletter" in their inbox.

A cool thing about using a service like MailChimp, Constant Contact, or Campaign Monitor is that you can track clicks on your links, view stats, send auto responders, etc. They all have their benefits and costs typically depend on how many users are on your list or your sending volume.

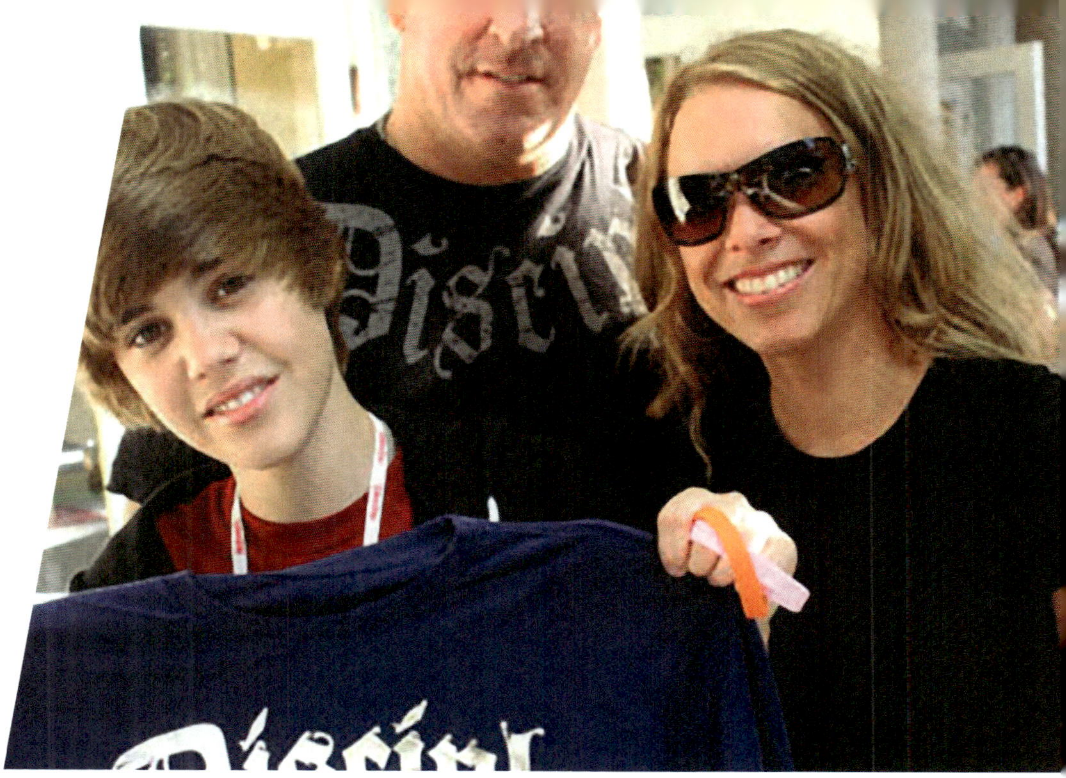

Justin Bieber holds up a design I did for Disciple.

Sponsoring Bands & Celebrities

A good way to get your name out there is to sponsor bands and other "famous" people. I remember in the "clothing company boom" of 2006–07, so many bands I was into were rocking new indie apparel lines like Heartcore, Bleeding Star, Rockett, etc. I'd flip through the pages of *Alternative Press* and I'd notice in some band photos they'd all be wearing a certain brand. They were likely sponsored by the company. That means that the brand has given the band members free shirts to wear in exchange for exposure.

When you're just starting out, this type of exposure could be huge. When fans of the bands see them wearing your tees, there's a good chance they might seek out your brand for themselves. The band adds another attraction to your line. It shows you are part of their culture and fans recognize that. It associates you with a particular scene or niche and that helps customers and fans identify with your brand. It puts you on their radar.

Four Tips to a Successful Sponsorship

1. **Find bands and celebrities who will rep your gear for free.** Until you can afford to pay cash AND tees, this is your best bet. Lots of bands will be happy just to get free clothes. Find celebrities, athletes, or other public figures who share a similar audience as your brand and reach out to them.
2. **Make sure you get photos** of the band members rocking your gear. You want to use these photos for your website or social media profiles to add credibility to your brand. They could be posed press shots or live photos. It doesn't matter if they're professional or not. You just need proof they are supporting your brand.
3. **Pick bands that match your aesthetic.** If your shirts feature zombies and gore, find bands that are into that stuff too. If your shirts are simple and cute and targeted toward tweens, look for an up and coming pop star. If they're true fans of your brand, they won't just wear your tees, they'll love talking about them.
4. **Find Video Bloggers to rep your brand.** They're in front of the camera a lot and often have a large viewership. If you've found someone with a popular YouTube channel, it couldn't hurt to toss them some free gear in exchange for exposure. I remember in 2006 when ***Stride Gum sponsored Dancing Matt's Youtube videos***.

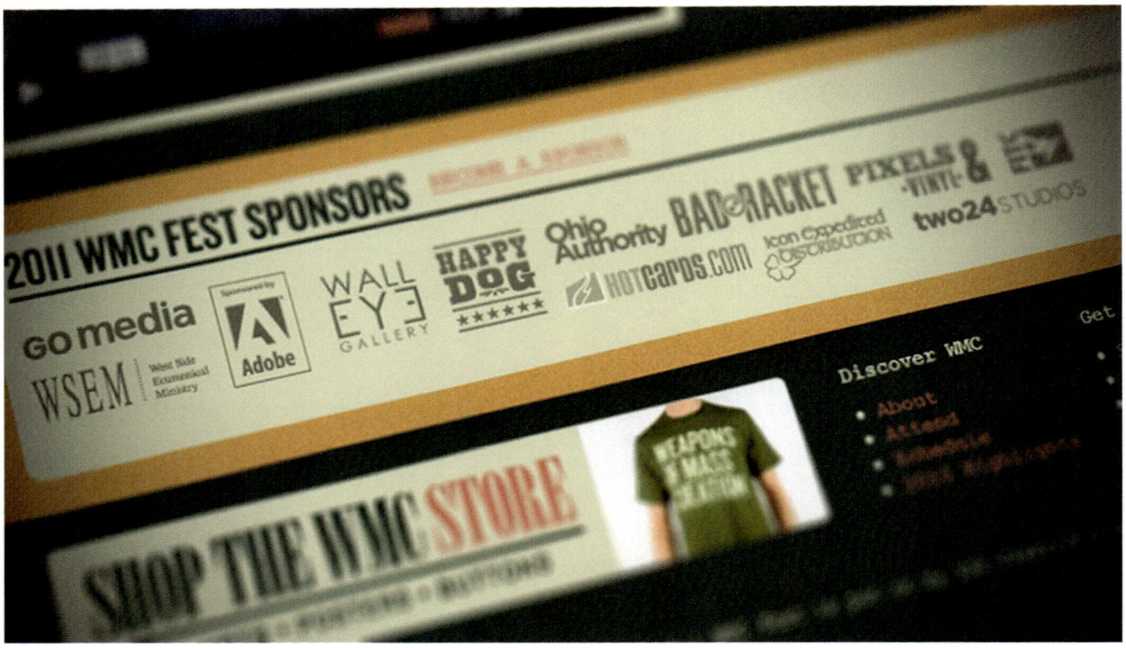

Sponsoring events, such as Weapons of Mass Creation Fest, is a great way to get your brand out there in front of your target audience.

Sponsoring Events

There's a major punk rock music festival down in Gainesville, Florida every year simply called ***The Fest***. As of this writing it's finishing up its 9th year. Go Media has been a sponsor since 2007. I've done a t-shirt design for them the past three years in exchange for logo/link placement on all their materials and free tickets for me and my friends. Honestly, I sponsor them because I love what they're doing and I want to be a part of it. It's cool that I can associate my brand with something I like. It's also cool that other people who like The Fest are going to see the connection as well.

Events are perfect places to get brand exposure. From sponsorships to giveaways, you're guaranteed to find new customers.

You could find events that cater to the type of crowd you're looking to attract. Send them some free gear or do something good for them in exchange. Most events have sponsorship rates that you could pay as well. I know for my event ***Weapons of Mass Creation Fest***, we are looking for cool sponsors to help fund the event and to make the experience better for our attendees. I know firsthand how badly events need sponsors, so don't forget about this avenue for promoting your brand.

Ten Secrets to Driving Traffic to your Website

In my six years of experience working as a freelance designer and at Go Media, I have used a combination of all sorts of things to drive traffic to our websites. If there's one thing I seem to have a knack for it's this.

1. **Track your stats.** I use ***Google Analytics*** and *Clicky* real-time stats. It's critical to track your traffic and find out where your visitors are coming from. It's the only way you'll know what the heck is going on behind the scenes. You could also track your e-commerce stats and conversion rates. Are you getting thousands of visitors but hardly any sales? Maybe they're the wrong type of visitors or there could be a problem with your ordering process. Who knows, but any good marketer keeps a good eye on his or her stats.

2. **Ego Searching or Brand Monitoring.** I use ***Google Alerts*** to track mentions of my name/brand on the web. And ***SocialOomph*** for mentions on twitter. If someone mentions an article about me, I get notified via email. This is also helpful to keep tabs on your competitors or other keywords. You could use some more robust social media monitoring apps like ***Sprout*** or ***Radian6.***

3. **Create Content OTHER than your product.** We ***write articles and tutorials*** to drive traffic and generate interest and appreciation. In turn we can advertise our expertise and mention products we have for sale. What can you do to create great content (for your site or others) that can drive traffic back to your product?

4. **CSS Gallery Submission.** Right now, CSS Galleries are saturating the net. But you can pay a small fee to a site like ***MeeCSS*** and get automatically submitted to a ton of galleries. If your site is inspirational and well designed, you'll likely get featured and get a boost in traffic. I've done that to new sites I've launched and it seems to help.

5. **Pay for traffic.** We have paid money into ***StumbleUpon*** for guaranteed traffic and it works. However, you need good content otherwise users will quickly vote down and bury your site and your advertising dollars will be wasted. You could also pay to advertise your site on ad networks like ***BuySellAds***, ***The Deck***, ***Carbon***, etc. You can also pay Google or Facebook to advertise your products.

6. **Submit News.** We've received big traffic from sites that deliver news to the creative community. In the past we had our products featured on DesignIsKinky.com, PixelSurgeon, Motionographer, etc. Find sites that are big in your community or niche and contact the authors. Be real and legit and there's a chance you could be their latest news story!

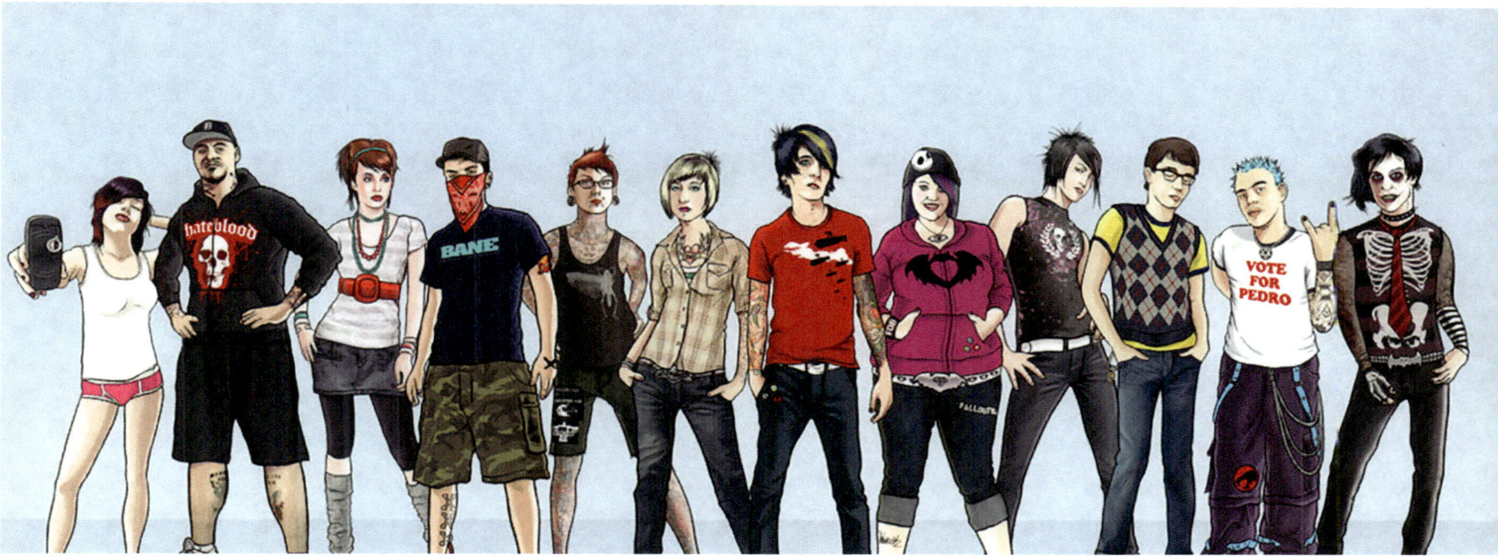

Rob Dobi makes fun of fashion trends with Your Scene Sucks. The site indirectly promotes his abilities as an illustrator while also turning people on to his clothing line Fullbleed. Great marketing idea.

7. **Link Exchanges/Blogroll.** Make friends with other sites and blogs similar to yours and get on their blogroll. You can swap links if that helps.

8. **Submit your designs.** Post your designs wherever people will see them! Communities like Mintees, Band Job, deviantArt, Threadless, Flickr, are all great places to get you some exposure. Basically if you set up an account and post your work, why not give it a go?

9. **Publicity Stunt/Viral Marketing.** Do something unique and memorable. Rob Dobi created a mini site called ***Your Scene Sucks*** where he mocks fashion trends with his clever illustrations. He makes sure to name drop his clothing brand Fullbleed on the site. Another brilliant marketing stunt he did was when Myspace was bought out by Fox News. He launched a temp site called MySpaceSoldOut.com (no longer live) and had an illustration of the founder "Tom" with a bag full of money and a snarky comment about all emo scenesters that seemed to populate the site. And after a few seconds it redirected to his Fullbleed store. The illustration went viral and he had a huge spike in traffic to his store. Did people buy? Not sure, but stuff like that couldn't hurt.

10. **Contests and Giveaways.** You could host your own contest or sponsor another. Give away your products to the winners and get some great exposure out of the deal. Do this enough and you'll start getting emails from other contest throwers asking you to donate some product. Trade products for exposure!

Additional Resources for Advertising and Marketing

- **7 Creative Ways to Advertise Your T-shirt Line**
- **How to Advertise and Market Your Apparel Brand**

To view websites cited in this book, please visit www.threadsnotdead.com/links.

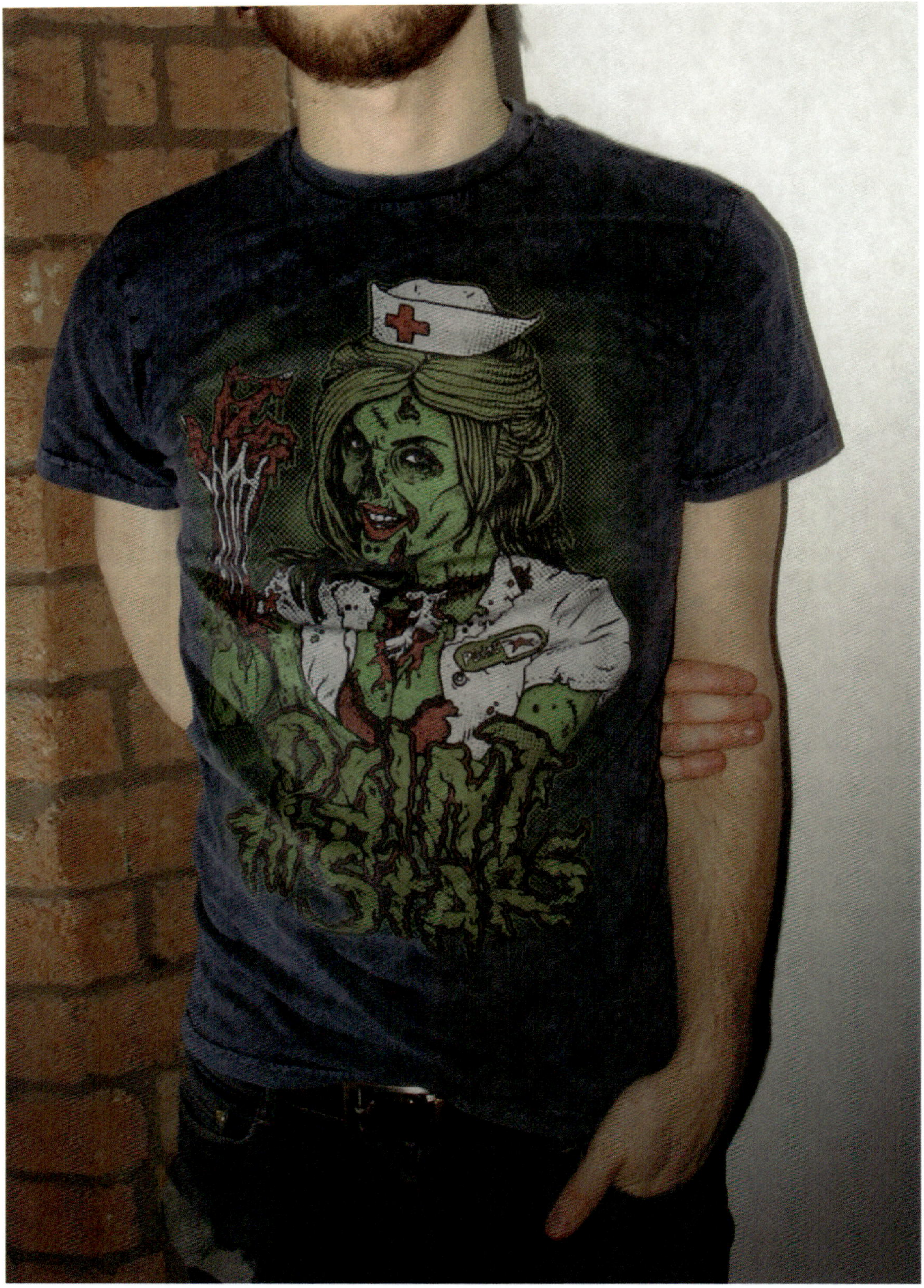

Blink-182 Tribute Tee by Jeff Finley for Paint the Stars

VII

SALES & FULFILLMENT

The barriers to selling your tees online have been destroyed and it's now easier than ever to do business. However, there are some things you should know.

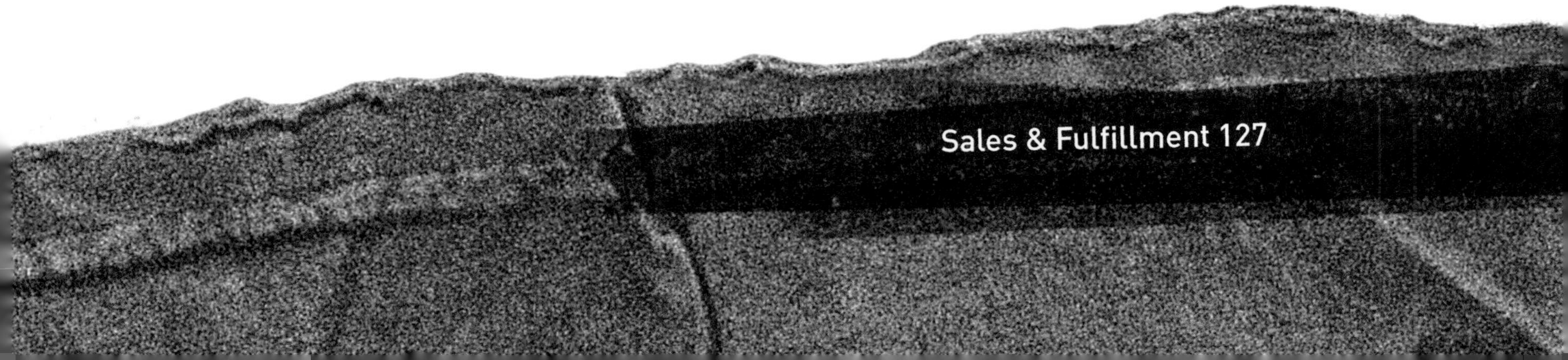

What You Need to Know about Selling Online

Domain Name

As a clothing brand, you'll be selling tees online and offline. For online, you need your own site with your own domain name. I feel like this is as obvious as putting a coat on when you go outside in the winter.

Getting your own domain costs roughly $10/year. You could reserve that through **GoDaddy.com** and be done with it. You could use your brand name like **cureapparelco.com** or get something creative like findthecure.com or curerocks.com. Other areas to register your domain: **Network Solutions**, **Blue Host**, or **Yahoo**.

Hosting

Hosting ranges from free to wildly expensive. You could always start out on social media sites like Facebook, Myspace, or whatever is hot at the time. It doesn't cost a thing to reach people and show off your goods. Alternatively you could host a free blog at **wordpress.com**, **blogger.com**, or **tumblr.com**. Another baby step up and you'll pay a small fee at **virb.com** or **squarespace.com** to build a more custom site. These are all hosted solutions.

If you're serious (which you should be) think about hosting your own site for more control. You could use **Rackspace** or **SoftLayer** like we do at Go Media. I know a lot of people that use **Media Temple** or **HostGator** as well. These hosting plans can range from $4.95/month to a few thousand per month for a managed and dedicated server. I suggest you do your research, read hosting reviews, and judge for yourself.

E-Commerce

For free and cheap e-commerce, everyone seems to use **Big Cartel** when they're just starting out. Big Cartel is an amazingly simple storefront to sell your goods. It doesn't get much easier than that. They charge a flat monthly fee and don't take a cut of your sales. You could also use a site like **Storenvy** or **IndieMerchStore** to start selling your stuff without a whole lot of technical knowledge. For these, you simply need a **PayPal** account and you can start getting paid!

However, if you want more control over your sales, stats, customers, and promotions, you might want to consider upgrading to a more robust e-Commerce solution like **Magento**, **Zen Cart**, **CS Cart**, **osCommerce**, **Shopify**, **Volusion**, etc. There are literally hundreds of choices, but those are some of the major ones. These solutions usually require a merchant account and some technical expertise to get it off the ground. I recommend this once you already have a growing customer base. A merchant account is a type of bank account that allows businesses to accept payments by debit or credit cards.

Accepting Credit Cards Online

You can accept credit cards easily with PayPal, but most professional brands have the ability to accept cards directly on their site. **PayPal Website Payments Pro** is one option. Another option is to apply for a merchant account like **Merchant Warehouse** (we have used them in the past) and a credit card processor like **Authorize.net**.

It's a lot cheaper and easier than you think to have your own site with your own web presence.

The biggest benefit to using these systems is that you can get more sales by accepting credit cards on your site. It creates a seamless experience for your customer. The cons are that they charge a lot of fees and you, the seller, are responsible for dealing with fraud and chargebacks. Like hosting and domain registration, there are many providers. I say **read reviews** and judge for yourself.

SSL Certificates

One important requirement for selling your goods on your own site is an SSL Certificate. This means that your customer's data is secure and encrypted when they're shopping on your site. When they enter their credit card information, they don't want to risk their information leaking out through an unsecure and untrusted connection. You can learn more and get hooked up with an **SSL Certificates at GoDaddy** for cheap.

I recommend reading discussions from other brands regarding **e-Commerce and your t-shirt biz**.

Shipping & Fulfillment

I remember when I got my first order back in 2005 after I launched my own line of "Mylkhead" t-shirts. Mylkhead was the alias I went by while freelancing and this was my first batch of t-shirts. I was so excited when I got my first order! I had to think fast and find a way to mail the t-shirt to my first customer.

All I did was run to a big box store like Wal-Mart and grab a bunch of padded envelopes that looked big enough to hold a t-shirt. I wrote the customer's address on the package with a sharpie marker and wrote my own return address (my house) on it too. I threw in some Mylkhead stickers and buttons, printed out their order from PayPal and wrote a hand-written thank you note on it. I sealed the whole thing up, took it to the post office and sent it priority mail. Then I gleefully skipped out of the post office and went on my way. My wife Kim wrote down their order on a spreadsheet and checked off that we shipped it. Done and done!

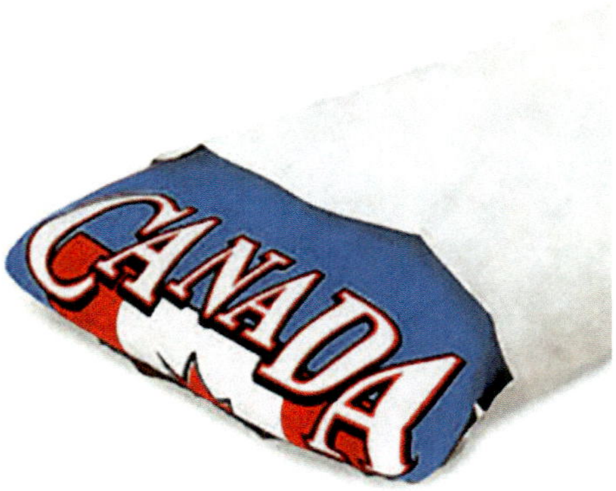

Uline.com offers some handy options for shipping t-shirts. These Poly Mailers are quite popular and allow you to put stickers on them for branding.

Most first timers do it themselves like I just described. This is totally cool and it's what I would recommend if you're just starting out. There's no need to get a UPS or FedEx shipping account and schedule pickups or use a third party distributor at this stage.

If things go right, you'll get more and more orders. Soon it becomes quite a bit of work just to keep up with the demand. Even 10–20 shirts a week is a lot of work! I remember Rob Dobi posting a photo of a week's worth of Fullbleed orders making a giant pile on his bed! Damn!

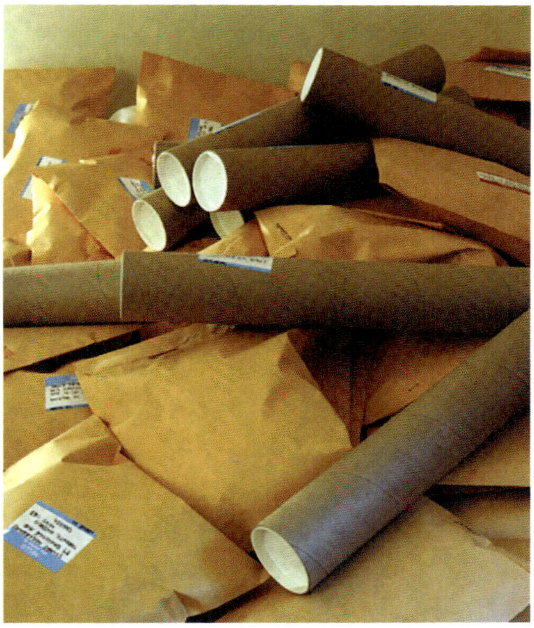

Rob Dobi shipped all his Fullbleed orders himself. If you get popular, you might have a stack like this on your bed!

Five Self Shipping Tips

1. Uline has **cheap mailers** that are good quality
2. Get a **shipping scale** to weigh your packages
3. You can use PayPal to print labels and generate tracking codes
4. Ship products within 1–3 days of orders to keep customers happy
5. Don't charge a lot for shipping! $3–$5 is enough for a t-shirt unless you are shipping internationally. More on this in a second.

Shipping with Paypal

I found a specific tutorial on **shipping your products with PayPal** if you're looking for more detailed information.

Third Party Fulfillment

When you get a lot of orders, you might want to hire a friend or someone else to help you. But after that, you might consider hiring a third party company to handle everything for you. This costs more but it can save you a ton of time.

A quick example you might be familiar with are companies like **MerchLine** or **Indie Merchandising**. Illustrator **Dan Mumford** uses them for his clothing line. You ship them your entire inventory and they handle the entire order fulfillment. They charge a fee, but you get to concentrate on making better designs and marketing.

Beyond those options are **Shipwire** or **Fulfillment by Amazon** just to name a few. I have never used these services myself, but I did research these options a few years ago when considering using it for our **Fail Sticker** business (which we have since sold to MerchLine).

I recommend giving third party fulfillment services a look once you start getting orders you can't keep up with.

International Orders

It's not uncommon to have a large demand from an international audience. From our experience, Go Media's **blog** and **store** attract a lot of international customers and we find ourselves spending lots of money shipping things across the world. Of course, we make sure to raise the shipping price to cover those costs.

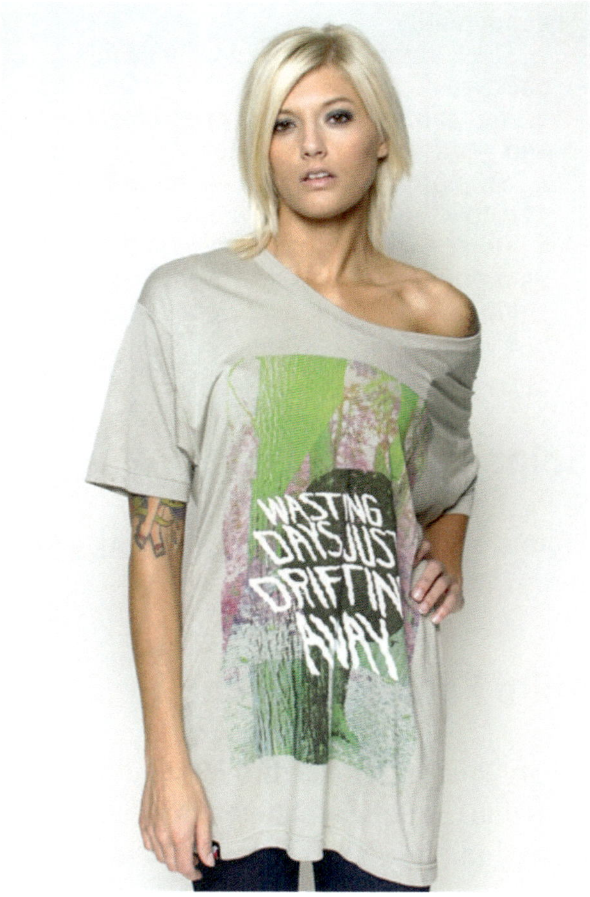

Shirt by Glamour Kills

One extra step in shipping international orders is filling out **customs forms** (in the US at least). If you have the demand for international orders check out **Endicia** or **Stamps.com**. Both have features to automatically fill out customs forms for you.

Now don't get overwhelmed. Selling your tees is fun! Don't worry about problems you don't have yet. This guide is just to make you aware of what lies ahead. When brands succeed and grow, it can sometimes be difficult. It's called growing pains. But growing up must mean that you're doing well! So don't sweat it, people just like you are doing it.

Dave Pearson from Paint the Stars said he didn't really take things seriously until he started seeing international demand. "Our breakthrough moment was probably when we started hearing from international stores who wanted to sell our stuff. We never even imagined our brand would get recognized outside of our hometown, let alone outside of the country. This really inspired us to step up our game and made us realize that we were on to something. It all got very serious after that, whereas before that, we were having a bit of a jolly and just taking it for what it was."

Shipping with UPS or FedEx

These are the two major shipping carriers in the US. You can sign up for business accounts with both of them and offer your customers more shipping options. One of the cool things is they can stop by every day and pick up packages from you.

At Go Media, we signed up with UPS for daily pickups but unfortunately didn't have the volume to make it worth the costs. We found that there were many days we didn't have any items to ship and it was a wasted trip for our UPS driver. We have since canceled the daily pickup and now schedule one-time pickups whenever we need to. There is a fee charged for pickups, so to avoid this fee you can always just go right to the UPS store or dropbox to drop off your packages.

To view websites cited in this book, please visit www.threadsnotdead.com/links.

Selling Offline at Events and Trade Shows

One of the best ways to get your clothing line out there is to set up shop at events. This usually refers to reserving some table space to sell your tees. There are typically costs involved as most events charge a fee to vendors. The fees vary depending on how big the event is. Selling at events can be pricey, but it's fun. You can meet your fans face to face, network and meet new people, and sell a bunch of tees in one place. Here are some good tips before you venture out.

Types of Events

You would expect to see apparel companies at the big apparel trade shows like Magic which we'll get into in the next chapter. And you might often see apparel companies setting up shop at major music festivals like Warped Tour, SXSW, or Bamboozle. Don't forget about craft fairs, film festivals, expos for various niches, etc. Try to think of events where there might not be a lot of other apparel brands competing with you. For example, Johnny Cupcakes could set up at a baking conference or something about cooking. Or maybe Cure Apparel could sell their tees at a Diabetes Race. If you were attending a horror film convention, you might expect to see a brand like Fright-Rags or Electric Zombie there. I recommend planning out your events a year in advance and budget accordingly.

Expect to Spend Some Money

Like I said, events are super fun, but can be pricey. Be prepared to spend some cash. In addition to travel and food expenses, you will need to pay for vendor fees to reserve a booth or table space at the event. At SXSW last year, they had a "launch package" for startups that ran $5,000. This included floor space at their Interactive Trade Show and two sponsored posts on the SXSW Facebook and Twitter accounts. Quite pricey indeed. At Weapons of Mass Creation Fest, we charged $100/day for a table or booth. You'll notice that most vendors at these events have a nice branded banner at the very least. They might have a tent with their logo on it and various other signage or displays that help them get noticed. You'll need to stock up on inventory, swag like stickers and buttons to giveaway, flyers, brochures, catalogs, etc. You are going to need to stock your table full of eye-catching goodies! And if that wasn't enough, you can even hire **D-List celebrities** to stand by your booth and attract attention.

Be Prepared and Organized

It can be a crazy hectic mess while selling at an event. Something will get lost or go wrong, it's inevitable. But with good preparation, you can minimize disasters. Prepare for this by running through the scenarios beforehand. Remember to think about the customer's experience. A visitor will notice your booth, approach it, and want to easily see your tees and prices. Do you take credit cards or cash only? Make sure visitors can see this info clearly. How are you displaying your tees? On a board behind you or laid flat out on a table? Are you going to bring shelves or storage totes to keep your inventory? How are you keeping track of orders? Money? We'll get to that in a minute.

Get there early

How long does it take you to set up? Practice this at home first! I can't stress enough getting to the event as early as possible to set up and make sure your booth is looking spectacular.

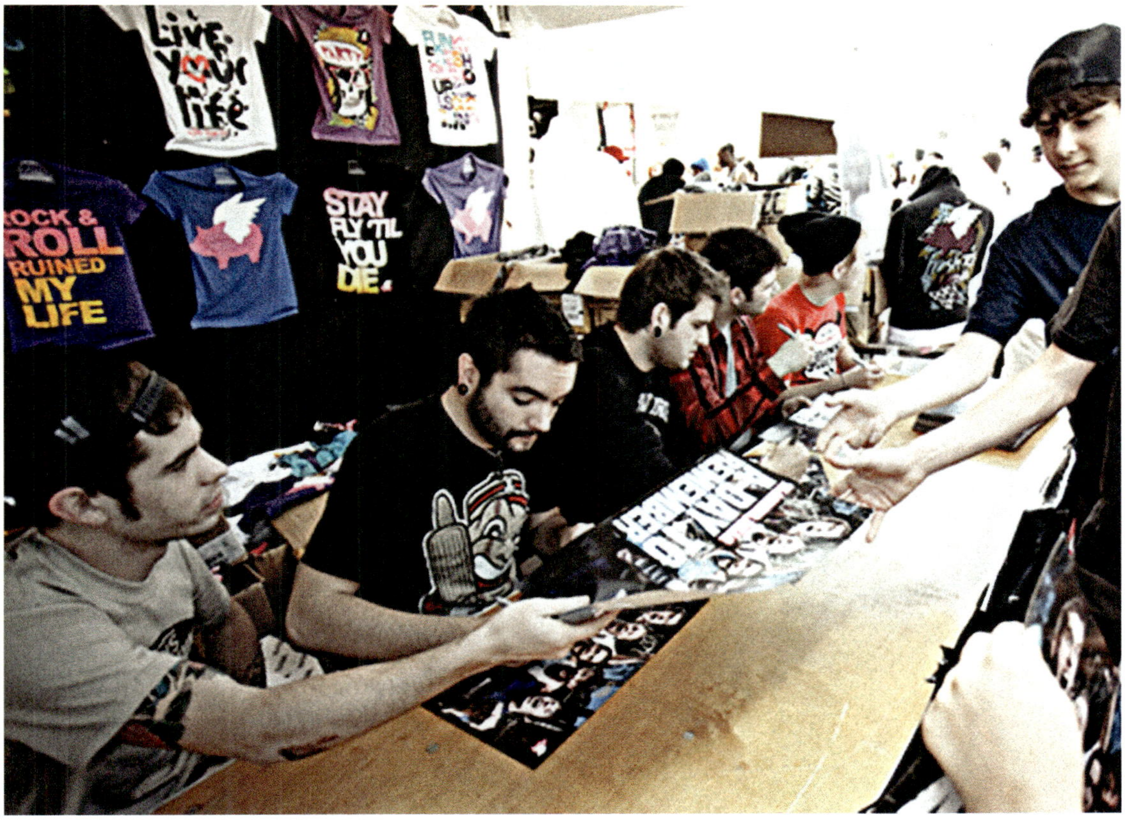

The Glamour Kills booth at Bamboozle 2009

Giveaways and Freebies

People like to go to trade shows or conferences because there is SO MUCH free stuff going around. Visitors are swinging by booths filling up their goodie bags with freebies from table to table. You better have something good! Make it unique, something that they show their friends. I think branded stickers and buttons are always nice, but do something fun!

Gather Contact Information

There's nothing worse than going home from an event realizing you never got anyone's contact information. You want to find a way to tastefully collect visitor's email addresses so you can add them to your mailing list. Eric Terry of **Linty Fresh** says he has people fill out a little card for a raffle. On the card they can check a box if they want to receive their newsletter. The people that opt in this way are usually pretty enthusiastic about your brand and you should stay in touch with them on perhaps a more personal basis.

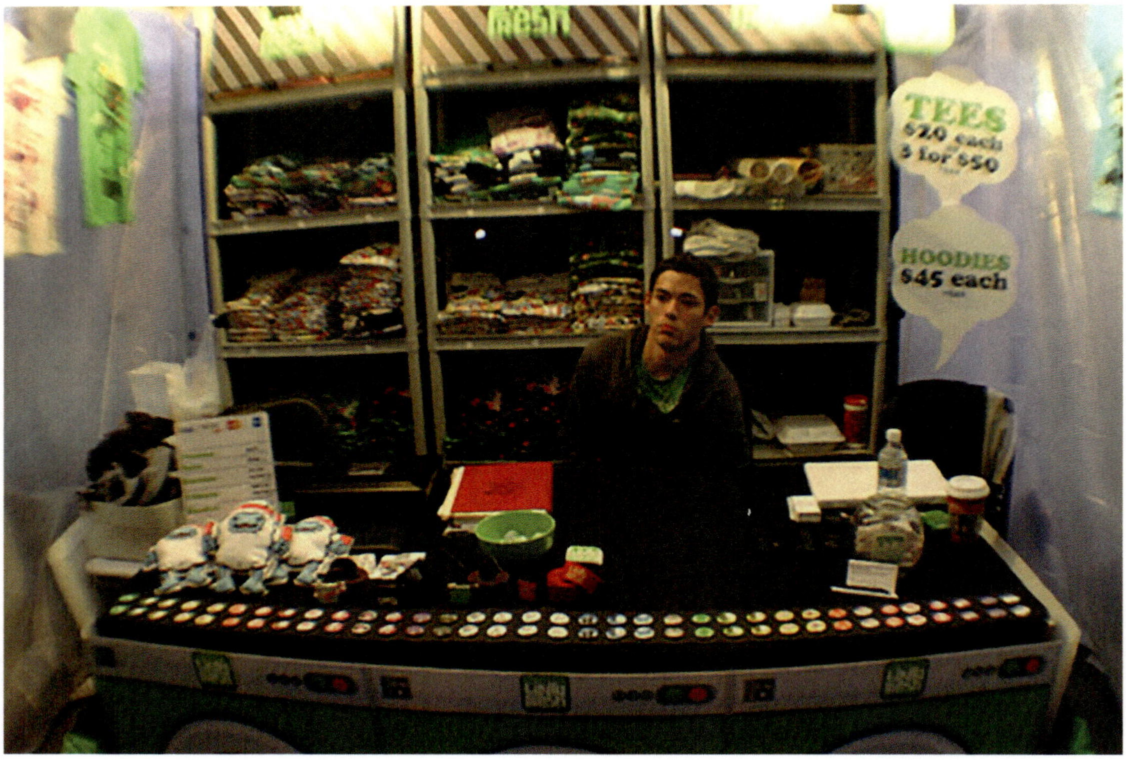

Eric from Linty Fresh does it big with his booth.

Peacocking / Building Buzz

I learned the term Peacocking from Neil Strauss's book *The Game* about the secret underworld of pickup artists. It explained that wearing a crazy hat or a giant gold necklace would get you more attention from the opposite sex. It seemed like a corny cliché, but somehow it worked. As funny as it sounds, doing remarkable, crazy, or funny things at trade shows builds buzz and certainly makes you stand out. When I go to events, I'll notice booths try to get bigger, louder, and more in your face than ever. With flashing lights, booming sound, and even dancing girls! They're all shouting LOOK AT ME! That kind of attention whoring works but there are less shameful ways of drawing attention.

For example, while I was at Siggraph in 2007, the Gnomon Workshop taught classes and gave demonstrations on big flat screen TVs. The Adobe booth had 30" Cintiq monitors all around so visitors could draw on their screens. There was some user interaction going on! Think of ways to involve visitors or get them to stop and watch. Demonstrations, classes, workshops, tutorials, and performances are great.

Money and Payment

Are you going to accept credit cards or cash only? By taking credit cards, you can get more sales as almost everyone uses their credit or debit card these days. Not everyone carries cash on them. But I think it's still a surprise to most visitors that a vendor is even able to take credit cards. There is also the trust factor. If your booth looks shady and amateur, people may not feel safe swiping their card with you. However, if you look pro, people might expect you to take cards. Keep in mind, accepting credit cards comes with its own price and per-transaction fees. You can purchase **a credit card swiping machine** or even use your iPhone with apps like **Swipe**, or **Square**.

If you're taking cash, make sure you have enough to make change the whole day. Keep your cash in a secure and lockable cash drawer and make sure a trustworthy person can keep an eye on it at all times. It's obvious but don't walk away from it; it could get stolen! Designate someone to be responsible for managing your cash at all times!

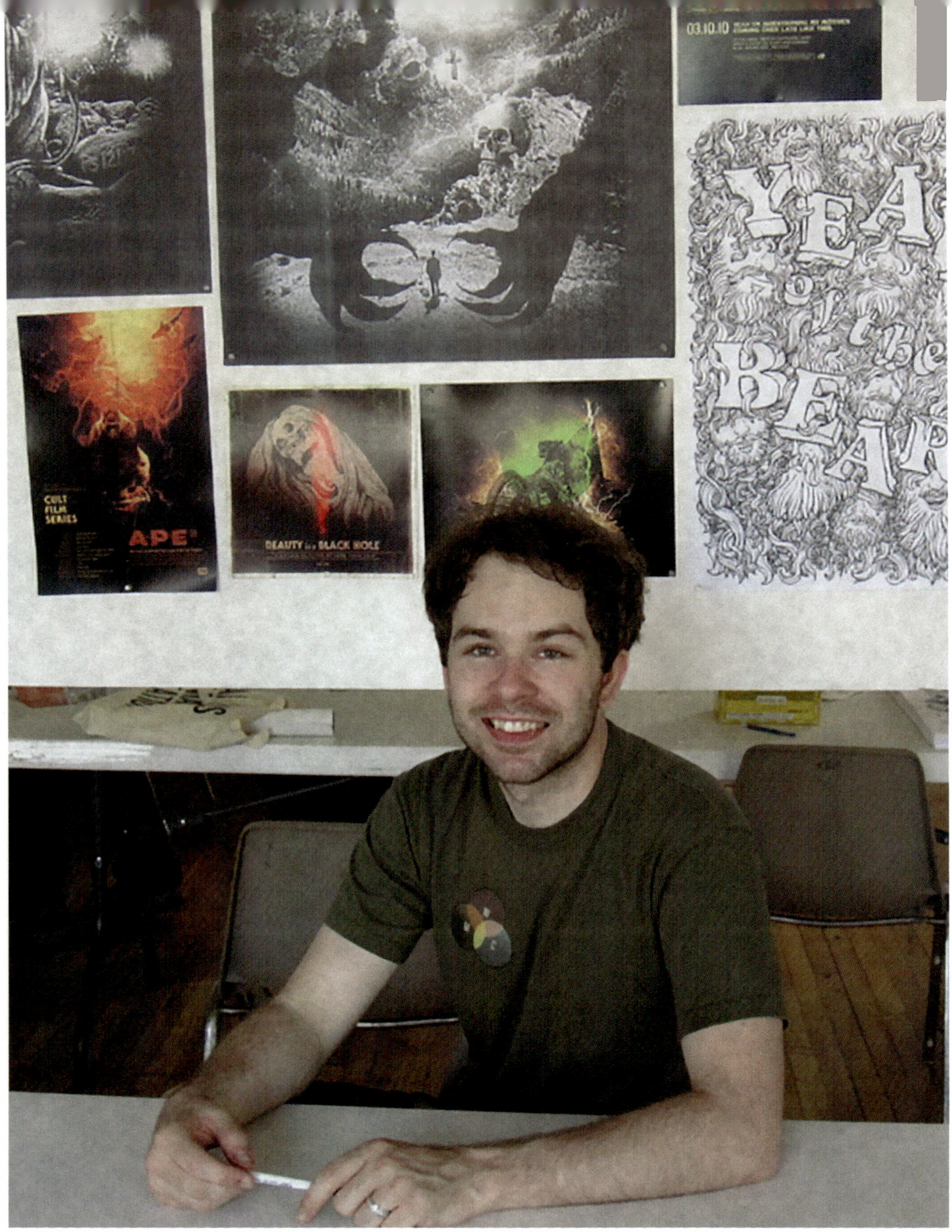

This is me after two long days at Weapons of Mass Creation Fest 2010

Network and Be Friendly

It's important to be approachable, friendly, and fun at events. You're there to meet people and have a good time. Don't be overly salesy or pushy when visitors are eyeing up your goods, that's a big turn off. Let them look and be available if they have questions. Don't be afraid to say hello or start up a conversation with someone. You might not get a sale, but you will still make an impression.

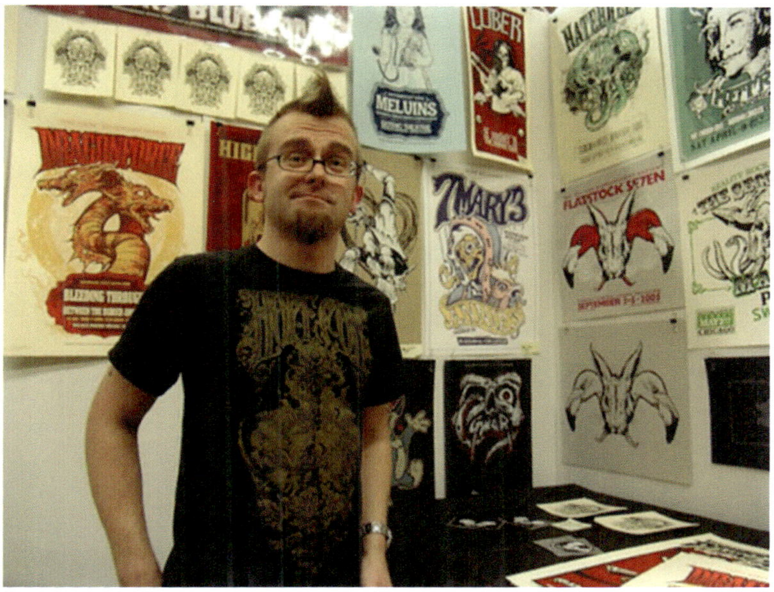

Justin Kamerer being friendly and showing off his mad skills at Flatstock. Photo by Kodiak Press.

More Tips for Selling at Events

- Come up with a gimmick or publicity stunt
- Encourage social media use with #hashtags
- Collaborate with other nearby vendors for cross promos
- Bring your own lighting setup
- Set up your booth in a high traffic location (intersections), avoid dead zones
- Provide seating or places for people to rest at your booth
- Keep things simple, show your best stuff
- Take pics with your visitors, post to social media
- Seed the crowd with free shirts, get people walking around with your tees
- Get the host or a band to mention your booth or temporary discount

Further Reading:

- **Make your booth stand out at trade shows**
- **Video: IATT Craft Fair Tips**

To view websites cited in this book, please visit www.threadsnotdead.com/links.

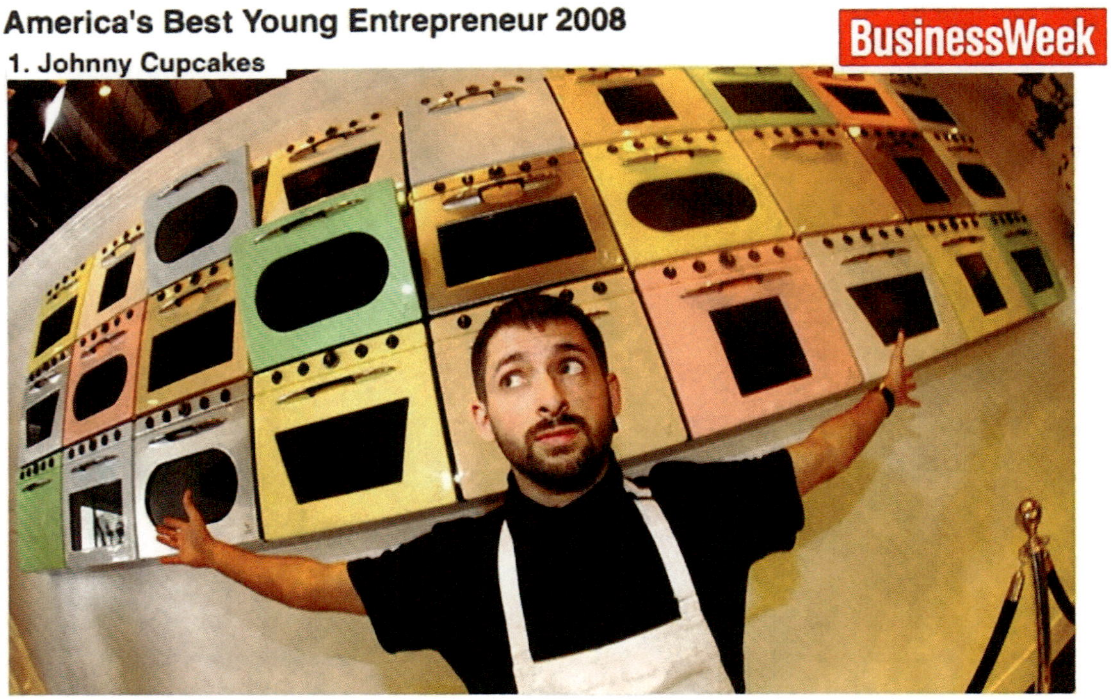

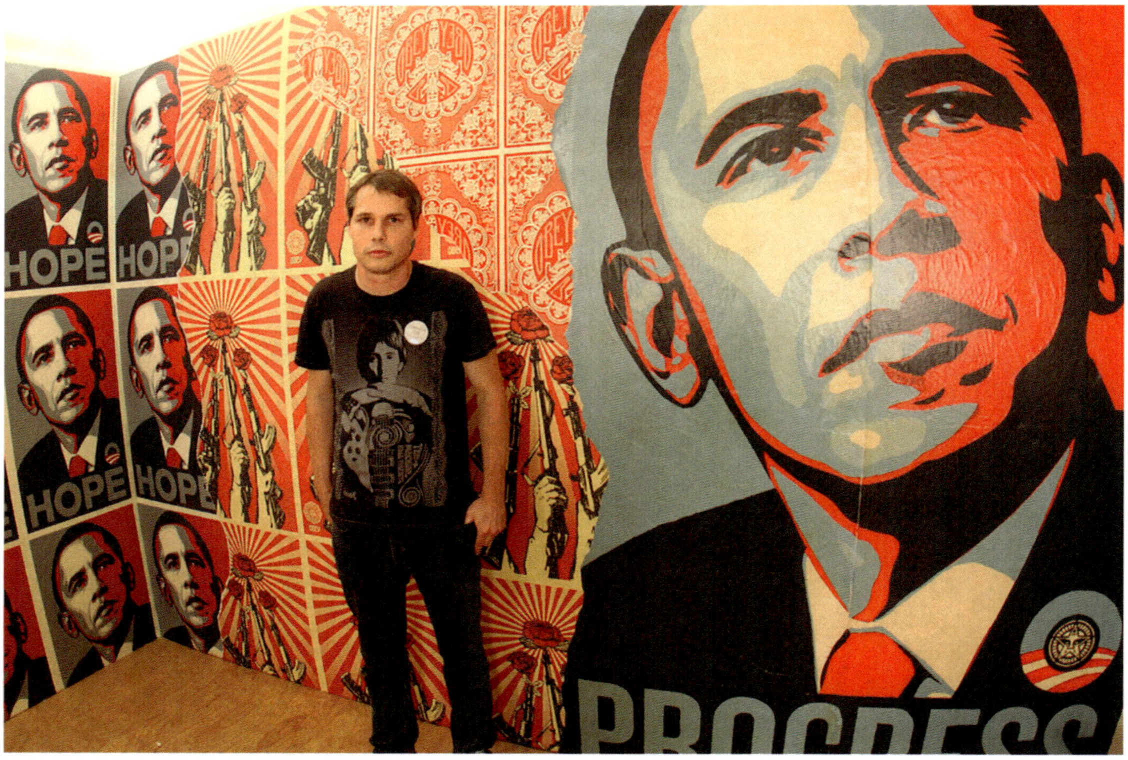

Johnny Cupcakes (top) and Shepard Fairey are two examples of designers that have "gone big-time" with their brand.

VIII

GOING BIG-TIME

Now is the time to ask yourself the big question. Do you really want to do this? Really?

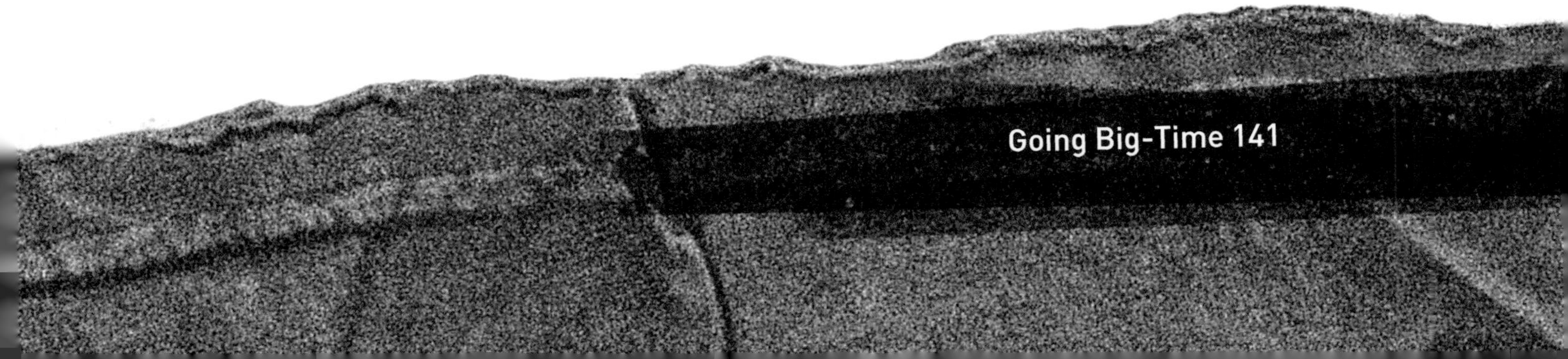

Never Say Die

Going big-time requires hustle and dedication and a never-say-die attitude. It's not for everyone. You should ask yourself how much of your life you are willing to dedicate to your brand because it's going to require lots of long hours and sleepless nights to get there.

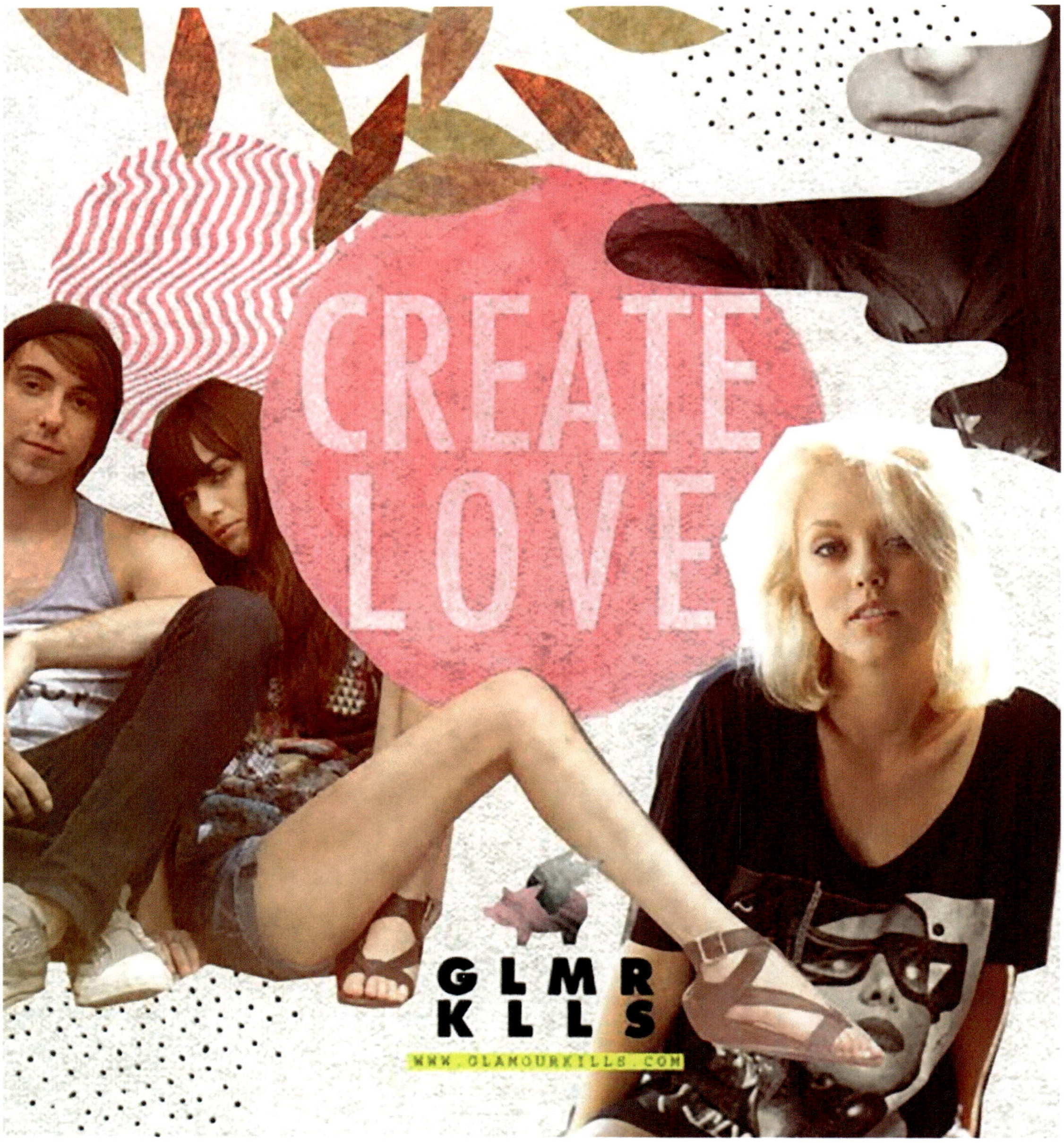

Glamour Kills magazine ad by Mike Zimmerman

"The thing I wish I had done from the start was run my clothing company as more of a business. In the beginning I was designing, printing, and shipping all the shirts. Now I don't do any of that. I know designers that are better than me that I get to design my ideas."

— *JON KRUSE, MEDIOCORE CLOTHING*

Most of the successful "big-time" brands will tell you it wasn't easy getting to where they are and that there's no formula for success. But you've got to be willing to tough it out, deal with rejection, and be ready to ride the roller coaster. You must also have the capabilities to manufacture hundreds or thousands of shirts. For those wanting to go beyond the side project phase and go big-time, read on.

Getting Help: Outsourcing and Employees

At some point you'll realize your t-shirt line is taking off. You're getting popular and shirts are steadily selling. You have had to restock shirts multiple times and you find yourself spending more time keeping up with demand and less time innovating. You might have considered hiring some help so you can focus on designing or building your brand.

Things you can outsource:

- Art and Design
- Printing or Manufacturing
- Website Design and Upkeep
- Advertising and Marketing
- Order Fulfillment
- Payroll, Accounting, Legal Stuff
- Customer Service
- Just about anything

Outsourcing

A lot of clothing companies will first start by outsourcing their designs to other artists. If you're an artist, it's sometimes difficult to let go of the reins. But if you've been doing this for a while and want to take it big-time, consider working or collaborating with other talented artists to keep your line fresh and relevant so you can focus on other things like marketing, branding, sales, etc. It's also good to use artists who have a big name or a following because that equals good exposure for your brand.

There are lots of things you can outsource. What are the aspects of your clothing company that you don't enjoy doing or aren't good at? Get other passionate people to do it for you. You can focus on what you do best.

However, the more you outsource, the more you take yourself out of your business. That's not necessarily a bad thing. That means you don't always have to be the one doing everything in order for your business to succeed. That's a tough concept for designers to grasp as they can't imagine taking themselves out of their own brand. **Marc Ecko**, for example, isn't the only one designing his t-shirts or responding to emails. He's built an enterprise around his vision and has taken it big-time.

Employees

The next step towards growing your clothing company is hiring employees. They can help with order fulfillment, website upkeep, social media, or some additional design work like ads or flyers. Maybe you want to bring in someone who can take charge of your marketing? They could spend their time spreading the word or negotiating sponsorships or ad rates in magazines. Or maybe you need a dedicated customer service person to answer emails in a timely manner while you're out negotiating a deal with a department store. Don't forget, if you've got employees, they need to be paid! This is where payroll and taxes come in.

Payroll and Taxes

You could pay your freelancers however they prefer, but your in-house employees are different. You could pay them in cash under the table, but you want to be legit and do things the right way. If you want to go big-time, you need to do it right.

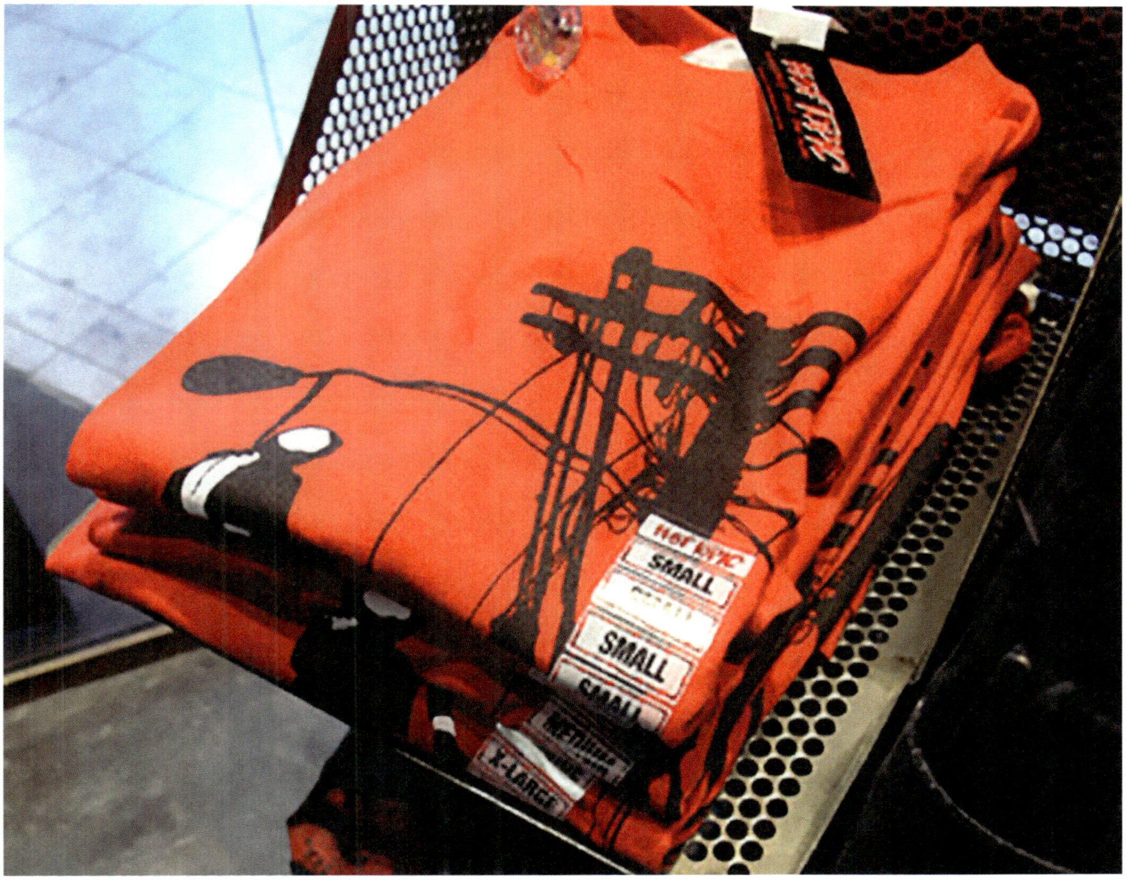

Rob Dobi had his Fullbleed line of t-shirts on the shelves at Hot Topic a few years ago

At Go Media, we use **PayCor** to manage our payroll. It automatically takes out the required taxes for each employee and gives them W2s at the end of the year (for the US). I don't know all the ins and outs of running payroll, but using a provider like **PayCor** or **PayChex** makes it easy to be legit and takes a lot of the guesswork out of it.

How to Get into Retail Stores

For a lot of brands, the holy grain of going big-time is getting into well-known retail shops. There's certainly an appeal to being able go into your local mall and see your brand on the racks. How do you get there? Here are some general tips for breaking into retail.

Be Proven. Your line needs to have a history of selling well. If you consistently sell out online or have built up a large fan base online, this increases your chances of getting into a retail shop. If all you have are mockups and no history of selling anything, you need to prove yourself first. It's like a band trying to get signed to a major label and play big shows when they can't sell out the local pub down the street.

Be retail-ready. This includes hang tags, custom poly bags or packaging, printed shirt tags, etc. You need to look put-together in order to be taken seriously by retail stores. Johnny Cupcakes often reminds people at his talks that those that pay extra attention to these little details are the ones that stand out and are successful.

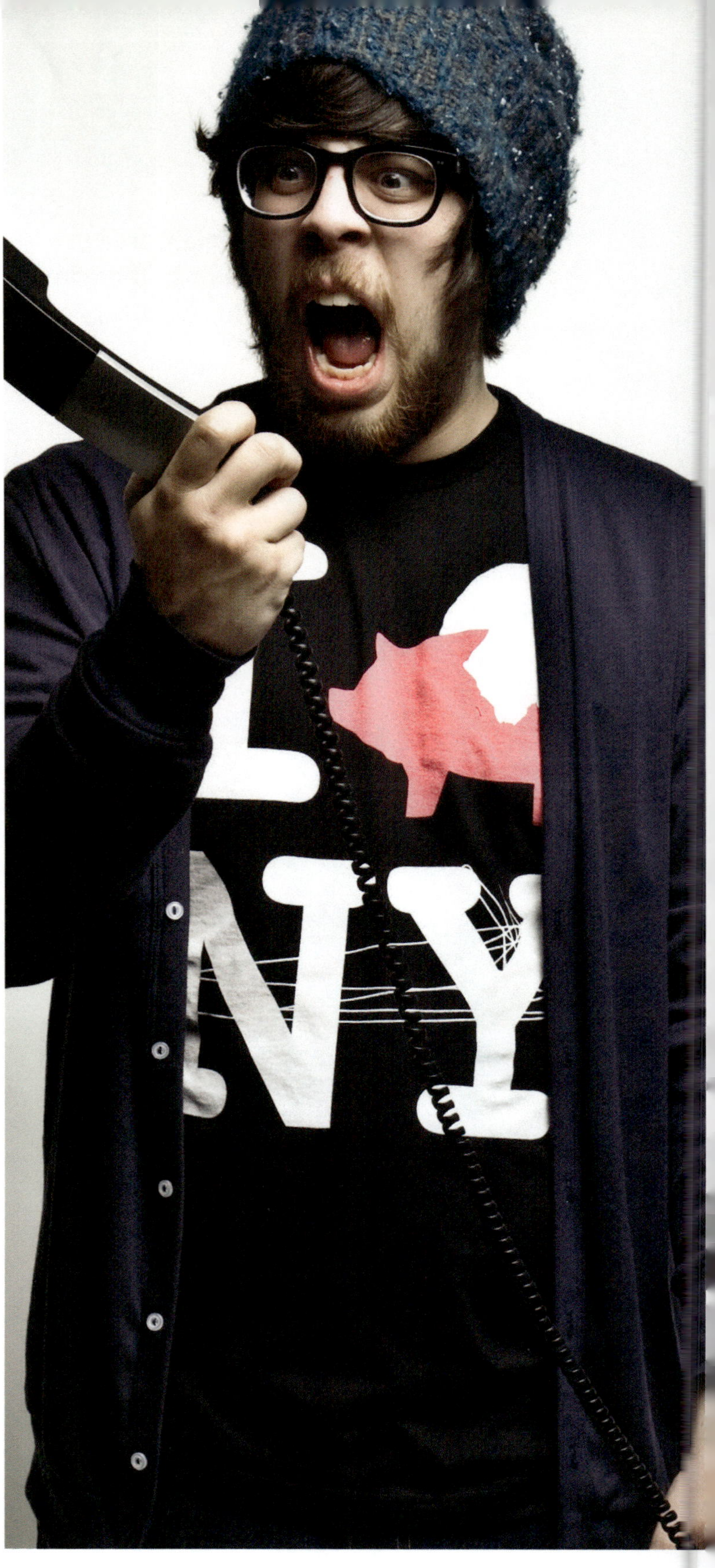

Mark Capicotto started Glamour Kills in his basement, and is now selling tees all over the world.

Have a line sheet or lookbook. A line sheet is basically a PDF of your t-shirt line with product info and photos. Include info about your brand, the names of the shirts, t-shirt color and specs, item number, prices, sizing, and other specs unique to your product.

Do your homework. Find out what stores you want to be in and get all the information you can about them. Make sure your brand fits the style and will look good with the rest of the products they sell.

Talk to the buyers. Find out who makes the buying decisions and set up an appointment to show them your samples. The employees at your local retail shop are not likely the ones making decisions.

Talk to other brands who have made it. Learn from their experience! Walk into the stores you want to be in and write down the names of the brands you find. Do your homework and look up contact information for them and introduce yourself. Be polite and see if you can set up an interview with them to discuss their experiences. If you have trouble finding information about a brand, it might be because they're a **store brand** under a different name. For example, I saw a brand called Aces & Eights at JCPenney once and couldn't find a damn thing about them online. From what I gathered, it was just JCPenney putting out a line of tees under that name.

Go to Trade Shows like **Magic** or **Pool**. You can meet a lot of retail buyers and talk to brand owners and consumers alike. You can really get a feel for what the current trends are at these events. Eventually, setting up your own booth should be on your annual to do list. There are others like **Agenda**, **ASR**, and Threadshow.

Hire a Sales Rep. Find someone who has experience selling apparel to retail buyers. They do this for a living and are likely better at it than you. They also already have the contacts that everyone wants but doesn't have. Some stores already have relationships with certain reps and buy from them often.

Bring samples. Retail buyers and sales reps like to be able see the actual products before they make a decision. It makes sense right? They like to feel the garment and test the quality and fit. This also gives your buyer a chance to notice all of your attention to detail!

Be professional yet personable. This is common sense in the industry. Buyers are attracted to people that know their product inside and out and can speak about it with passion and conviction. They buy from people they are comfortable with. If you can't manage to clean up and persuade someone to want your tees, then get a sales rep.

Be persistent and follow up. When you contact a store, rep, or buyer, don't be surprised if you don't hear back. These people can have hundreds of brands trying to get into their store! Make a spreadsheet of all the people you are contacting and when you need to follow up. Make sure you follow up and be persistent. Just don't be annoying and if they say no, it usually means no. Don't nag anyone, you don't want to damage your reputation.

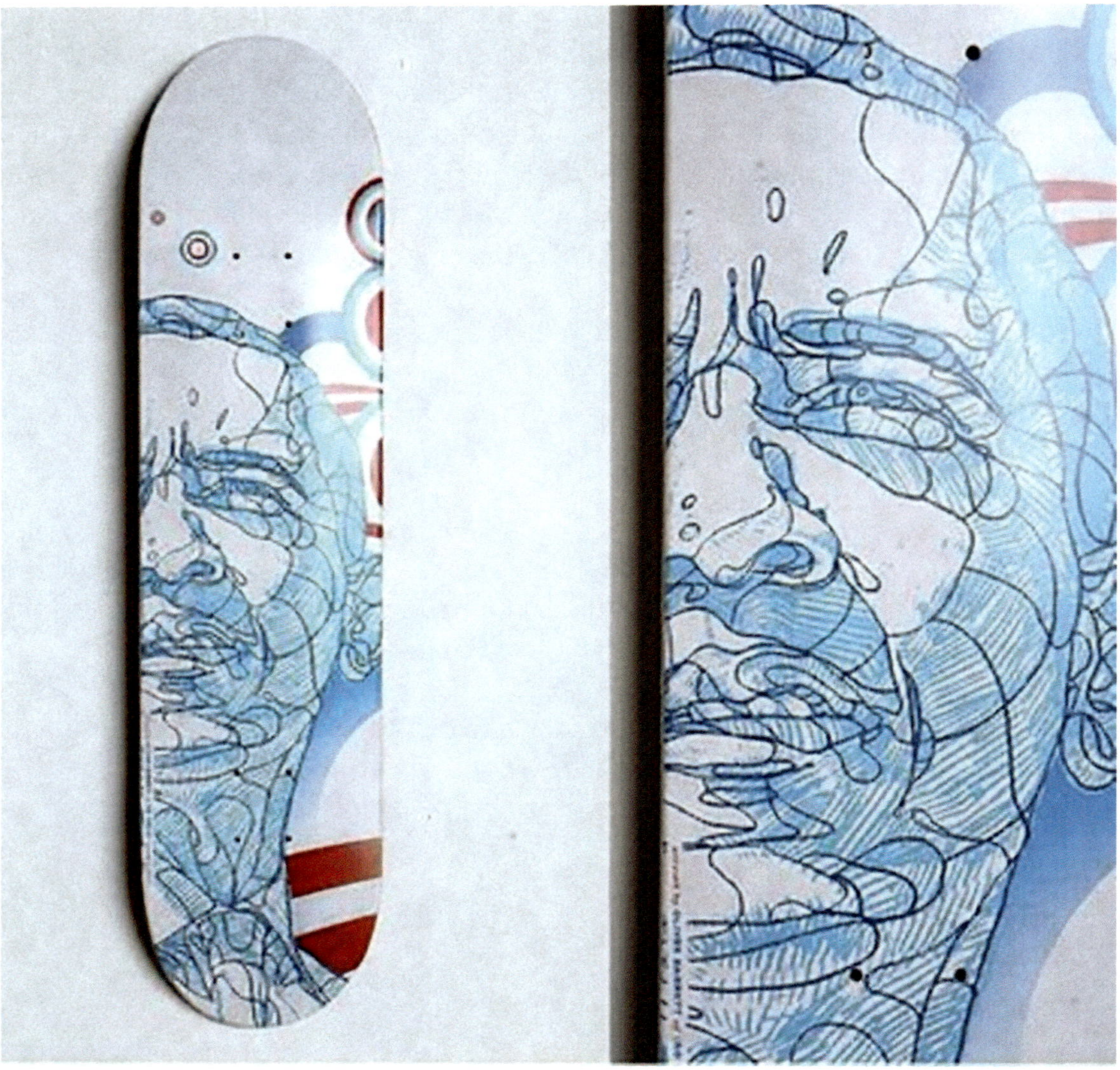

This skate deck designed by Oliver Barrett was sold at Urban Outfitters

Sell at Local Boutiques and Consignment Shops

You can swing by your local clothing boutiques and ask if you could sell your line on consignment. The terms vary, but you only get paid if the shirts sell. The shop gets to keep a percentage. This is a good way to get your feet wet selling in stores. There's no guarantee of making any money, but you can test the waters and get your brand name out there a little bit. You'll need to find shops that sell to the type of consumer you are looking for. Do your tees fit in with the boutique?

If you find that your tees are selling locally, then you can consider moving on to more national stores.

Sell at National Chains and Department Stores

If you want to sell your stuff at Hot Topic, H&M, or other chain stores like that, you'll need to talk to their regional sales reps. You can find them at the major apparel trade shows looking at hot new brands to buy up.

However, if you've got a large following online, these stores may find you through word of mouth. Urban Outfitters contacted Go Media asking to purchase a bunch of Obama skate decks that Oliver Barrett designed. We agreed on a price, signed the deal, and **saw the deck in their stores**. It was kind of a lucky shot there, but his design was timely and fit with what they were looking for.

Working with Distributors

Dave from Paint the Stars says, "Distributors are a great way to get your brand into places that you might not be able to reach independently." They can also help you with manufacturing and producing your tees. Getting a distribution deal is like getting a record deal, which is one way to get more exposure and sales.

Dave says he's had good and bad experiences with distributors. "We've found ourselves bound by some pretty unreasonable contracts that have only benefited the distributor and left us with nothing but a bunch of empty promises." He warns, "It's easy to get drawn in with promises of brand exposure, marketing you never dreamed of, and crazy production. So make sure you go through every minor detail of a contract before you sign it."

Through their roller coaster experience, they have decided to start their own distribution company called **Breakout Distribution** to help themselves and other indie brands take it to the next level without a lot of the fine print from major distros.

Further Reading:

- **Threads tagged "retailers" on T-Shirt Forums**
- **The High Cost of Doing Business with WalMart**
- **How Fashion Designers Break into Boutiques**

To view websites cited in this book, please visit www.threadsnotdead.com/links.

Become a Household Name

Quick, name three Apparel Companies that you know of off the top of your head and write them down. Who did you list? I listed Affliction, Johnny Cupcakes, and Billabong. I could have listed a lot more and rattled off all the chain stores in the mall like American Eagle, Hollister, Gap, A&F, Old Navy, etc. But that's too easy. Those brands are household names. You've reached household name status when your brand is instantly recognizable by a mass audience. I think we all know why those "mall brands" are household names, because they're in every body's backyard so to speak. You really can't get away from them because you're always reminded that they exist through mass exposure and advertising. Being a household name doesn't happen overnight and it doesn't necessarily mean you're the best brand out there. It just means everyone knows about you. We all know Coke and Pepsi exist. We all know Nike and Reebok exist but we might buy different brands regardless.

So let's go back and talk about the "indie" brands that I mentioned above.

Now take a minute and think why those were the first ones you thought of? What makes someone remember a brand immediately like this? Let's talk about each of the three brands and see why they are household indie brands in my mind.

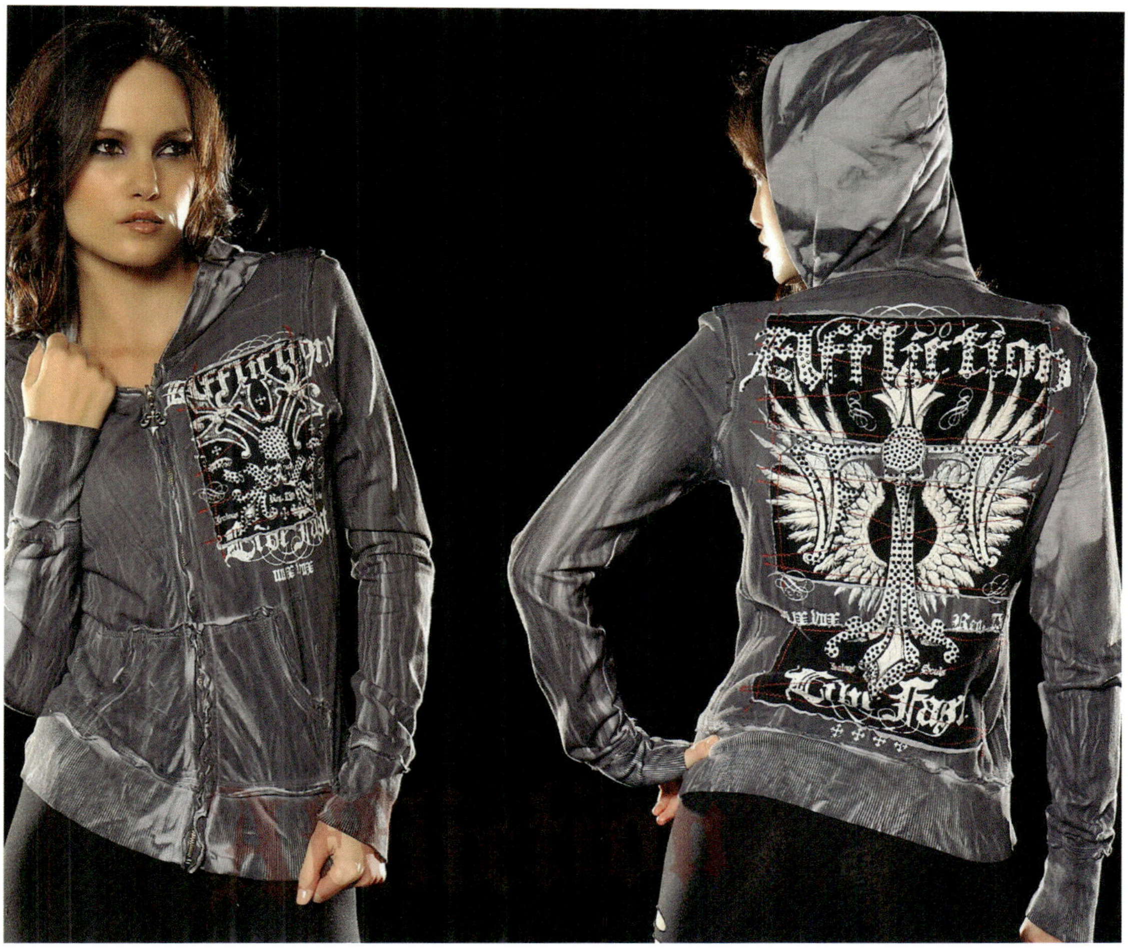

Affliction has become a household name because of the surge in popularity of Mixed Martial Arts and celebrity endorsements

Affliction

Affliction has become a household name around here because we constantly hear about them from new leads. Like I said before, we get lots of emails from new startup clothing companies citing Affliction as an influence. When we're constantly reminded of a brand for one reason or another it stays in our mind and becomes a standard. While the trend of "make it look like Affliction" is fading, it's still omnipresent in my mind whenever I think of a clothing company.

But why are these new startups name dropping Affliction more than other brands? Obviously they're getting their name out there and riding the wave of the MMA and UFC explosion. Mixed Martial Arts is becoming the new boxing; the new WWF. Affliction has cornered the market by sponsoring the biggest names and advertising in loads. They are being sold in department stores like JCPenney and Macy's. They took off first and inspired a legion of wannabes trying to ride their coattails. By getting to a market first, you cement yourself as the de facto standard, a household name.

Johnny Cupcakes

Johnny Cupcakes is another household name for me. Almost everyone I interviewed for this book lists JC as an influence or as an example of what a clothing company should do to be successful. I think Johnny is an inspiration because he came from our peers. He was "one of us" so to speak. He just seemed to hustle a little harder.

He started out selling t-shirts out of his car at shows and his friends gobbled them up. His rise to success is one of the most inspiring stories you'll read. He may not be known to your neighbors down the street or be competing for market share with Abercrombie, but in my own little slice of the world he's big-time. And that's all you need as a brand, to be seen as "big-time" in the minds and hearts of a smaller niche.

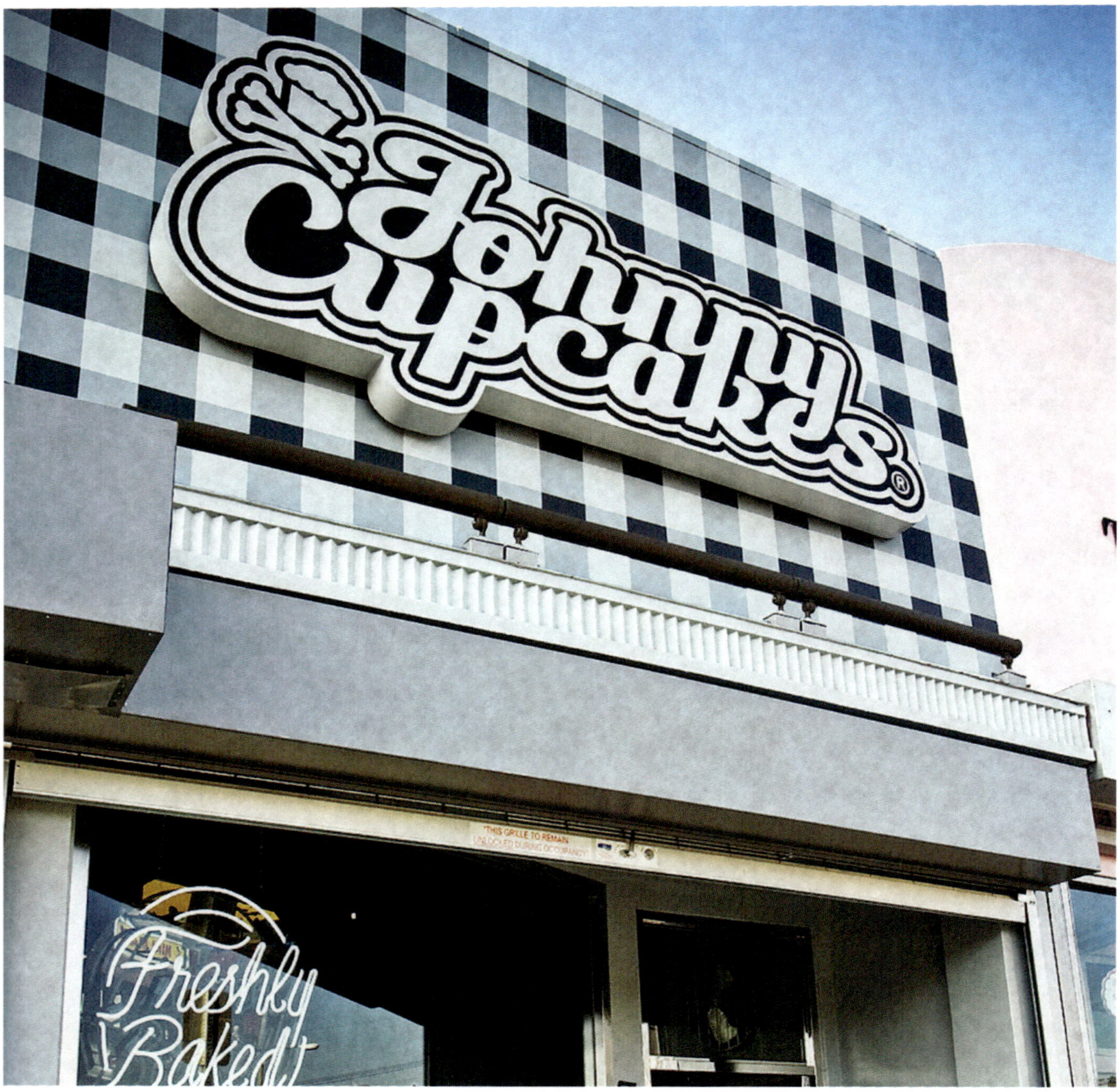

Billabong

Billabong is a household name for me as well because I can't keep myself from referring to them when I think of surf/skate apparel brands. Walk into any PacSun store in the mall and you'll be sure to see the Billabong name. In my humble Midwestern upbringing in the 90s, Billabong was what every wannabe skater kid was wearing. It was obvious that it struck a chord with those kids.

Another reason they're a household name for me is it symbolized an attainable "big brand" that I could design for. I saw other designers like Hydro 74 with Billabong designs in his portfolio and it gave me the inkling of hope that I could do it too. So whenever I thought about reaching the next level, it always seemed that Billabong popped up in my mind as a way to break out of obscure indie brands and into more mainstream brands. I never did do a design for them, but then again I haven't proactively gone after it. Maybe one day.

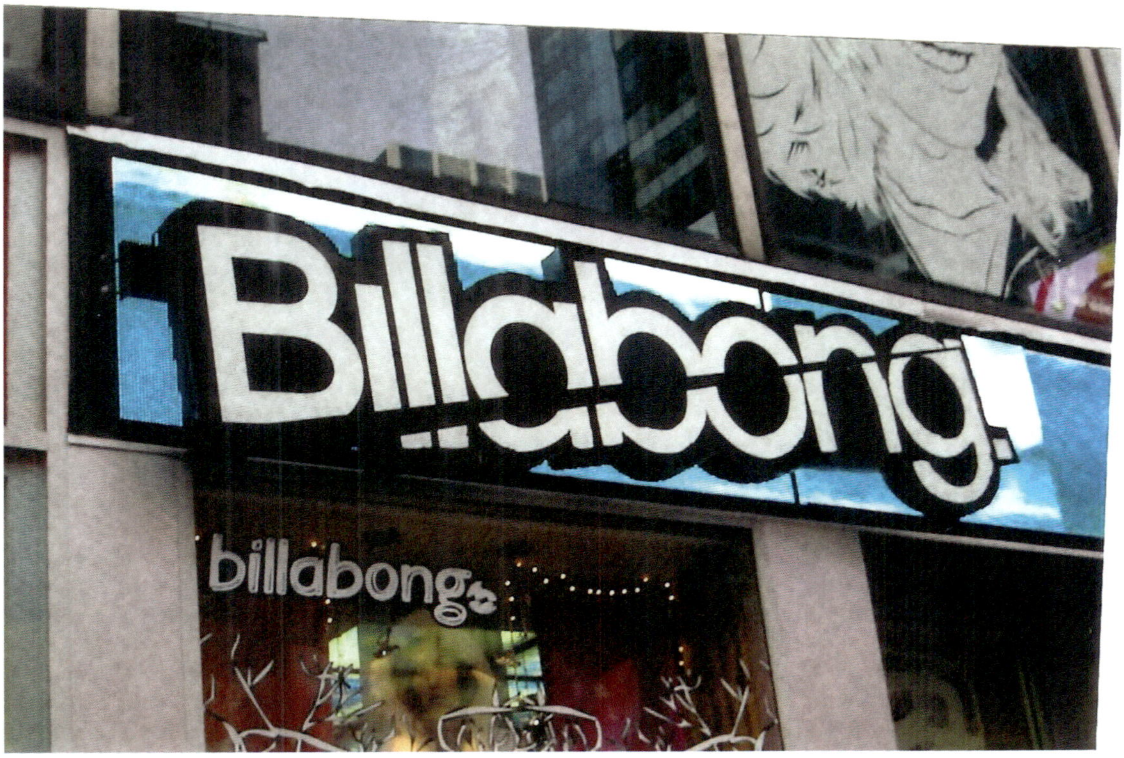

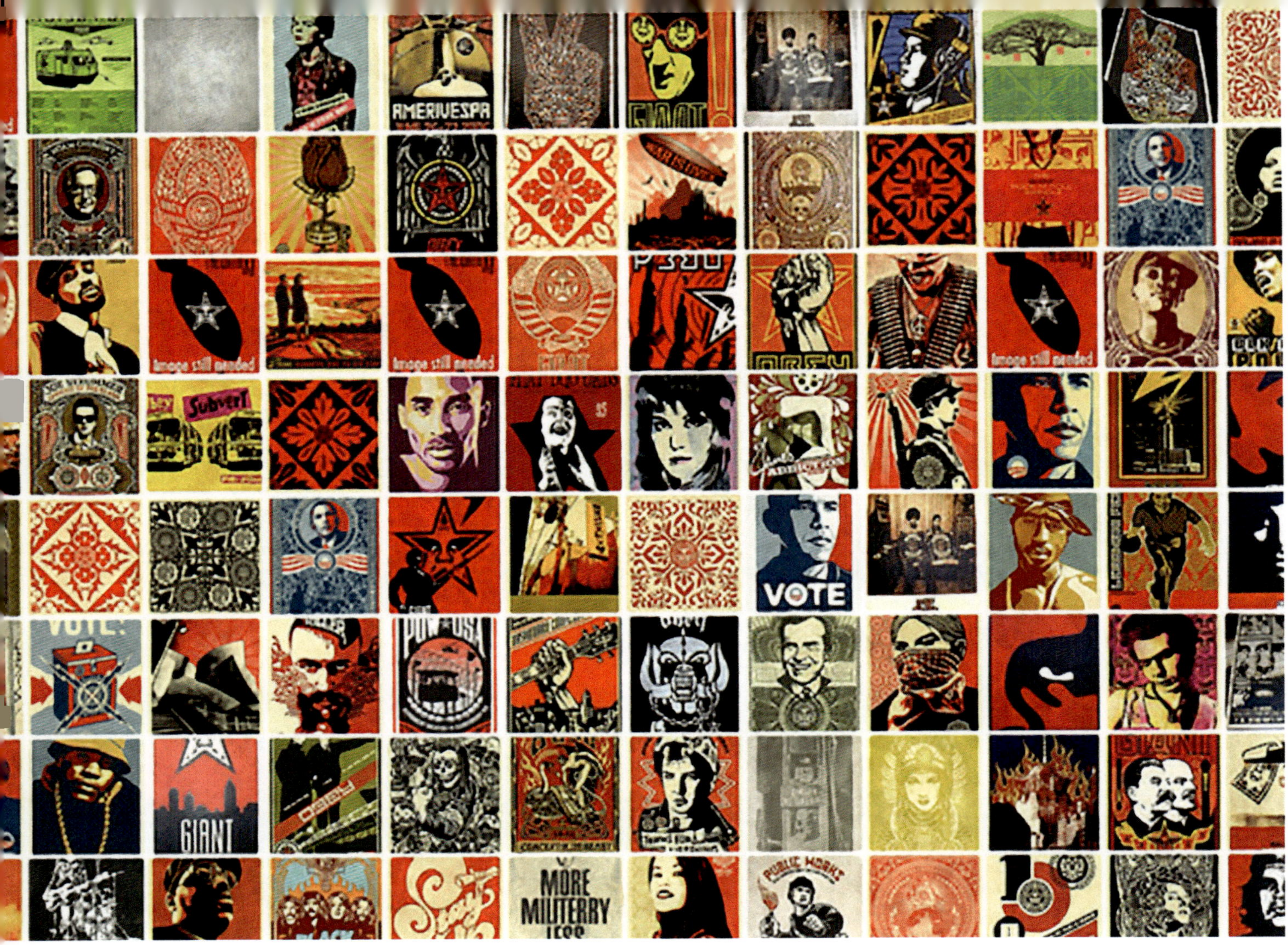

If you want to talk about leaving a legacy, look no further than Shepard Fairey.

Three Steps a Household Name

- **Be First.** If you're first to a market or first to do something a certain way you're in. You have a prime opportunity to take advantage of it. If you're not first, you can be the first one to do it bigger and better than everyone else.
- **Be memorable.** Be worth talking about. There's got to be a reason why people tell their friends about your brand or cite you as an inspiration in their life.
- **Be everywhere.** Be all over the web, tv, print, retail, trade shows, concerts, events, etc. The more times you are seen, the more people will think of you first. That's why brands spend a ridiculous amount of money on advertising. McDonald's is already well-known, but they continue to beat people over the head with their advertising. It will likely cost you lots of money too if you want to be everywhere, but that's the price you pay.

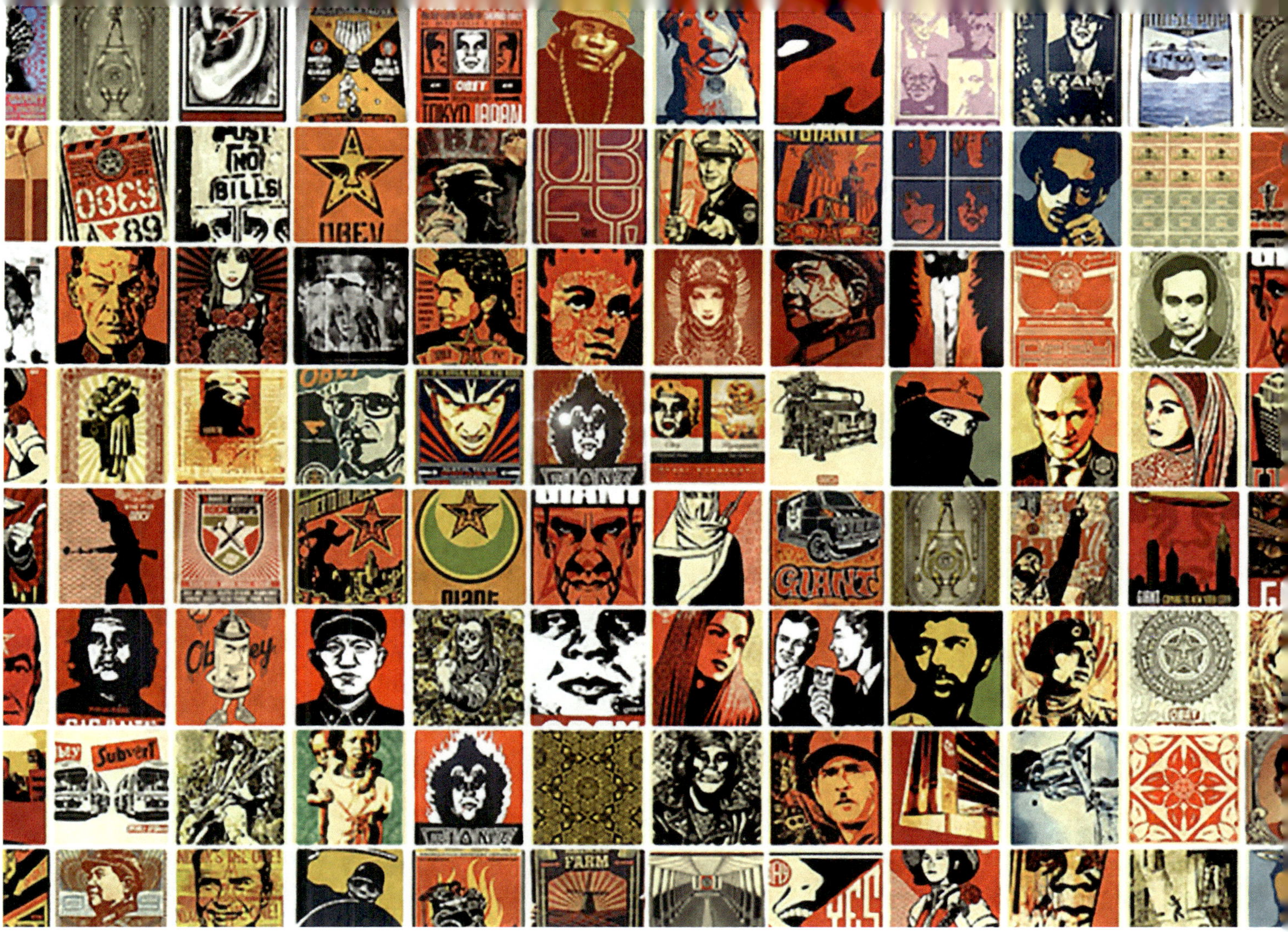

Leaving a Legacy

My recommendation is to find a niche and own it. Do something remarkable for that niche and do it bigger and better than everyone else. Give that niche something valuable that they can't let go of. Let your brand become part of their lives that they remember for a lifetime. Be an inspiration. Your brand could be the reason why people get involved with a certain lifestyle. That's the kind of legacy you want to leave behind.

To view websites cited in this book, please visit www.threadsnotdead.com/links.

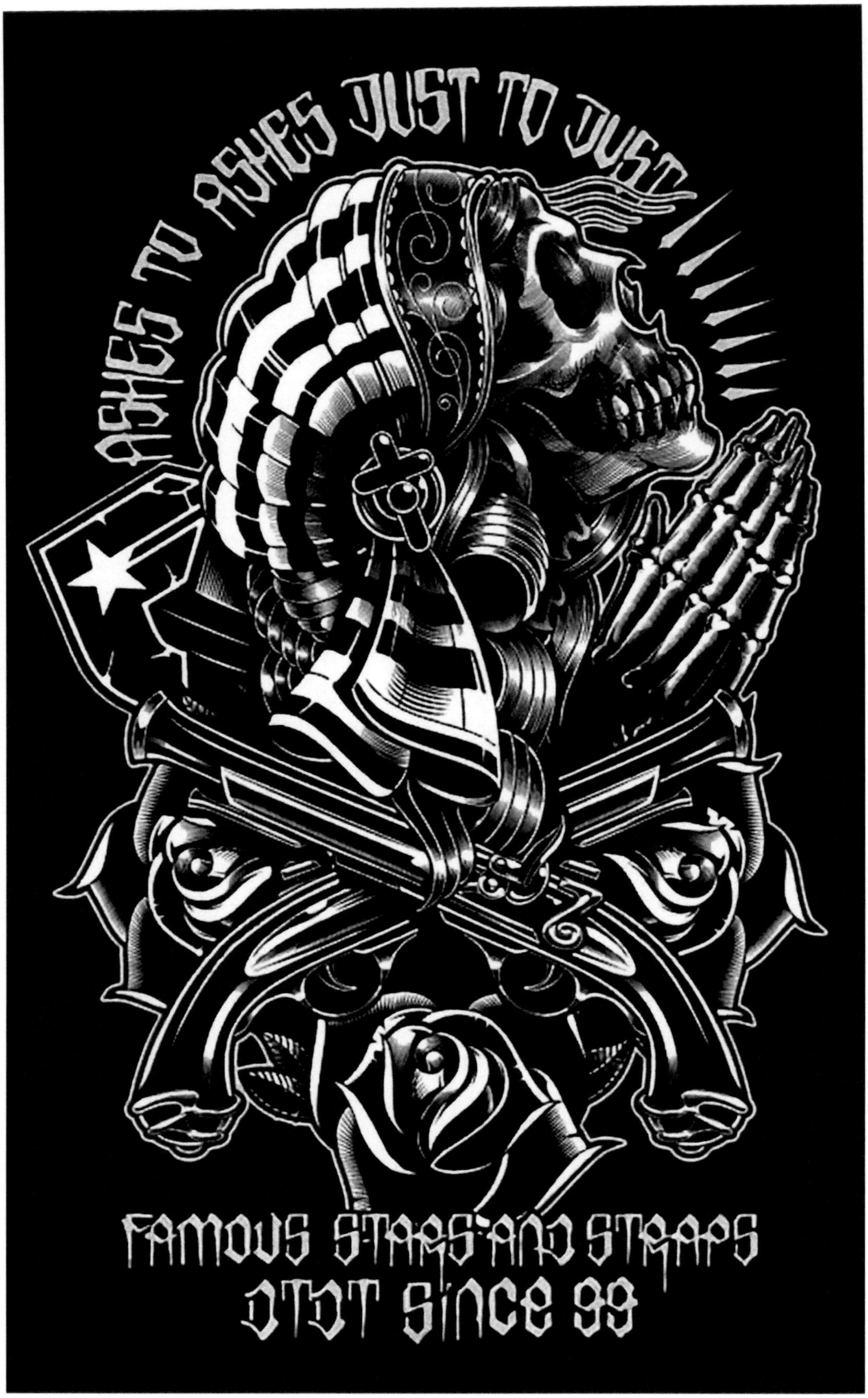

Illustration for Famous Stars and Straps by Maxx242

IX

CONCLUSION & NEXT ACTIONS

You've made it to the end! That's quite an achievement if you ask me. There was a lot of information to digest and it can be overwhelming if you look at it all as one big to do list. Don't sweat it.

Working on your own brand and clothing line is a very fun and rewarding experience. It's a wonderful journey as you will see. If you have any feedback for me regarding this book, please email me at jeff@gomedia.us.

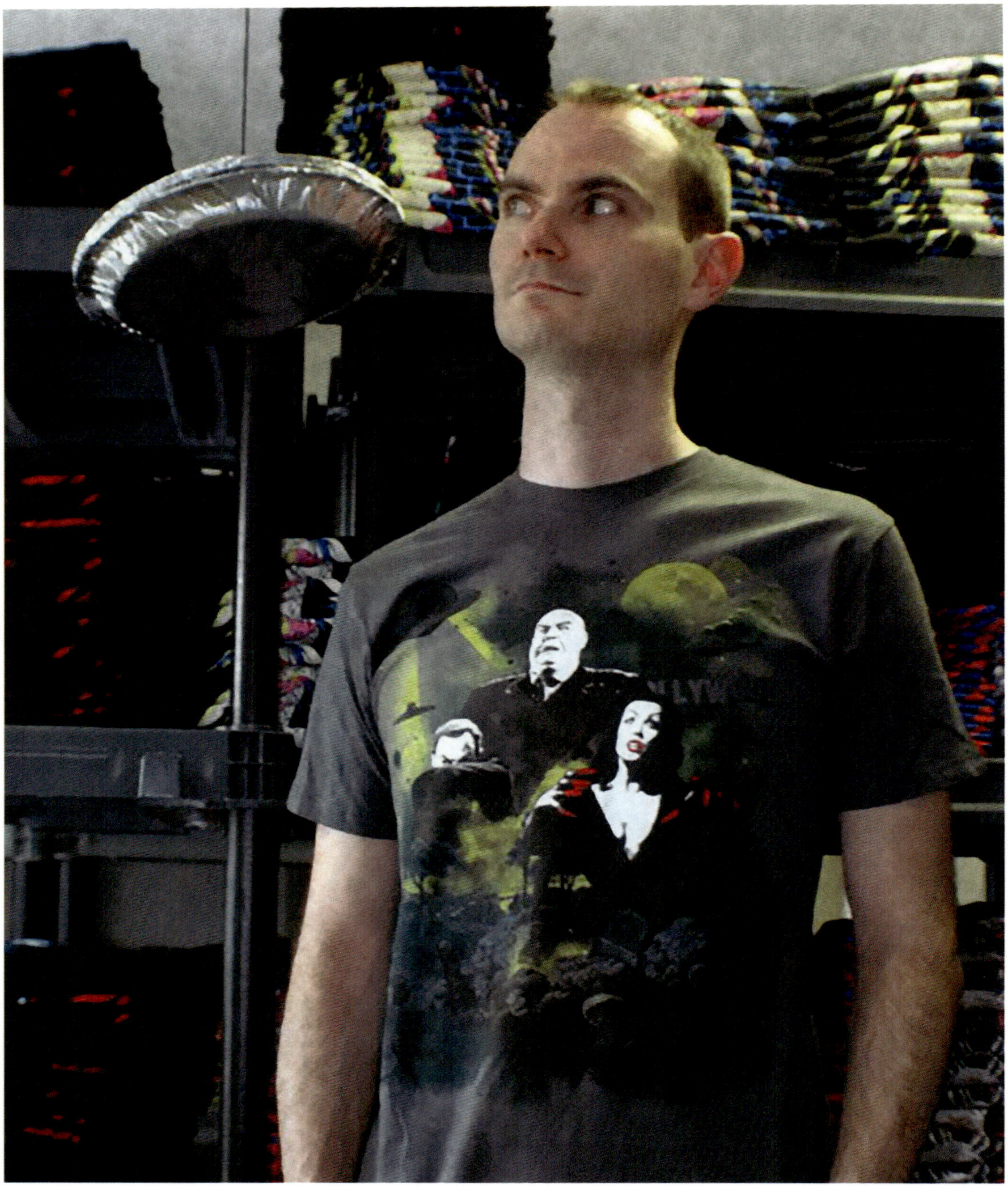

Ben Scrivens of Fright-Rags

Don't Overthink It

Remember why you got into this field? It's fun and rewarding. Designer Brandon Rike reminds us, "I also roll my eyes at the constant "over-talking" of an industry that is as simple as making cool graphics for bands [and apparel companies]. Let's not act like we're philosophers, let's just make good art."

Start! Don't Put it Off

This is a great strategy employed by the most successful people. What they've realized is that they don't need a five-year business plan. They have an idea and they take the first baby step to get things rolling.

I asked Ben Scrivens from Fright-Rags what he recommends for you to do and he says, "Start. As simple as that sounds, it's the one thing that holds people back the most. They get caught up in minutiae like copyrighting everything they do, or getting a trademark, or worried about their ideas getting stolen even before they have sold a single t-shirt. So my advice is to start right now. Dive in and figure it out while you're in it. Hell, I didn't even have a DBA until I received a check for $12,000 from Hot Topic and couldn't even cash it because it had my company name on it!"

Don't Worry about Problems You Don't Have

Matt Wigham of Big Cartel says, "Don't worry yet about how you're going to fulfill hundreds of orders per day, how you're going to run an affiliate program, or how you're going to scale your website to accomplish all the ideas you might have one day. If your products suck, none of that is going to matter. Stay focused on what matters [when you're small] and that's your designs."

Focus on what you Do Best

Ben from Fright-Rags says, "I find our best successes come from when we focus on the things we know we can succeed at, which is usually what we're most passionate about. When those things align, magical things happen. And cutting out all the distractions helps you do just that." Mark from Glamour Kills adds, "Figure out your style. Get to know it and embrace it. Don't try and do things because Johnny Cupcakes or Obey is doing it and it's popular at the moment. Find your niche and stick to it. Some of the best and long-running brands have their own aesthetic and still roll with the times, never straying from their own unique style and vision."

Hard Work Will Pay Off

"Get over yourself, and do the work. Don't be lazy. Laziness will not succeed," says Brandon Rike. Furthermore, Kelly Kiernan of Cure Apparel recalls what the owner of a car dealership once told him, "While you're 'jerking off' someone else is busting their ass for the things you want." The owner stressed the importance being proactive and persistent. Kelly says, "He made a huge impression on me. Until that conversation I never realized that you need to actively pursue your goals. If you really want something, work for it. You can get it with desire, dedication and persistence." Industry veteran Jamie Tallerico agrees, "Work hard! There are always people out there who really want it. Talent only goes so far."

Stay focused. Don't get involved in distractions that keep you from your goals. Enjoy the fruits of your labor but don't get lazy. Maxx242 says, "I try really hard not to let

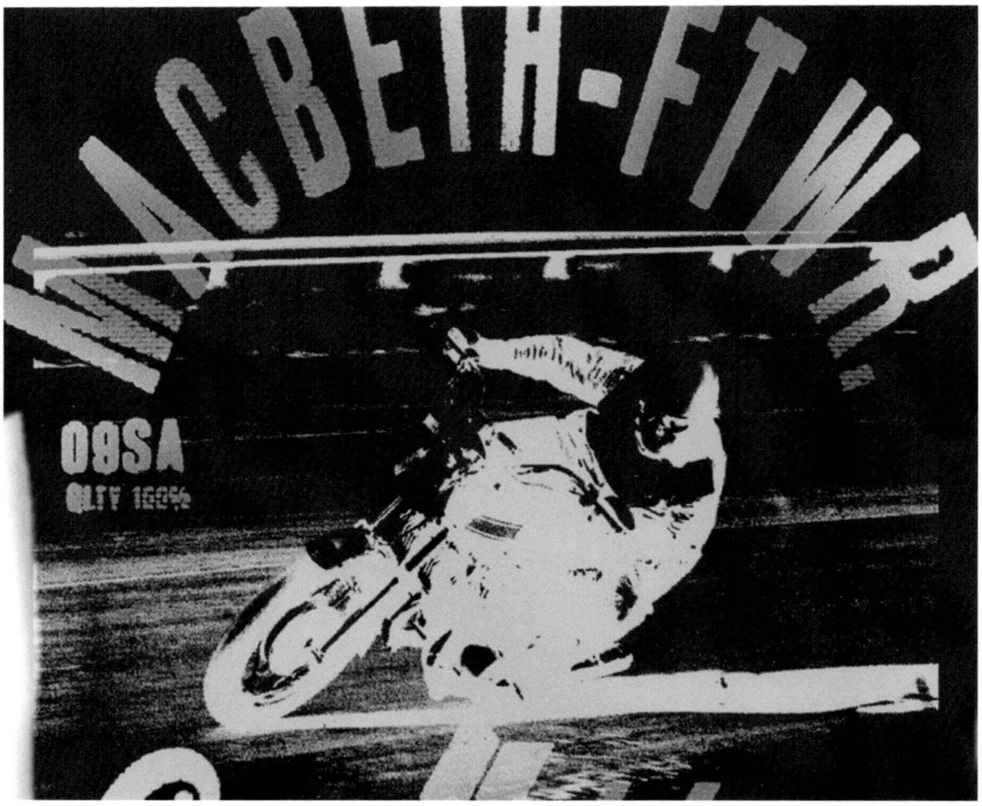

Design for Macbeth Footwear by Jamie Tallerico

a lot of distraction come along. I don't drink or smoke, I don't go out a lot. If I'm not at my desk drawing or in front of my computer, I'm spending time with my family. Do what you love, and do it a lot. Always look for artistic growth, we all have growing to do."

Get Involved in the Community

Adam Hendle from IATT says, "My biggest piece of advice would be to get involved in the community. There are so many helpful people, sites and resources at your fingertips that are there to help you. The absolute worst thing you can do is stay dormant. If you want people to take notice of you and your art you need to be visible."

Kelly Kiernan suggests "Making it a habit of stopping by sites like Emptees [or Mintees] and getting involved in blogs and forums." Dave Pearson from Paint the Stars adds, "It's a great tool for designers and a lot of people owe a large chunk of their success to that website. I know that I probably wouldn't have been hired half as many times without having a presence on that site."

Know Your History

There's nothing that irks industry veterans more than ignorant newbies that don't understand and appreciate the history and culture of design. Whatever niche you're in, do your research and be a "student of the game."

Justin Kamerer (Angryblue) says, "As a designer, I think it's important to submerge yourself in pop-culture and the pop-culture from eras gone. Understanding what makes certain illustrations or typography represent an era and why, is really valuable for having versatility in your portfolio. What makes those designs tick? What lettering styles made soviet posters or french deco posters have the style that only they have? Once you understand those, you can take them and pervert them for your own deviant needs."

Thanks to all the unselfish designers and entrepreneurs for helping me come up with great content and ideas for this book. Specifically Jon Kruse, Adam Hendle, Mark Capicotto, Kelly Kiernan, Dave Pearson, Matt Wigham, Marc Hemeon, Munk One, LT Magnotto, RikkiB, Jamie Tallerico, Simon Hartmann, Richard Minino, Justin Kamerer, Ben Scrivens, Brandon Rike, and Maxx242.

Ways to Connect

If you have feedback, questions, or would like to say thanks, you can **email me** or find me on **twitter**. You might also want to check out my **video tutorials**.

Share Your Story

Post a blog about your experience after reading this book and tell me about it. I might want to link to your story as inspiration for others. It's also some good exposure for you.

To view websites cited in this book, please visit www.threadsnotdead.com/links.

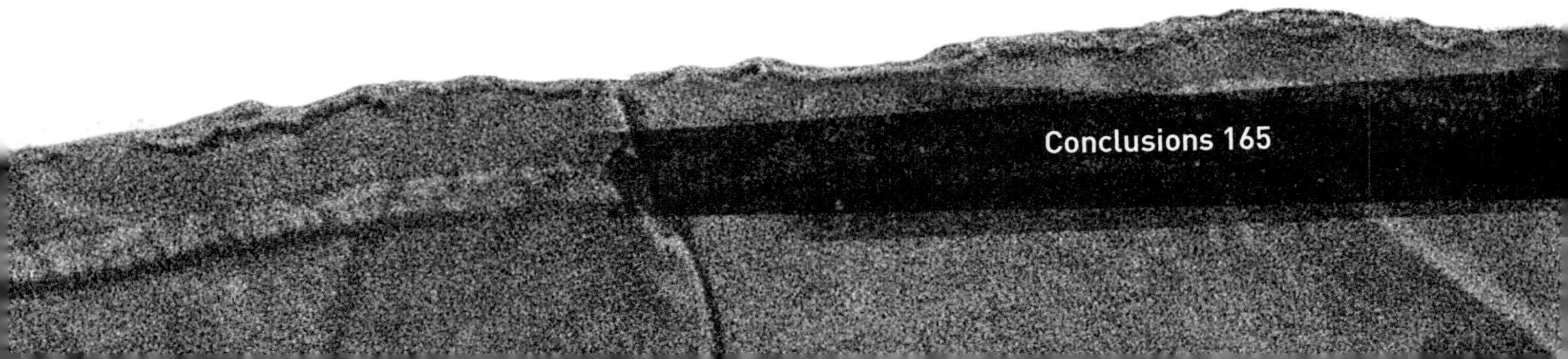

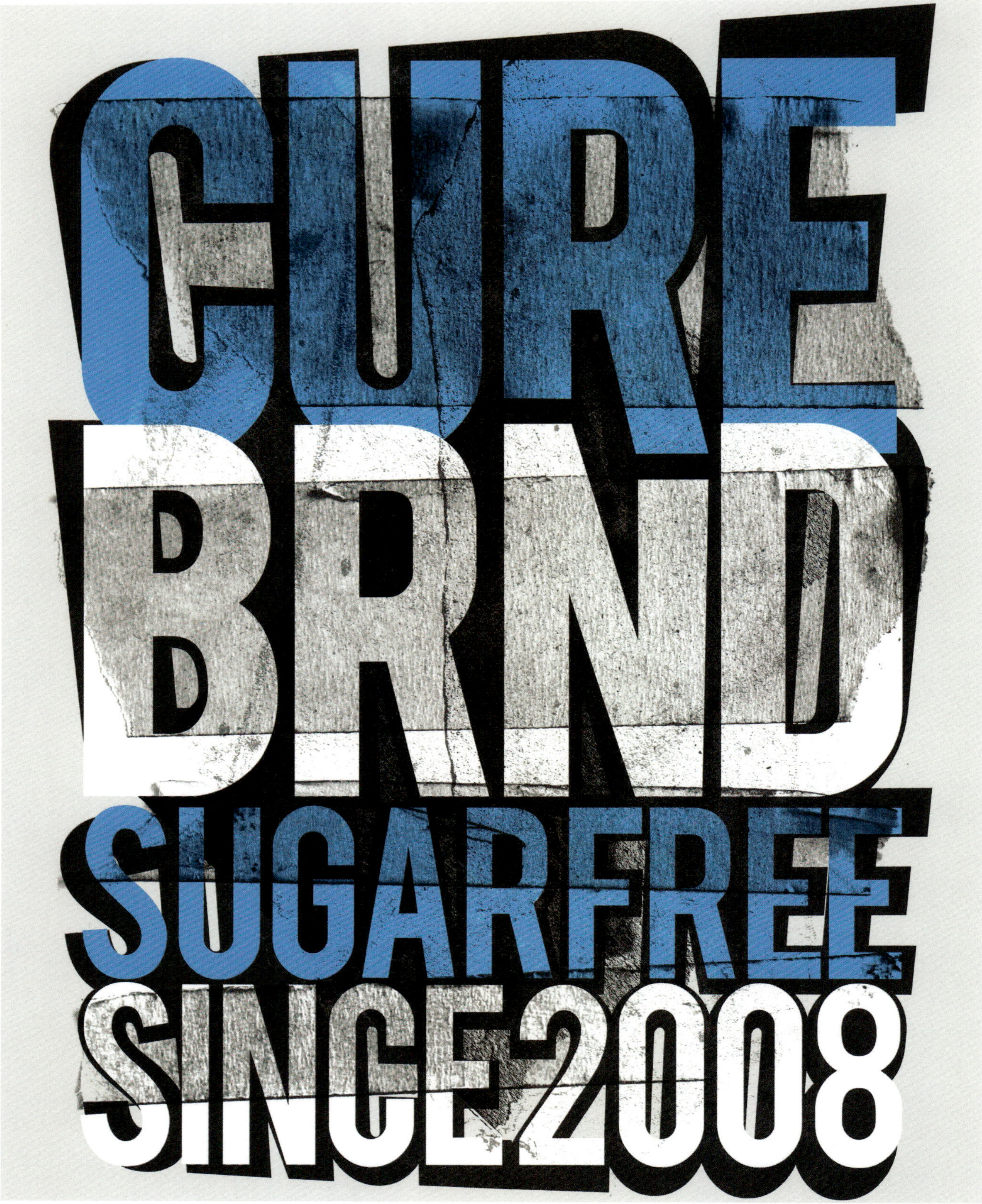

Kelly Kiernan designed this tee for his brand Cure Apparel

X

CASE STUDIES & INTERVIEWS

This is the part of the book that I put down my author hat and let some of my peers tell you their advice and stories. Some of them had specific advice to give while others told stories of their own experiences. I will let them speak for themselves.

Matt Wigham

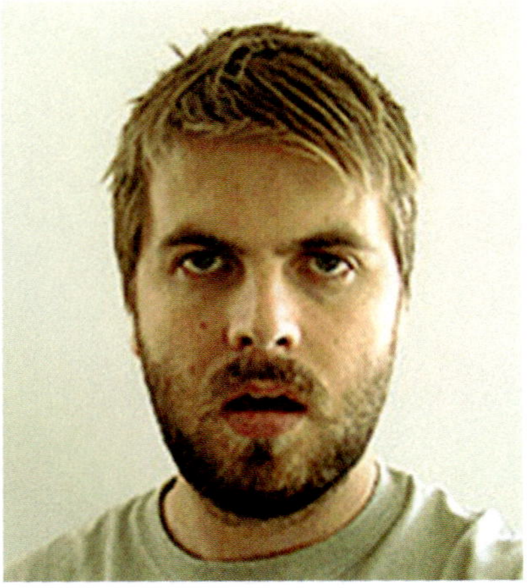

Over the years I've seen apparel companies come and go. I've seen designers go from no sales to thousands. I've seen them evolve from laughable beginners to widely respected experts. Most importantly, I've seen them make a living, or even just a few extra bucks, doing what they love.

At Indie Labs, each of our sites and services is tailored to help artists in different ways. Big Cartel, our online shopping cart service, has helped thousands of apparel companies get off the ground. Emptees, our website devoted to the art of t-shirt design, has helped designers of all sizes show off their work, get feedback from fellow designers, and make connections in the industry. And our newest service, Pulley, which is a way for artists to sell their digital products, is used by apparel designers to sell the other stuff they make, like vector artwork, illustrations, and more.

Our work has introduced us to some truly amazing designers, and we've seen them build their brands from the ground up. Here are a few things I think are critical to new designers, and things we've learned from those who've pulled it off.

Stay Focused on your Core Business

When you're just starting out as a new business, you're probably doing it on nights and weekends, with little to no money, and that makes it critical to stay focused on what really matters most to your business — your designs.

Don't worry yet about how you're going to fulfill hundreds of orders per day, how you're going to run an affiliate program, or how you're going to scale your website to accomplish all the ideas you might have one day. If your products suck, none of that is going to matter.

There are plenty of people and services that you can leverage to get the ball rolling, so the best thing you can do is create some great products and just get them out there. After that, things will evolve naturally, and if you're lucky enough to have growing pains later, you'll be better equipped to handle them.

Good photography is the secret sauce

When showing off your products online or in print, be sure to use beautiful and consistent photos. Even if you need to hire someone, it's worth it. You can have the best designs in the world, but they can only look as good as the photos they're in. Use a solid photographer, great models, consistent cropping, maybe some subtle branding, and your designs will look like a million bucks.

> *"Don't worry about how you're going to fulfill hundreds of orders per day... If your products suck, none of that is going to matter."* —MATT WIGHAM, BIG CARTEL

Promote like a human, not a robot

Everyone hates spam, and people thinking you're a spammer can be the nail in your business's coffin. Find organic ways to connect with potential customers. Try to honestly engage with them, don't just slap some flashing banner on their website, or send some email with no "unsubscribe" link to the first address you find. That's just lazy. Growing a customer base isn't easy, but when it's done right you can build off of it for years. Stick with it.

Building a business takes time.

Many of the apparel companies you see may seem like overnight successes, but you're likely missing the whole story. These companies have paid their dues, and it took them a while to learn what they know, and get where they are today. Accept the fact that you won't know what you're doing early on, but keep at it, and look forward to the journey of developing your own style and brand. We've seen so many of our customers and friends become successful businesses that I'm convinced you can do it too. The hardest step is the first, so just get started, stick with it, and enjoy the ride.

Munk One

I am 30 years old and have been in the business for over 11 years. I began at a large screen printing company working in the art/separation department as quality control of films. During this time I took some basic classes at the local college and learned as much as I could from the artists around me at work, eventually joining their ranks. I decided to become an autodidact and not to continue with college. Instead, I was learning on the job through books, magazines, the Internet, and practice. After years of working as an employee for apparel companies and improving my skills and knowledge of the business, I took the leap into self-employment as a freelance illustrator and fine artist. Working for myself has also been a learning experience that has allowed me to really put my creative yet analytical personality to full use.

"To help put you ahead, I would recommend learning and perfecting drawing and design skills instead of just using software as a crutch."

—MUNK ONE

I don't think I have had one particular breakthrough moment. I think it's more of a steady output of quality work that people tend to recognize. Some people are drawn to my work with certain bands while others are drawn to the zombies, clothing line work or the paintings.

Inspirations

My inspirations are always in a state of flux so right now the artists that make me want to create are French figure painters like Jules Joseph Lefebvre and William-Adolphe Bouguereau. Contemporary artists like Mark Fredrickson, Emek, Mark Ryden, Brian Ewing, Aaron Horkey, Jeff Soto, Hydro74, Maxx242, OG Abel, Louis Diaz, Mike Giant, and The Mac.

I think my way of standing out is to just be myself and not be tied down to one particular style or way of working. I always try to push each design to be the best it can be, while also pushing myself artistically. My website is my main tool of promotion and I have tried to make it as interesting and personal as I can while maintaining the focus on my art. The videos section has been a great tool as well.

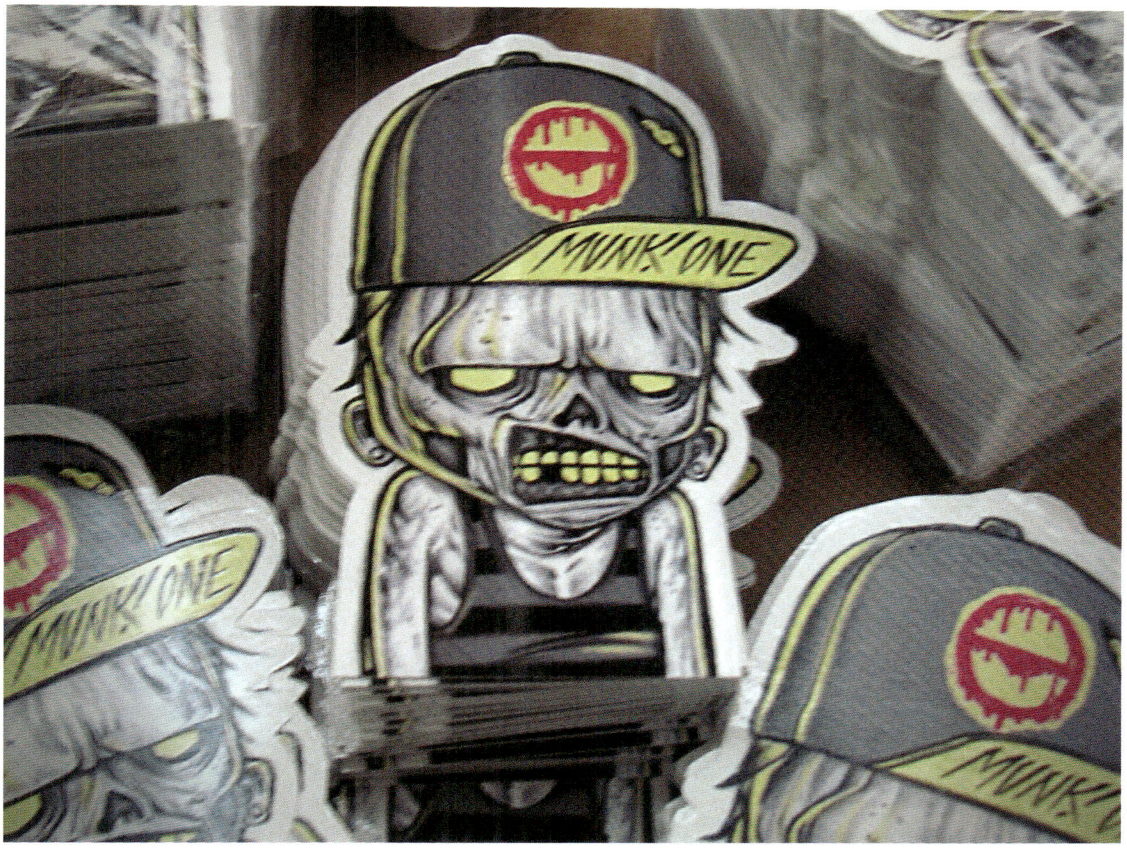

Don't Use Software as a Crutch

Right now it's almost too easy to use computer programs to skip the basic design skills artists should have. Looking at even the simplest design I can tell if someone can actually draw and has the skills to lay something original out. To help put you ahead, I would recommend learning and perfecting drawing and design skills instead of just using software as a crutch. I would also recommend learning about business and copyrights if you are working for yourself.

Perseverance

My career so far has been defined by hard work, perseverance, experimentation, continuous learning not only about art but also the business, and having a good time. I've also been lucky enough to work with good people who help promote me as an artist and not just as a hired hand.

Rob Dobi

I am a 29-year-old maker of visual things from Connecticut. I grew up wanting to be a comic book illustrator, eventually attending the Rhode Island School of Design with those same aspirations. Sometime during my last year I realized comics weren't for me and I wanted to take my art in another direction. I started doing illustrations based off of people in various music scenes but wasn't sure how to market it or what the appeal would be.

One day in 2003 a friend happened to introduce me to a band I was a fan of called Thursday. The band took a peek at my portfolio and liked what they saw. Soon their management emailed me and asked if I could send over some potential t-shirt designs. Having never really done any freelance work or merch design before I had no idea what I was getting myself into. Sure, I had been wearing band merch for years, but I didn't really understand the business side of it. I threw together something like 15 t-shirt ideas within the span of a few days. To my surprise the band actually wanted a few and printed them for a tour they were about to set out on. When I saw people wearing something I designed at a concert for the first time, I thought I might be onto something.

"When I saw people wearing something I designed at a concert for the first time, I thought I might be onto something." —ROB DOBI

Soon I started getting emails from other bands whom Thursday referred me to and I would design work for them. Eventually those bands happened to recommend me to other bands until one day I came to the realization that I kind of carved a niche for myself as a t-shirt designer pretty much by accident. I spent the next few years designing merchandise for bands and eventually started my own line of wearable merchandise [Fullbleed] based around the same aesthetics I was creating for those musicians.

Seven years later and I am still working in the music industry and creating my own personal work along the same lines.

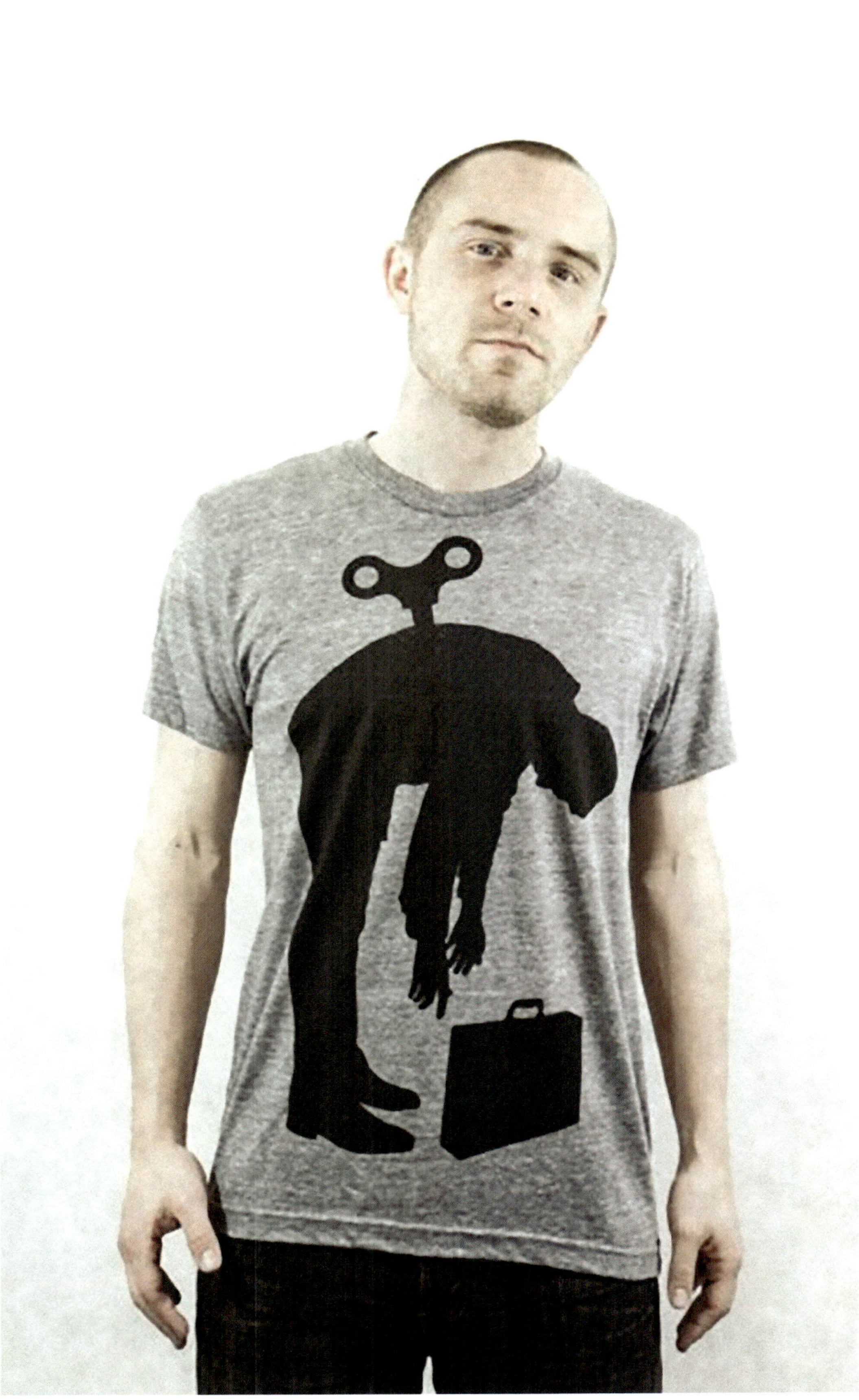

Dave Pearson

My name is Dave Pearson, I'm from Lincoln, England, I'm 25 and I'm the co-owner of Paint the Stars Clothing and Breakout Distribution Ltd. I'm also a freelance designer. I've been in the apparel industry for about five years.

Just Winging It

I'd be lying if I said that we started PTS with a long-term goal. I have the utmost respect for people who can say that they started their brand with a five-year plan and made it happen, but in our case it was the fact that my friend Martin and I were super bored in our little hometown one day and needed a creative outlet that wasn't playing in a terrible band.

I've been into art since I was a kid and was dipping my toe in the design pool and had done a couple of t-shirt designs for fun. Martin was a year into a degree in Media and I was helping him with some Photoshop techniques for his coursework, which he instead used to mess around with designing t-shirts. As we were both messing around with designing shirts we decided one day to start a project and design

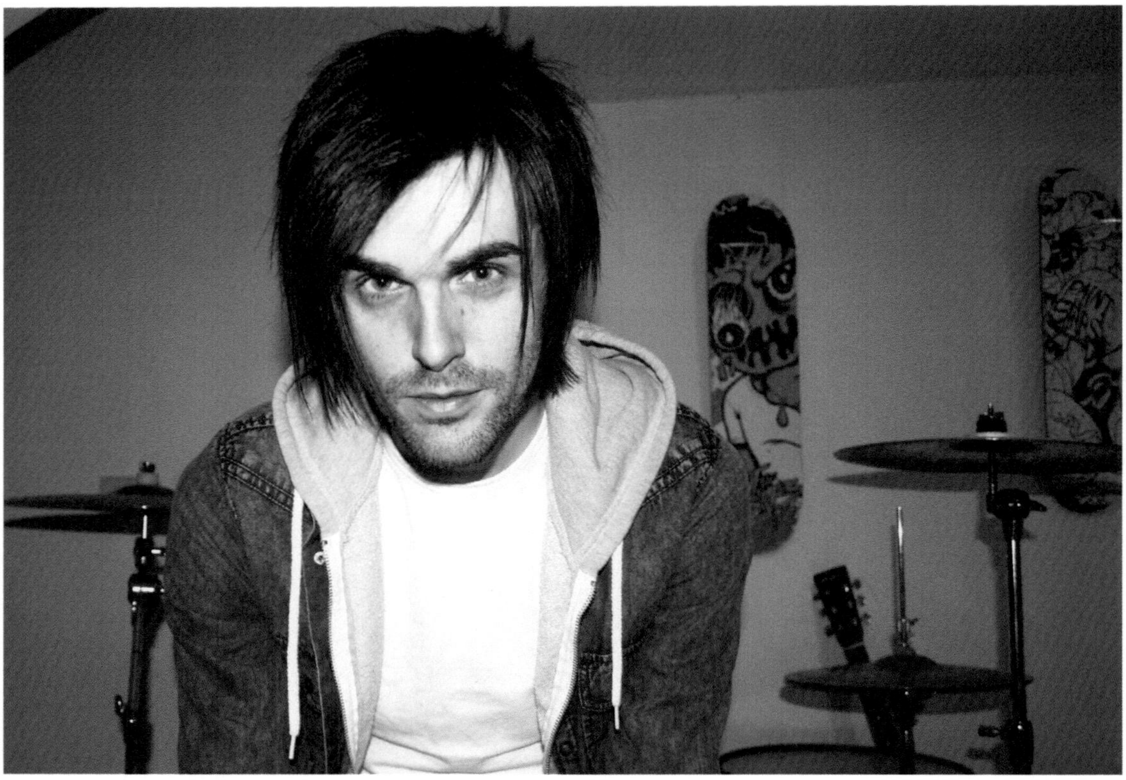

some clothing that we would wear, as we couldn't see anything else out there that grabbed us. We put a few (awful, awful) designs together, mocked them up, sent them to some stores to see what they thought and they all put in a bunch of orders which paid for our first print run. The tees (somehow) sold well which got us a solid fan-base, and the rest is history!

"I think it's pretty cool that two dudes who don't have a clue about designing for the apparel industry can wing it and be reasonably successful." —DAVE PEARSON, PAINT THE STARS

I remember having a conversation with Martin at the time and saying, "We'll give this two years, we'll more than likely be a flash in the pan, so two years is realistic. Maybe we'll come out of the other side with some business experience, some good times, and maybe a little bit of money if we're lucky." We weren't naive or arrogant enough to think we'd still be around after five years, but things just seemed to get crazier and bigger with each year, so we're genuinely humbled that it's worked out and that all of the hard work has paid off and that we're still here.

I think it's pretty cool that two dudes who don't have a clue about designing for the apparel industry can wing it and make a genuine go of a project and be reasonably successful, because to me that says that there's hope for everyone, and I'm always quick to draw on that point to reassure anyone who doubts themselves or thinks that it is an impossible goal.

Breakthrough Moment

Our breakthrough moment was probably when we started hearing from international stores who wanted to sell out stuff, because we never even imagined our brand would get recognized outside of our hometown, let alone outside of the country. This really inspired us to step up our game and made us realize that we were on to something. It all got very serious after that whereas before that we were having a bit of a jolly and just taking it for what it was.

Inspirations

Back in 2005 there were nowhere near as many brands around as there are today, and a lot of that has to do with the Internet and the way the music industry has grown to rely quite heavily on merchandise as there is a direct correlation between music, music merchandise, and music-inspired apparel. Back then it was all about the likes of Rockett (who are still awesome), Heartcore Clothing and Ordinary Clothing. They were all making a good go of it, so we looked up to those guys and that kind of status is what we were aiming for when we started out.

Before them, Blink-182 was still the biggest part of our lives (they probably still are), so all we knew of brands was Atticus and Famous Stars & Straps. We probably even drew some inspiration from them just because of how much Blink influenced us! If we could have put our name on some super-baggy Dickies or those really shit two-stripe baggy jeans with a bike chain hanging from the pocket, we probably would have!

These days there are so many brands around who inspire us and the market is so much more competitive. Which I think is great as it means everyone is battling to raise the bar. I'm sure a lot of people will say that Johnny Cupcakes is a huge inspiration. What Johnny Earle has done with that brand is phenomenal. Everything about his branding and marketing, attention to detail, his retail stores, the way he runs his business, the way he interacts and gives back to his customers...it just has the whole apparel community in awe. He's not a chancer like us, we've had some lucky breaks and have fallen into a lot of this as well as throwing in some hard work, but he's worked his ass off every day to get to where he is, harder than almost anyone in our industry, and he's known where he wants to be from the start. I'd love to get the standard of our branding somewhere near that one day.

Electric Zombie are really on top of their game at the moment too. Kyle's branding is tight and he's really putting his all into the attention to detail of his products and extras for customers, as are a lot of brands these days. You don't just get a t-shirt when you buy one anymore, you get a ton of creative goodies. That TMNT line EZ did was one of the best lines I've seen in years and it stunned everyone in the community. Pizza box packaging?! Genius!

Artists-wise there are too many inspirations to mention. Michael Shantz has carved out a great niche with that style of his. The way he captures humour with subtle lines and expressions in a way that can't be imitated is awesome. Chris Sandlin (Sock-Munkee) has really settled into his own style now as well. His linework is outstanding and we love working with him.

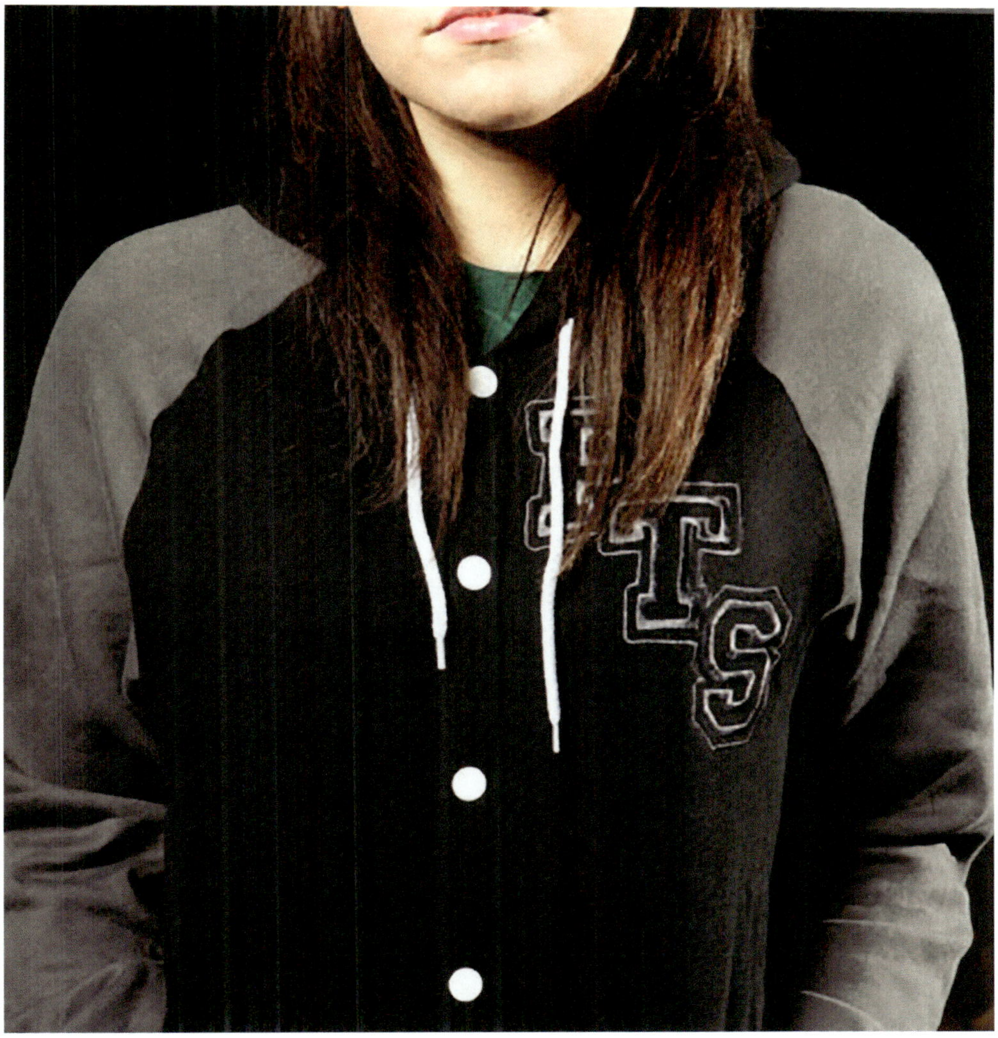

PTS Custom Jacket

Chad Lenjer is another dude who kills it every time. The fact that each design he does is a masterpiece in its own right is awesome. Chad is an artist in every sense of the word. His work wouldn't be out of place in an art gallery. Jon Contino is one of my favourite designers around at the moment. His work is timeless, classic and so versatile. I'm looking forward to working with him more. The Black Axe dudes are an awesome design collective, we love working with them. They all bring something to the table and you know when you hire them you're going to get something special and they really get what our brand is about.

Standing Out

We were quite lucky that we started when we did, because in late 2006 there was a bit of a MySpace boom, and it seemed like hundreds of brands just popped up overnight and started doing exactly what we and other companies like us were doing, which was great as it showed what a powerful tool MySpace was and it inspired a lot of kids to get into business and be creative which is great, but it definitely diluted the talent pool because of the sheer number of them that were out there. Fortunately, by the time that happened we had already built up a dedicated following, which is probably one of the reasons why we survived that washout as a lot of those brands died off after a little while. When that happened it really hit home that we needed to stand out more, so we thought about what we could do to not get lost among this sea of splatters, diamonds and knuckledusters.

We figured that if we put more emphasis on custom garments and pushing the boundaries of the production process then it would give us an edge and would make us harder to imitate. We also put in place an 'all killer no filler rule', we wanted to make sure that all of our ideas were well thought out and that we weren't just throw-

> *"It's a bit like a band signing to a major label. The record labels are always going to say, 'Hey, remember that hit single you wrote? Well I want a 12 track album full of songs exactly like that.'"* —DAVE PEARSON

ing loads of shit at the fan and hoping some of it stuck. We've got a big folder of unused/cut designs and we'd rather take the hit on paying for those than put them in a line that they don't fit in.

Self-Promotion

We've done a lot of good and bad promotion, but it's something that we feel is important and if you get it right can have a good impact on your sales and your profile. One of the things we do when we're going to see bands that we like is take a bunch of cus-

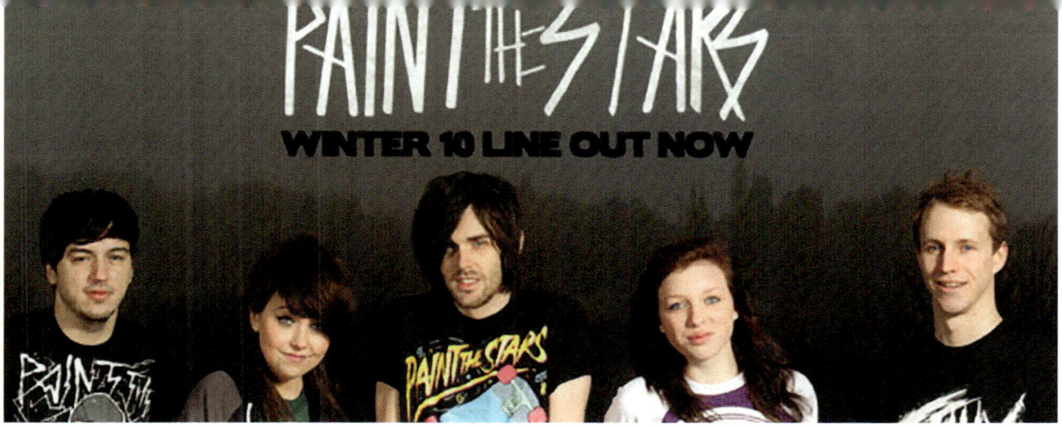

tom-shaped stickers or drink mats — cool little knick-knacks that people could keep — with our website and discount codes on them and just hand them out to people.

Giveaways are another great way to promote your business, and having customers post photos of themselves in your clothing is a great way to make people feel closer to the brand and more involved, and it's something they'll tell their friends about and can create a domino effect. We did try the avenue of band sponsorship, but it's tough to put in place. Glamour Kills do a great job of that, but they're quite notorious for sponsoring everyone! It does wonders for their brand though, so good for them.

What Would We Do Differently?

There's a bunch of things we'd probably do differently if we could do it all over again, but I think it's important to make mistakes so that you can learn from them. The majority of our bad decisions have been creative ones. We've put out some bad designs that I'm not proud of in retrospect, but that's growing up I guess. I remember reading an interview by Jesse Lacey of the band Brand New who are one of my favourite bands, and he said he found it really hard to listen to his old albums without feeling embarrassed because he can't relate to the person he was when he wrote those songs anymore because he'd grown up. And that's why you have to look forward instead of regretting things you've done. Business-wise we've made some good and bad decisions. We signed to a major distributor a couple of years ago, Europe's biggest music merchandise distributor in fact. It was a big deal. While it opened up a lot of doors for us, we did feel like we were working for "the man" and we did find ourselves questioning the ethics quite often because we didn't share the same goals.

It's a bit like a band signing to a major label. The record labels are always going to say, "Hey, remember that hit single you wrote? Well I want a 12 track album full of songs exactly like that." It's all good if you can look at yourself in the mirror and say, "I haven't sold out," but there was definitely a point when I couldn't do that...

probably around the time we did the Dark Knight collab, that was ridiculous, a great opportunity, but completely ridiculous.

Carve Out Your Own Style

Figure out what it is that you do best and really focus on carving out your own style. All of the best designers out there can be identified by their work. You can always spot a Finley, a Lenjer, a Sandlin, a Godmachine, a Henson, or a Shantz from a mile away, and I think that the fact that they each have their own style is what makes these guys successful. So I would say find your style, do a ton of work and pick the best of it, set up an online portfolio and start networking and make yourself known.

Emptees is a great tool for designers and a lot of people owe a large chunk of their success to that website, I know that I probably wouldn't have been hired half as many times as a designer as I have without having a presence on that site. Also, do some research and some reading — make sure you know what the industry standards are in terms of artwork specifications, client relations and business practices. It's not all about being great at drawing; you need to know how to run your business, because that is what you are, a business.

You need to know what companies expect from a designer, how much to charge and how to produce the goods and above all how you put each of those factors together as a professional service, because that's what your clients will remember when they've finished working with you.

Nobody wants to work with some cowboy who doesn't know what they're doing. It's up to you to make sure you come across the right way and at least seem to know what you're talking about.

Trends

There have been some pretty cool trends that have passed and some horrendously bad ones. Trends are something that I don't think anyone likes to admit that they actively follow, but in this industry it's difficult to avoid. You always find yourself as a designer being asked to draw a certain way or a certain subject matter, and as a brand you find yourself seeing something you like and feel you can improve, so by all accounts you are following trends, even if you're not consciously aware of it.

Two tees from the Paint the Stars winter line

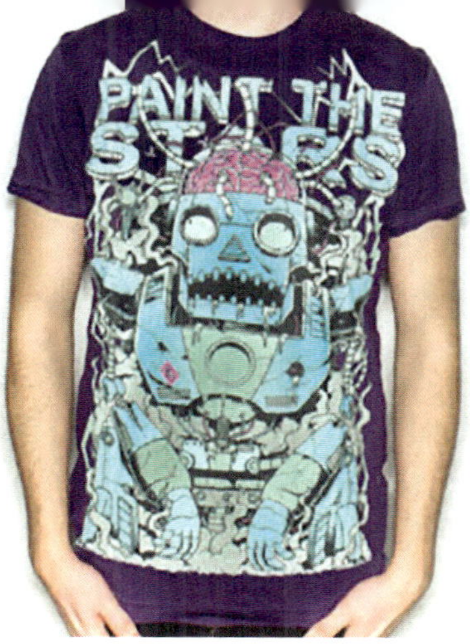

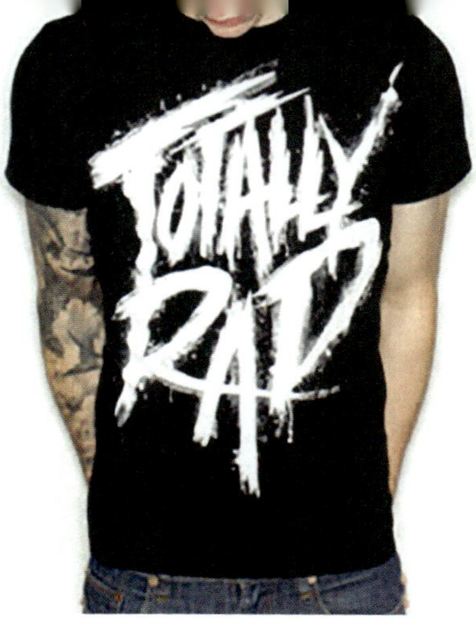

When we started there were a lot of guns, diamonds, knuckle dusters, broken hearts and splatters around. Bleeding Star Clothing were pioneers of that and could well have been the catalyst for it. Devin from Bleeding Star has always been an impressive designer, and kids loved it and a lot of brands went with similar themes when they saw how much he was killing it. Darkside Clothing from the UK are still plugging that particular trend, so there must still be people out there wanting it.

After that I seem to remember the "Nu Rave" trend hitting, everyone was doing those Wham!-style "Choose Life" capital letter text tees. I'm proud to say we never did any of those (although Martin wanted to do one that said "Butts & Dicks since 86" for a joke, but we didn't think anyone would get it). There was a "100% hand-drawn" (heh) revolution a couple of years ago — that was all childish scribbled designs and it was super popular for a while and a lot of brands and bands were going down that route.

It hasn't aged too well though, we had a couple of those kinds of designs and now they look like my three-year-old niece drew them. There have been a lot of subject matters that have been popular over the years too. I've seen dinosaurs, unicorns, skulls (lots of skulls), boomboxes, sharks, all sorts of stuff. Some of it is embarrassing, but ask your parents and they'll tell you that the 80s was embarrassing, hell, the 90s was embarrassing. My mum made me and my brothers wear matching shellsuits once. The point is anything you look back on can be embarrassing in one way or another, but everyone will say the same thing about it, "That's what we did back then."

Trends come and go. That's fashion. I don't think anyone should worry too much about the timelessness of their work. If you ever want to know what trend has just been in just take a look at what Criminal Damage are pushing at the time. They usually have whatever was popular a couple of months after the ball has dropped! Haha. Just kidding. They're a solid brand though...huge brand.

LT Magnotto

My name is LT Magnotto, I am 26 years old and have been making color separations for apparel screen printing full-time for the past six years. Like most designers, I had no idea how involved the screen printing process was. I was 20 years old, working part time at the YMCA doing before- and after-school childcare in order to pay for college. I was enrolled in the "Multimedia" program at the time which was teaching me everything from photo restoration to Flash animation.

Derek Hess and Jakprints

I picked up some hours working with local artist Derek Hess to design what was to be a new clothing line that features his art. We now all know it today as Strhess Clothing. I realized a few sessions in that I really didn't know anything about screen printing, and that if I were designing for it, that I should probably educate myself on the process. I figured that by knowing and understanding it better, that it would help me design better. Luckily, Derek's studio was directly above a small (at the time) screen printing company called Jakprints.

The owner Jacob at the time was doing all of the color separations himself. He had a real backwards approach to Photoshop to say the least. I was really intrigued by the way that he used the program and his wild methods of extracting colors. Jacob had no formal training in the program and had figured out how to use it in his own way. Jakprints was growing fast and Jacob was no longer able to juggle separating for two shifts of production and all of the travel involved in owning a growing business and he offered me the job.

Sink or Swim!

It was a terrifying time in my life. I feel like it was one of those moments where I was thrown into a pool for the first time and just told to start swimming. That being said, I was able to really learn the process through trial and error and develop my own methods. I wasn't really the most popular dude in the shop at that point.

You have to remember is that separations are step one in a long process. When I screw up, there are a whole line of people who now have to redo everything! New films need to be made, screens need to be coated, then exposed, blown out, dried, taped up, lined up on the press, ink loaded, and then printed. Repeat this process

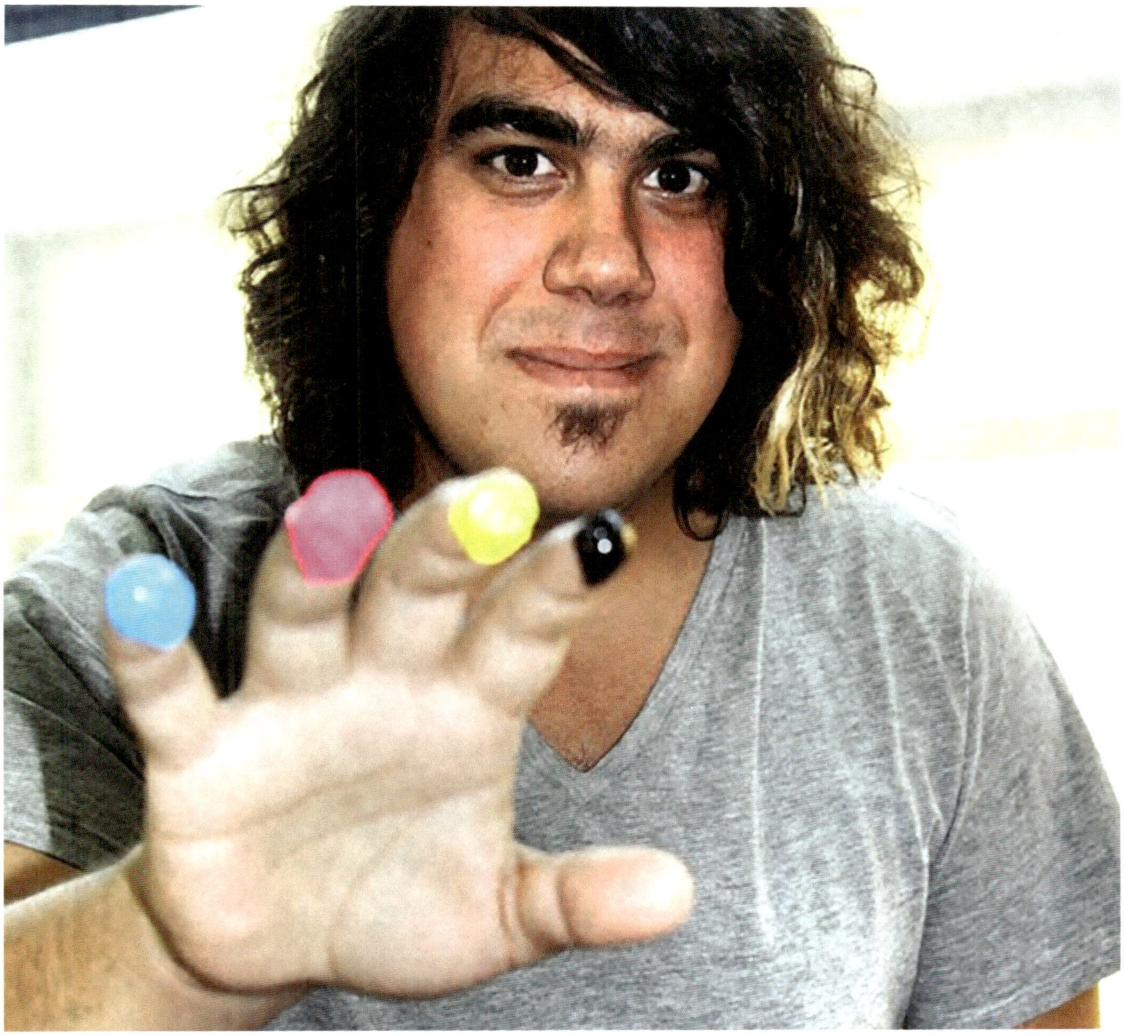

LT Magnotto has earned a reputation for being one of the best color separators in the biz

ten times a day because there is a noob behind the wheel and I bet you will get the idea of the vibe in the shop. Sink or swim!

When you get into wild color separations and simulated process printing, you are essentially painting on the t-shirt. There is no true way to view in Photoshop how the colors are going to simulate with each other or how Pantone 102 C isn't going to simulate the way you wanted it to with Pantone 185 C. Six years and thousands of dollars in destroyed t-shirts later, I'm doing full color simulated process separations for t-shirts that hang in stores at the mall.

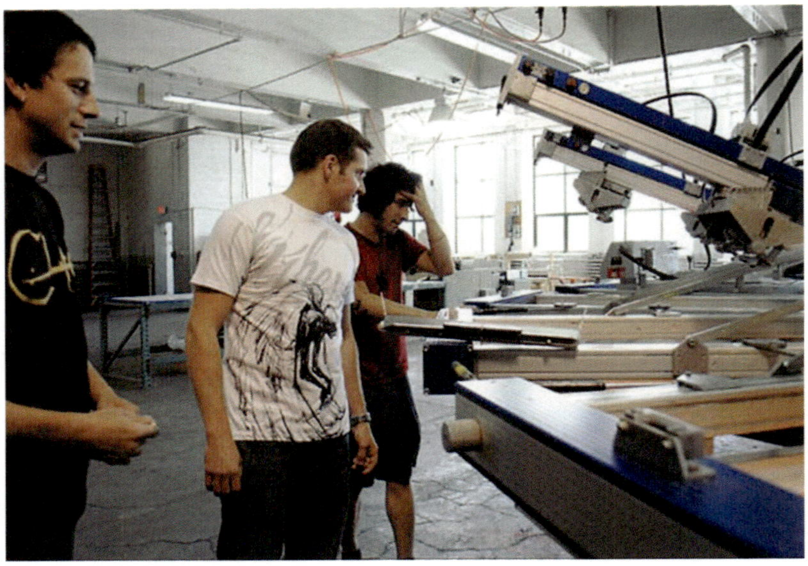

The screen printing press at Jakprints

Respect the Printing Process

If I could give any advice to designers it is to try and have realistic expectations and respect for the printing process. There are no screen printing robots (yet) printing your shirts, chances are its just your average starving artist or tattooed band guy plopping solid coated Pantone-matched plastisol ink into your screens. The same guy is exposing and blowing each and every halftone dot out of the screen.

My biggest pet peeve with designers who take a stab at printing is bitmapping! Stop it! Let the professionals handle your halftoning and angles! Most designers when they bitmap an image have no clue what their printer's capabilities are. The size of your halftone dot is determining the mesh that your image can be burned on and sometimes the dots can't even be held! Your standard shop is going to be able to print in the range of 35 LPI–65 LPI. Please keep that in mind when designing with halftone dots. Any dot smaller than 65 more than likely will not be held on press.

If you plan on designing for apparel printing, please invest in a Solid Coated Pantone book. This is the only way to truly control your design from point A to completion. I deal with snooty designers all of the time who are unhappy with their print because their orange on their calibrated monitor happened to look yellow on my calibrated monitor. The chances of your screen looking the same as someone else's is slim to none. All of this can be avoided simply by calling out your Pantone colors. Pantone 109 in your book looks exactly like Pantone 109 in my book. Problem solved, everyone is happy.

Trend Watching

I have seen it all. When I first started, I rarely ever had to output anything more than 12 inches wide and everything was plastisol. Yesterday I output a film that was 28 inches wide and discharge ink. For a while foiling was the hottest thing ever. I was creating separations with foil prints five times a day. Now, I see a foil job once every three weeks.

"Have realistic expectations and respect for the printing process." —LT MAGNOTTO

The trend that seems to be sticking around is over-sized printing. Everyone wants the biggest and softest print they can have. But nobody wants the imperfections that come along with it. T-shirts have seams, and when you go over them, it creates problems. The trick is to design your graphics with these imperfections in mind. Distress areas that you know are going to be near seams, so that when the ink gets distressed from trying to print over gnarly hems, nobody will think twice about the final product.

Also, it is important to know about your print processes. Standard printing at 99% of your shops will be printed using Plastisol inks. These are inks that are plastic-based and colored using pigments. Then you have Discharge and Water-based printing. Discharge inks remove the pigment from the apparel and leave behind a smooth soft feel.

However there are limitations to these soft feel print methods. Discharge printing requires the ink to really penetrate the shirt, that being said, a lower mesh screen is needed. Lower mesh screens cannot hold small dot sizes thus limiting the detail that can be held on press. Also, discharge printing is not eco-friendly! Some brands of discharge ink have formaldehyde in it to keep if from exploding!

When printing full-color images on shirts, it is always best to stick with plastisol inks. The colors pop and more depth can be created simulating with the color of the t-shirt. Also, nine times out of ten a simulation is going to feel soft anyway because you are printing halftone dots and its not just a solid deposit of ink!

RikkiB

I'm RikkiB, I'm 29 and I've been making t-shirts since I discovered iron-ons and an old screen in school. I've always drawn in my spare time and made my own crappy t-shirts to fill my personal craftiness requirement.

When t-shirt competitions started showing up on the Internet I jumped at the chance. Then came opportunities from print-on-demand companies such as MySoti, and smaller tee companies looking for different designers. I love the t-shirt design community. Emptees was great for opinion and advice.

My Breakthrough Moment

It was being picked up by shirt.woot.com. It gave me some great publicity, but the community at DesignByHümans really got my name out there. I love them both for supporting me and the hundreds of other designers they help every day.

Standing Out

I'm probably a bit different from the others because I only design as a hobby — so I haven't gone out there with my name on a NES-themed YouTube video. I'd certainly not recommend against making something '"viral" but I would recommend making something awesome! I can only handle a small amount of design work in my spare time so I generally don't go looking for it. It still comes to me which is probably a combination of luck and promotion from awesome t-shirt competition sites.

My inspirations include Ray Fenwick, Ray Frenden, Jimiyo, Wotto, Godmachine... Their styles are different from mine, but I admire them and their attitudes.

If I Could Do Things Differently

I'd listen to people more. When you look back in a year, you'll see that the designs you loved were actually pretty shitty. And you'll recall that someone who knows told you that, but you didn't believe them. Get all the criticism and advice you can before putting your work out there with your name on it — especially online, because it never goes away.

I'd recommend joining a community like Emptees. Get some real advice and criticism, and use it to make your work better. Criticism can be harsh so get your thick skin on before you go there...and remember that you're better off improving your work in that kind of environment than in a real public forum.

Trends

Firstly, the distribution of t-shirt sales has gone from smaller stores to huge daily tee and competition websites, to print-on-demand. This has made it easy for anyone to be a designer, and harder for designers to get noticed. In actual design, the trends change almost weekly. One week it's wolves, then space, then robots, then bears, then huge prints, then small prints...

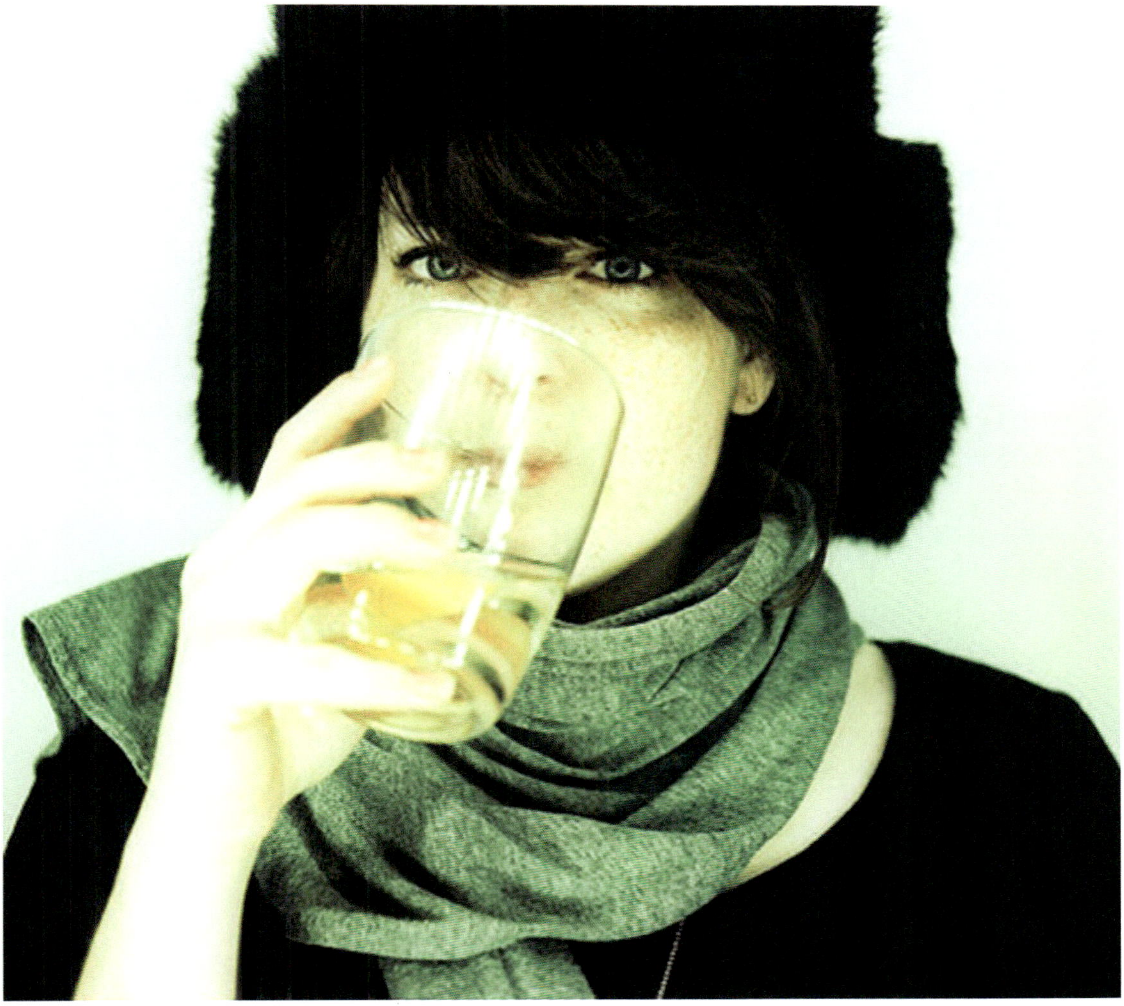

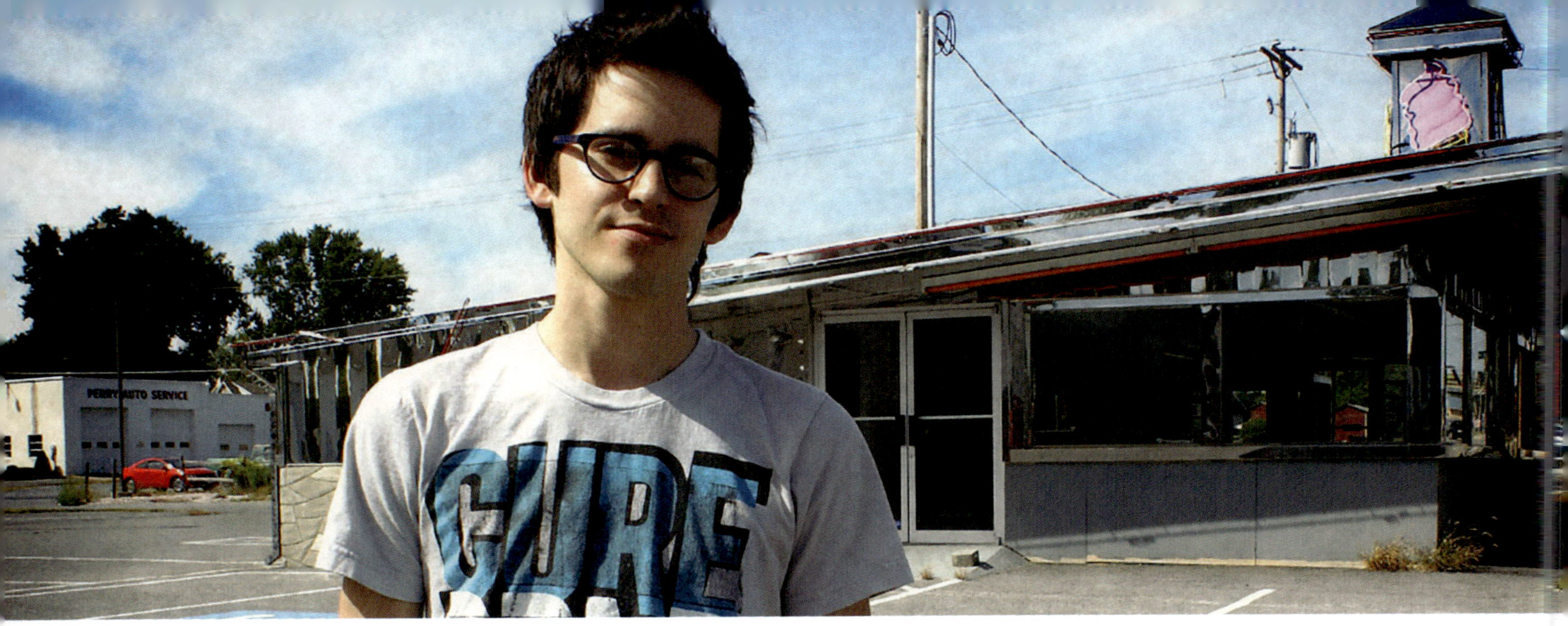

Kelly Kiernan

I am 21 years old and I started my clothing brand Cure Apparel in August of 2008. I've been plugging away at this for two years now, but have always had projects going on in art and music. I played guitar and vocals in a metal band throughout high school. We landed a record deal on the local independent label and put out an album. Naturally we needed shirts, stickers, and album artwork. At the time I had no idea that there were such things as professional graphic designers (seems silly now I know). I had Photoshop, so I started hacking away. As we got older my friends and I got jobs and girlfriends and the band fell apart.

I've always been the entrepreneurial type, so I needed a project to work on. While looking for shirts that related to diabetes (I have type 1), I realized I could start my own brand to reach out to the diabetic community. I was stoked on the idea and quickly discovered that there was an entire scene of clothing companies and designers...really talented people. I studied my favorite brands and used them as inspiration to work on my own. I'm still learning every day, and still trying to bring what is in my head to reality.

My Breakthrough Moment

There hasn't been one single breakthrough moment for me. It's been years of different realizations with surely more to come. I can say my first "aha" moment came when speaking to the owner of a Porsche dealership my mom works for. He emphasized the importance of hard work, and told me that while I'm "jerking off" someone else is busting their ass for the things I want. He stressed the importance being proactive and persistent.

He made a huge impression on me. Until that conversation I never realized that you need to actively pursue your goals. If you really want something, work for it. You can get it with desire, dedication and persistence. One thing I try to remember is that defeat is temporary. There are tons of inspirational stories about people who failed numerous times and hit many road blocks before some great success. Read about Edison, Ford, or Frederick Smith (founder of FedEx).

Inspirations

My biggest inspirations are Jeff Finley (Go Media), Kyle Crawford (Electric Zombie), and Jeff Sheldon (Ugmonk). I always watch what these guys are doing. They are up on (if not creating) the latest trends and really know what they're doing. I also keep an eye on more "corporate" companies too. I like Heritage 1981, Cardboard Robot and Glamour Kills. For me, inspiration is everything. I can't pull design ideas out of thin air, whether it's for a shirt or our web store background or whatever.

Standing Out

I never consciously thought about how I could stand out. I wanted cool shirts that related to diabetes and knew no one was making them. I think standing out can be as simple as just being yourself. We live in a diverse world where every single person is unique. Take the things that make you unique and magnify them.

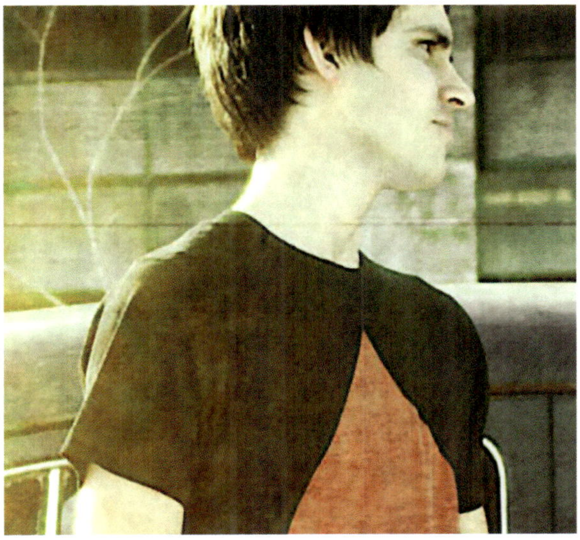

I've tried tons of things to promote the brand. Mostly I've been unimpressed, especially with paid advertising. Investing in the brand itself has actually been the most important thing. The general idea is to create something worth talking about. You want a person to see your work and think, "Man! I need to tell somebody about this!" People love finding cool stuff and telling their friends about it. What would get you excited about a brand or artist? What would you gladly hand over money for?

At first, a solid identity is more valuable than any advertising you can buy. Investing in your product is indirectly investing in promotion. Focus on your apparel, or artwork, or whatever you're working on. Make it the very best possible and people will notice. You can focus on fun promotional campaigns once your identity is taking shape and you've got some customers.

Believe in Yourself

I started in 2008 assuming that I wouldn't sell any shirts and no one would care about what I wanted to do. I started slowly and progressed even more slowly. I kept Cure as a hobby for more than a year before I changed my mind-set. I finally realized what a self-defeating habit all my negative thoughts were. I wish I could have sat down and said, "This is what I want, and I'm going to do this no matter what." I could have come up with a plan from the start. I could have done more research, saved investment money, and time. Instead, I halfheartedly stumbled along without conviction. If you don't believe in what you are doing, how can you expect anyone else to? Use your desire as fuel. Let it push you to make your work the very best possible.

> *"I wanted cool shirts that related to diabetes and knew no one was making them."* —KELLY KIERNAN

My main problem has always been my mind-set. If you have negative thoughts or a poor outlook, start by changing the way you think. Feed your own ego. See yourself where you want to be, not where you are now. If you want to be doing Metallica t-shirts picture yourself getting those jobs. You have to believe it.

Get Involved

Some more concrete things you can work on right away include networking and creating an online portfolio. Make a habit of stopping by sites like Emptees and getting involved in blogs and forums. If you don't already have social networking accounts, get to it! Interact with your favorite artists and blogs on twitter and Facebook. Approach local or independent labels and bands about doing some free or low-priced designs. Touring bands will jump at anyone willing to help them out with good designs. You'll build a portfolio and get your name out there, and eventually people will start coming to you. As far as portfolios go, I've seen some pretty cool stuff done on Cargo Collective. They have free and paid layout themes to choose from. Check out Workerman or Kyle Crawford's portfolios. Pretty slammin.

Last Word

Instead of rambling on about success, I'm going to suggest you read "Think and Grow Rich" by Napoleon Hill. The book discusses the qualities of some of the most powerful people in history, and basically dissects success into manageable pieces. I just read it recently, and the book has truly changed the way I think about and live life.

Jamie Tallerico

My name is Jamie Tallerico. I am 33 years old and have been in the business 11 years now. I am currently Senior Graphic Designer at American Eagle Outfitters. I have been Senior Graphic Designer at Abercrombie & Fitch, Clothing/Graphic Designer at Atticus Clothing, and Art Director at XVALA Denim.

My first real apparel job was with XVALA Denim. My friend Jeff started a denim company and asked me to design the website, promotional items and some t-shirts. After about a month of working with him we decided to partner full-time. I was with XVALA for about one and a half years. It was an awesome time. We did a ton of stuff besides clothes like put out a 7" record, painted murals and traveled. Probably one of the best jobs I have had.

The Blink-182 Connection

During that time I was doing a ton of band freelance, specifically for Motion City Soundtrack. They were into the stuff we were doing at XVALA and wearing it happily. When they were on tour with Blink-182, Mark Hoppus really was into my t-shirts. He soon gave me a call asking me to do some designs for Atticus Clothing. XVALA was winding down. People wanted Japanese denim at the time, not American-made denim. So Jeff and I decided to part.

I got offered a job at Atticus as a clothing/graphic designer. They were just getting established when I joined on. There were three of us designing men's and women's, plus all the marketing! It was an intense job, but I learned a ton. I was there for a few years. Then about 6 months after Blink had broken up, is when I decided to leave. Things got really weird then and the vibe was not so good.

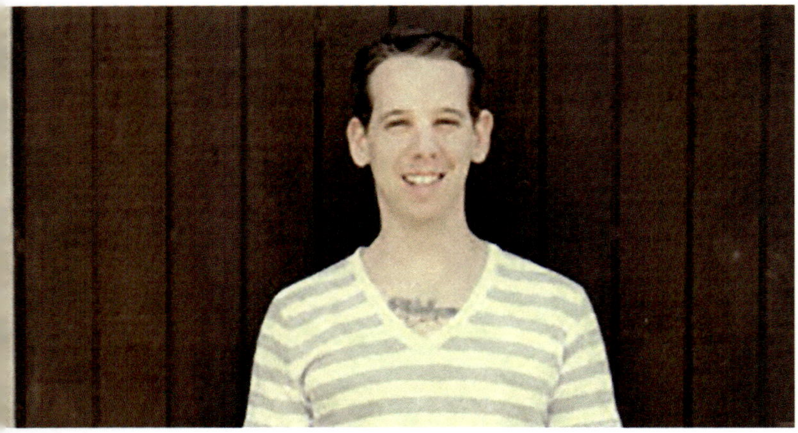

photo by Maggie Phipps

Going Mainstream: A&F and AE

So after a couple of months doing freelance I got a call from a recruiter at Abercrombie and Fitch. In 2007 we were leaving sunny San Diego and moving to Columbus, Ohio. I was there three years before moving to NYC for my current position at American Eagle Outfitters.

The Big Break

My big breakthrough moment happened at XVALA in 2003. It was there I knew I could make a career out of it. I had designed and built the XVALA website and submitted it to a bunch of graphic design blogs. (There weren't apparel-specific design sites then) The blog was called Newstoday. Now it's called QBN. Anyway, one of the buyers from Urban Outfitters saw our site, liked our stuff and called us up. They ordered t-shirts for all stores and denim for some. We were so pumped! I knew once I saw my shirts in an Urban store in Las Vegas that this could be a real career choice and not just a fun time. I haven't looked back since.

My Inspirations

Michael Leon, Steven Harrington, Wes Anderson, Spike Jonze, Michel Gondry, Mike Giant, Adam Hathorn, Greg Craola Simkins, Faile, Bast, Travis Millard, vintage t-shirts, thrift stores, flea markets, mid-century modern, Popeye, Richard Prince, Gilbert and George, all sorts of music, my dad and his work ethic. Man I could go on forever!

Be a Jack of All Trades

My strategy to stand out is to be a jack of all trades. I never wanted to confine myself to one style or one medium. I have always loved learning and love trying new things. It's been my willingness to explore, as well as my eagerness and enthusiasm to work on different projects. On the contrary, not having a specific style is hard. Sometimes it can feel like you don't have your own voice. I think there are pros and cons to having a style. It helped David Carson, but what is he really up to these days? I guess just never be afraid to go out of your comfort zone and try something without knowing anything about it. Just be open to whatever.

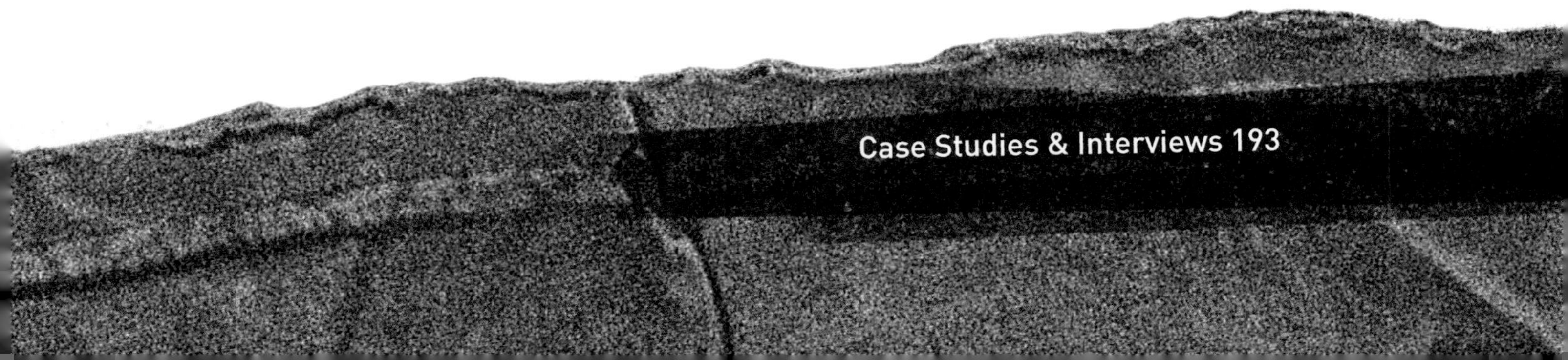

You Gotta Hustle

What I have done to give myself an edge is hustle. I am not the best artist out there. I know I am not the best graphic designer there is; but I will work till all ends of the night. I email people I am interested in working with, I design when I'm not designing. I draw all the time. I always have a sketchbook and some sort of camera on me! Network. Network. Network. I have done shitty paying spec work in the past just to do the project. Just because I was excited about it.

Spec Work

One thing I would say about spec work is: I have done it. I have done a ton of it. It seemed like in the early 2000s it was all spec. Some of it I enjoyed, made lifetime friends and good connections out of it. My Motion City Soundtrack jobs were spec and that turned into me being a designer at Atticus and I still talk to all those dudes to this day.

On the other hand, I never let anyone take advantage of me. If someone asked me for a $50 design, then I would give them something typed out in a font and made sure I did it within 20 minutes. Twenty minutes of my time would equal a $50 design. I don't do spec now, unless it were some amazing opportunity that I felt passionate about. I think spec work should be up to the designer, especially the prices. If companies want people to do spec, then the designer should say how much the art is worth. Not the other way around. It's your creation. You tell them how much you want for it. If it's amazing, they will agree to pay for it.

My Advice to You

Work hard, network, look for inspiration beyond the web, especially t-shirt-specific sites. Don't be afraid of rejection. Be easy to work with. Stay humble. Someone is always better than you at something. If you're truly passionate about what you do, it will show, people will notice. Don't be a follower. Just because people are buying neon zombie shirts with guts spilling out doesn't mean you have to make another one. Take the style of the time and put your own spin on it.

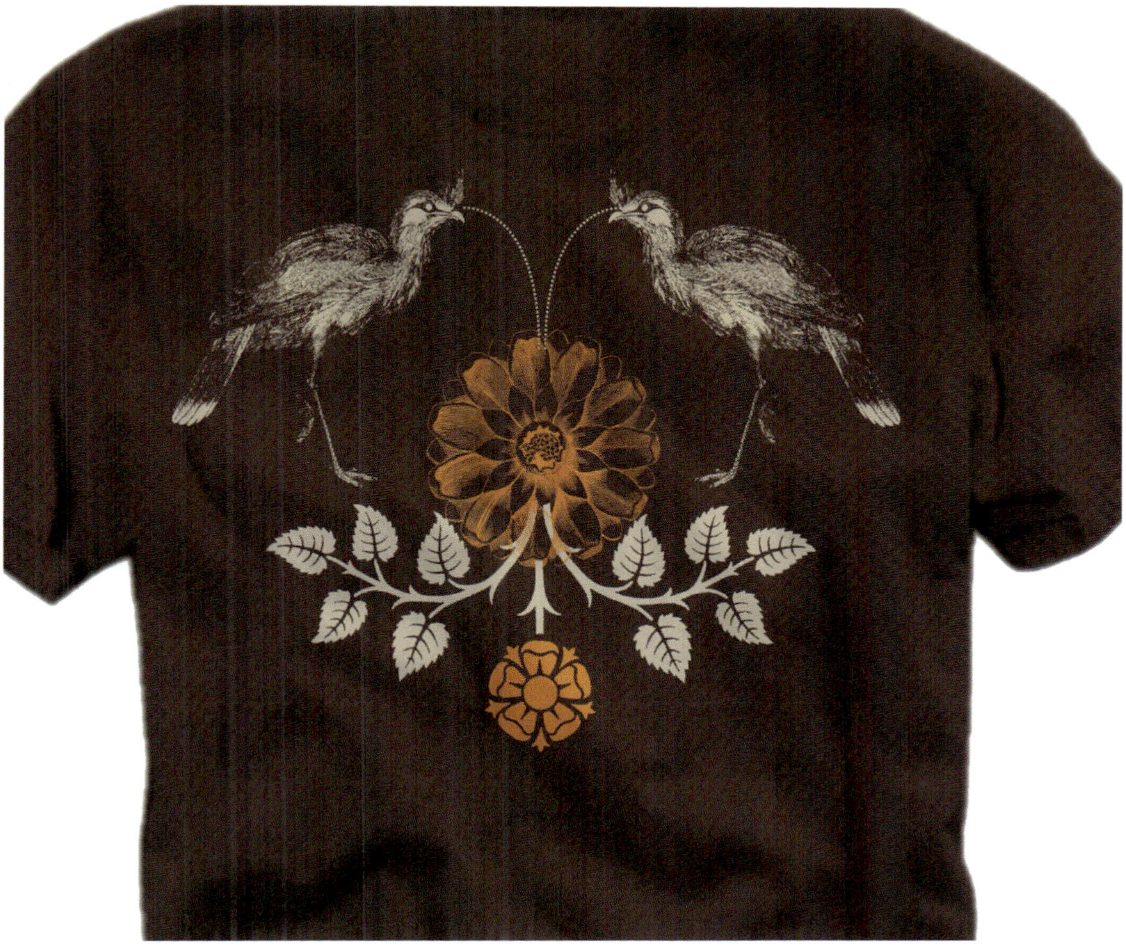

Design for XVLA by Jamie Tallerico

What you can do now is design and learn. I think blogs like Emptees and DesignByHümans are great resources for critiques and feedback. There are also millions of tutorials out there on the technical side of things. But you should always draw, look at the world with unfiltered eyes, (gets harder when you are older) and jump on anything you can get your hands on. Just keep hustling and designing. I've personally noticed some growth of young designers with heart. Their stuff started out kind of whatever, but over time they are getting better and better. Never rest, never feel settled.

Trends I Have Observed

Over the last ten years some trends have lasted longer and some are short lived. All-over prints were huge as was the whole Affliction craze and the neon gore zombie 80s style. Nautical has been big the last two years with brands like Mr. Freedom. Vintage surf style is starting to come in now. Vintage in general is always big. Cleaner easier graphics are making a comeback too. Photorealism was big for a bit. I have to do a lot of trend analysis at my job, so I see a ton of flash in the pans and small trends that stick.

The Appropriateness of Graphic Distressing

This is something I have had to deal with at the bigger companies who can afford washes and sprays on their garments. If a t-shirt straight out of the box is getting printed on, use less distressing on the art. Nothing is weirder than a crisp bright colored shirt with faded distress graphics. It just doesn't make sense. But if you have a faded sprayed down t-shirt add all the distress you want. Just keep in mind what the whole garment is going to look like when it's done. Don't just think about the art.

What's My Secret to Success?

The secret to my success is love of clothes, networking, hard work and a humble attitude. Be in love with what you do and it will show. Bug people you want to design for and when there are changes be cool about it. At least up to a point. Work hard! There are always people out there who really want it. Talent only goes so far.

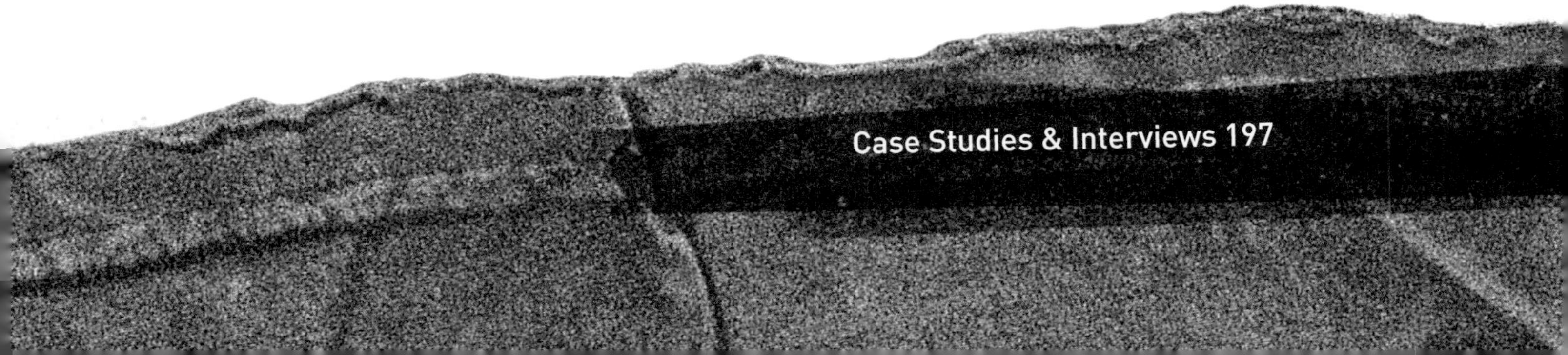

Richard Minino

I'm 31 and go by the name HorseBites. I've been doing this for about six years. I sort of fell into it by accident. I was just doing art for my own band (New Mexican Disaster Squad) and I caught the attention of some of my other friends' bands like Strike Anywhere and No Trigger. They wanted some art so I did it more for the fact of just being excited to do some merch for another band except for mine. Later my friend at Fueled by Ramen Records asked me to do a shirt for an "up and coming" band called Fall Out Boy and I got it approved. After that it was easier for people, including myself to take my art more seriously. Soon after, I quit my job of delivering pizzas for almost ten years and the rest is history.

My Breakthrough Moment

It was that Fall Out Boy shirt and also the Strike Anywhere layout I did. Doing the FOB shirt opened the doors to bigger named acts and Strike opened the doors to more of the underground scene. It was good to have my wings spread over such a huge playing field.

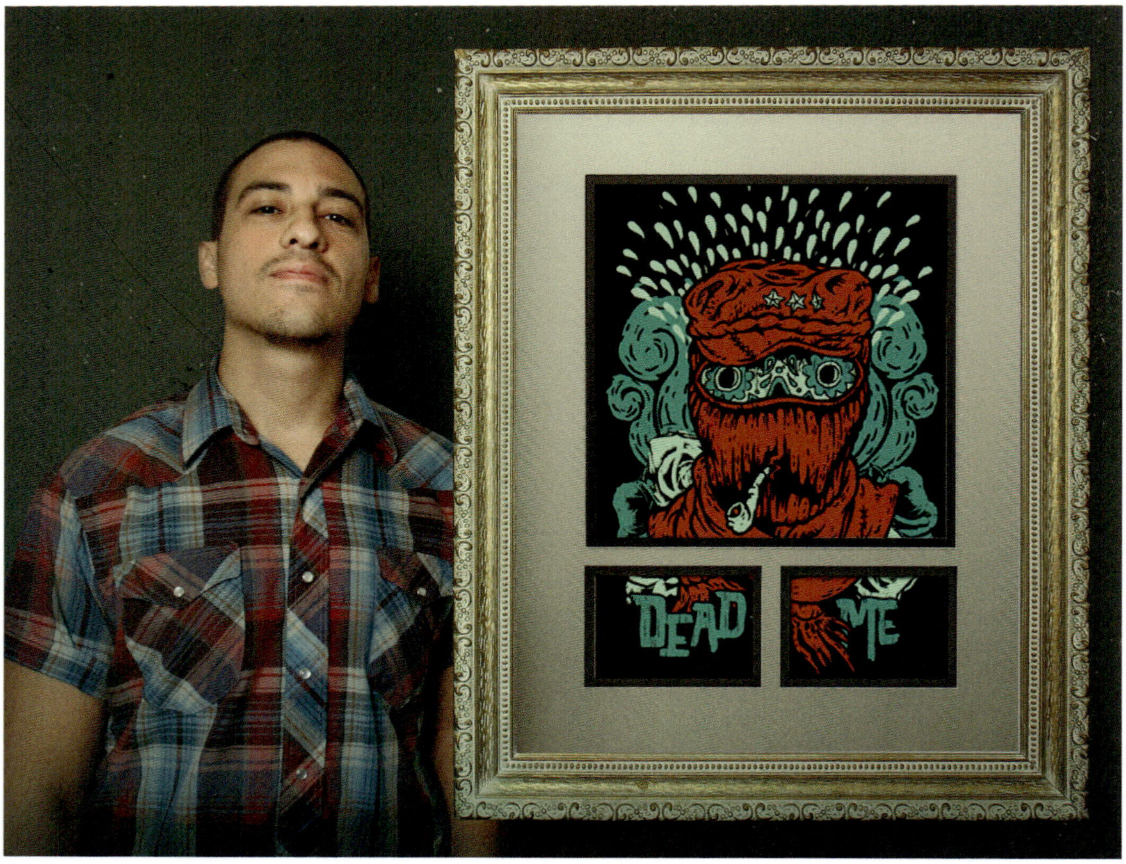

My Inspirations

I had a lot of inspirations and the list grows every day. It started out more with low-brow artists such as Ed Roth, Jim Phillips and other artists involved in the skate/surf/hot rod scene. Others include plenty of early Disney animators, Camille Rose Garcia, James Jean etc.

Be Yourself

My strategy has been strictly to just be myself. It's as easy as that. If you open up yourself to people, you build a personal relationship with them and they see the real things that inspire you and also the things that piss you off. Being real instead of some over-inflated robot is way more endearing.

> *"My strategy has been strictly to just be myself. It's as easy as that."*
>
> *—RICHARD MININO*

If you meet people that like you for who you are then they will say good things about you. This takes a lot of time and if you're impatient, this is not the career for you. Don't get into this field with hopes of making a lot of money. Think of it as "if I really am an artist, then I would do this regardless of money." Art for art's sake.

There's a bunch of trends that pass and come back all the time. I try not to pay too much attention to them because I don't want to be overwhelmed about whatever is new at the moment. It just makes me want to go against the grain anyway.

Don't Take Anything for Granted

As a designer you should never take anything for granted. You have to look at your situation as "I'm getting paid to create art." If that's not the craziest thing you've ever heard of as an artist then I don't know what is. The ability to use your creative talents and share with the whole world no matter what medium is such a rare gift and privilege that rarely anyone gets to experience. It's easy for me to get side-tracked and look at it as just a job but I have to slap myself in the head when I get like that.

Adam Hendle

My name is Adam Hendle and I have been running the independent clothing blog **iamthetrend.com** for almost two years now as well as just launching my second site **shirtlaunch.com**. When I started IATT, I was completely new to the blogging world and pretty much a novice in the indie clothing world. Before going much further I have to admit that I was pretty naïve when starting it.

If you go by-the-book, I pretty much did everything wrong when starting a website. I didn't do my homework to see who my competition was or really do any research about blogging and capturing market. The funny thing is looking back on that lack of knowledge and research. I view it as a blessing.

"Instead of putting my toe in the water first to test it out, I took one big running cannonball into the pool."

—ADAM HENDLE, IAMTHETREND.COM

By the Seat of My Pants

I learned everything on fly from how to publish blog posts, to how to contact clothing labels, artists, bands, etc. The biggest thing I learned from all of that was you just have to go for it. Unfortunately there is no magic switch that you can just turn on when your website or blog goes live that just drives tons of traffic through your door; you have to put in the effort and hours to gain respect, recognition and a following. If you want to be successful you have to throw your inhibitions aside and keep your eyes on the prize.

As I mentioned earlier I think the not knowing how much competition was out there for me was a good thing. I didn't worry about what others were doing, I just did my own deal and I really believe this kept my site unique. The moment you start peeking at your neighbor's work is when you start losing your identity.

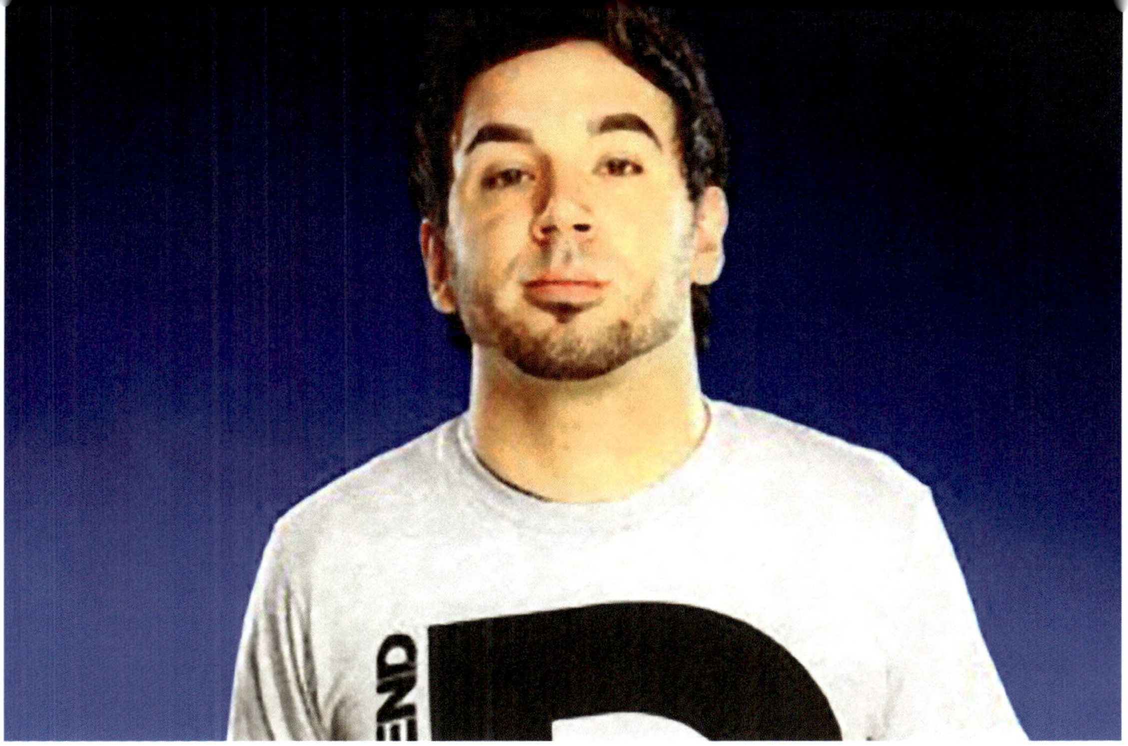

Already almost two years deep into running IATT, I still have a ton to learn, and to me that is one of the most exciting parts. As an artist, musician, blogger, etc., You have to embrace the unknown and try and learn something every day.

My Breakthrough Moment

I think my breakthrough moment occurred about a year into running IATT. It was at that point that clothing labels, artists and bands really started coming to me asking to write about them. Site traffic also really started to pickup around this time allowing me to land some advertisers that help me keep the site running.

Offer Something Slightly Unique

My best strategy for standing out has just been to try and offer something slightly unique. In a world where basically everything has been done twice it's hard to create something that is completely unique, but by allowing yourself to show through in your art, music, or writing, your work becomes more unique.

My goal has always been to give a face to iamthetrend.com, when people read my site the last thing I want is for it to seem like this lifeless machine that just posts black-and-white articles. By keeping the writing on my site fun, relaxed, and approachable I really feel that my readers come to the site for information delivered to them by a friend as opposed to a lecture.

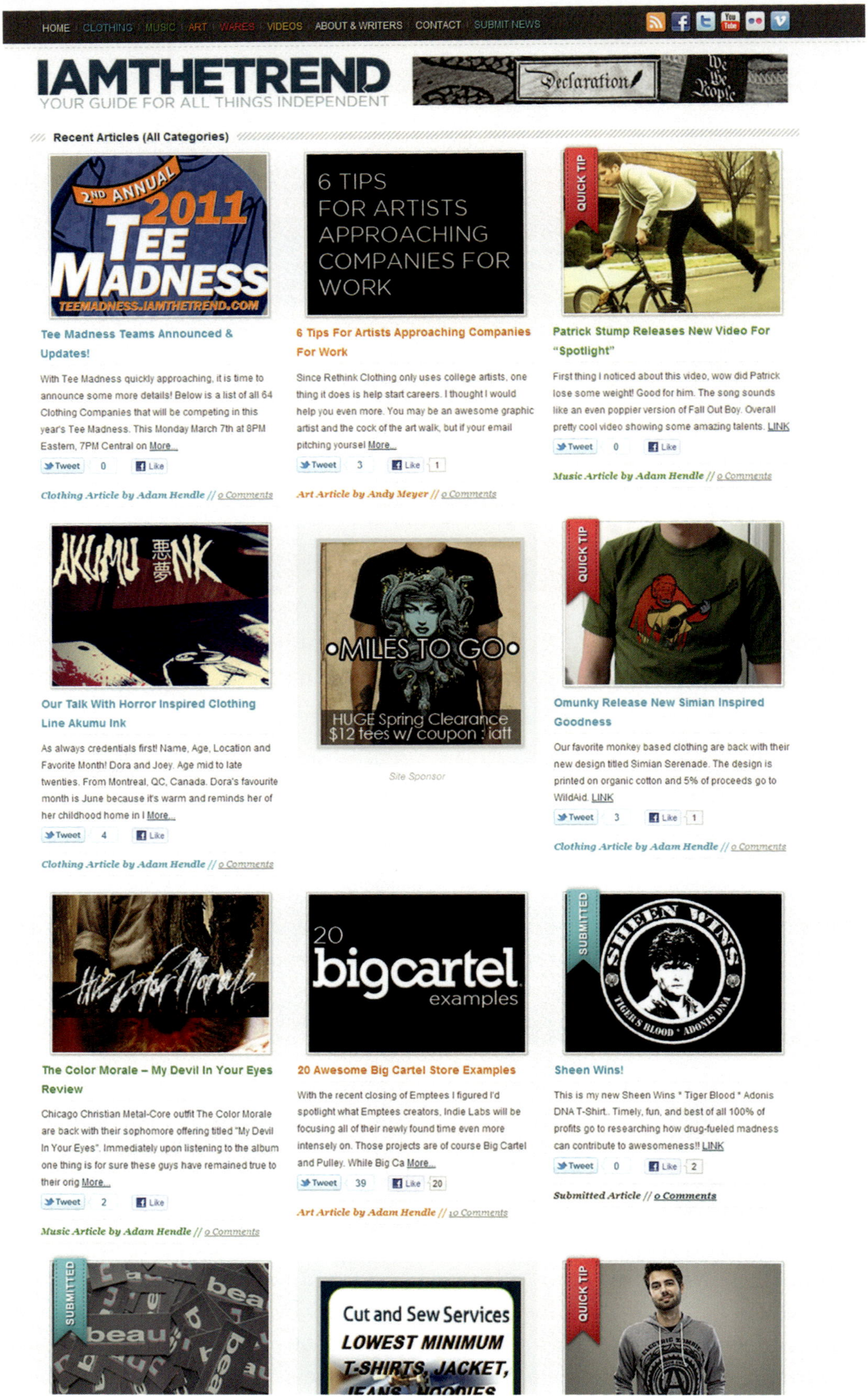

A screenshot of Adam's website iamthetrend.com

Connecting with the People

I have never really done any banner advertisements or traditional advertising. Instead I have opted to try and get in front of as many people on the Internet as possible. Taking part in forums such as Emptees.com and T-Shirtforums.com really allows you to connect with people. When you offer something of use and positivity into a community, people recognize that and spread the word about you to their peers.

Get in Front of the Camera

To promote myself I also run a web show called IATT.TV or iamthetrend.TV. This really allows me to put a face to my site while allowing me to personally interact with readers of my site. Through contests, reviews and information given on the show, I feel that has been a pretty instrumental part in IATT being successful. In a world where 20 hours of video are uploaded to YouTube.com every minute people it doesn't take a rocket scientist to figure out people like watching videos. No matter what media you are in, I strongly believe setting up a YouTube channel or putting together a live show can do nothing but help your cause.

My Biggest Piece of Advice

Get involved in the community. There are so many helpful people, sites and resources at your finger tips that are there to help you. The absolute worst thing you can do is stay dormant. If you want people to take notice of you and your art you need to be visible.

The Quality Shift

The first change that stands out to me is the attention now to quality. The days of indie clothing lines and bands selling designs on the cheapest blanks around are gone. People want a quality product and with brands such as American Apparel, Alstyle, Alternative Apparel and many others becoming readily available the small guys can now compete with the big guys. The playing field is getting pretty level now, and now is a very exciting time to being an indie clothing company or apparel designer!

Ben Scrivens

My name is Benjamin Scrivens and I am 32 years old. I started **Fright-Rags** in September of 2003, when I was just 25 years old. Let me preface this by saying I NEVER expected to be where I am today — but I did often dream of it.

I started Fright-Rags mainly as a way to do something creative in my spare time. My day job, while in graphic design, was not as fulfilling as I had wanted it to be. And I am the type of person that, if I'm not satisfied with something, I pretty much seek out anything and everything that will offer a way for me to channel my passions into something that challenges me. So I spent most of the summer of 2003 looking for just that...something I could do that gave me that sense of personal satisfaction.

Channeling the Passion

Horror was a natural place to start, as I have been an avid fan of horror films since the tender age of four. I had always been into them, and it was something I constantly went to for a source of entertainment, inspiration, etc. As for t-shirts, that was pretty natural as well. I've always been fond of "off the wall" shirts, and had collected quite a few while growing up. But, I never had any horror shirts. And when I started looking for them, I found many of the same types of tees out there...and ones I really didn't care for.

So, I thought I could do better and one day on my lunch break I started sketching out ideas for designs. The first idea was for our WWJD? shirt, which was a parody on

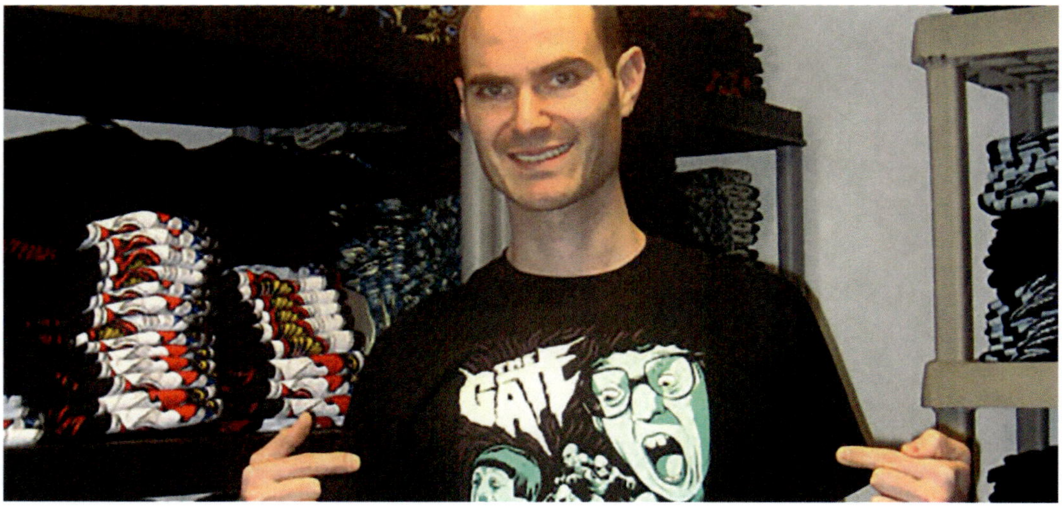

the "What Would Jesus Do?" craze...only, instead of the "J," I drew a hockey mask to signify "What Would Jason Do?" The idea seemed so simple that I assumed it had been done before. But after some research online, I couldn't find anyone with the same idea.

The next thing I did was show that and a couple other designs to some friends of mine on an online horror forum to get their opinion. Everyone seemed to like my designs, and many said they would purchase t-shirts if I produced them. Based on those reviews alone, I used my credit card to purchase $600 worth of shirts. Over Labor Day weekend in 2003, I came up with the name, basic logo, and first incarnation of the website to set it up to take pre-orders on the shirts I was waiting to get in.

Using Passion to Keep you Going

From then on, I just kept at it. Every dime I made on t-shirts went into printing more and releasing new designs. Since I already had a job, I wasn't relying on this for income...it was just something to do for fun. Not only did I have a passion for it, but the response from customers was gratifying and made me feel as though what I was doing actually had some impact on people. But I will admit it was slow-going.

If I didn't have that passion or customer feedback, I would have thrown in the towel years ago. In fact, I almost quit it a few times... A couple years after starting it, I had gotten married, moved into a house, and started thinking that I should spend my time differently. However, every single time the thought came into my head, an order would appear in my inbox. I took these moments as a sign to hang in there. And doing that has paid off in ways I could have never imagined. Granted, running a business is never easy, but I'm lucky enough to have made this my only "job" (I use the term loosely) and to have employed my friends as well.

My Breakthrough Moment

It came to me in January of 2005. I had been running the business for just over a year and while it was fun, it wasn't really growing all that much. I was stuck in traffic on my way home from work and started to think about my life, where I was at, and where I wanted to be. I knew that I no longer wanted to work at my current job and the only option was to update my portfolio and resume and start looking for another job. I also knew I would have to put Fright-Rags on the back-burner, or quit it altogether, if I were to really focus on getting a new job.

Then I asked myself a question, “If I could make the same amount of money with Fright-Rags as I could at a new job, which would I rather do?” After a few moments on thought, I said out loud, “Fright-Rags.” The answer seemed so simple and obvious, but actually hearing the words coming out of my mouth verbalized something I had been feeling for awhile but had never fully realized or expressed until that moment.

The fact is, I would not have been happy at another job. Sure, it might be fine for a few months, but it wouldn’t last. My passion was Fright-Rags. That’s where I knew my heart was and anything else paled in comparison. From that moment on, I decided that all my energy and focus would be on getting Fright-Rags to a point where I could do it full-time. However, it took three years until I was able walk into my boss’ office and announce my resignation. But during that time I never shifted my focus away from that one goal. I faced the brutal reality that I may never get to that point, but never lost hope that I would. And I owe it mainly to having that moment of clarity while I was stuck in traffic.

My Inspirations

In terms of business, many of my inspirations have come from learning what it takes to keep going when you think it’s time to give up. They also come from people and companies that have gone the opposite direction of what everyone else was doing, and did so with the determination to succeed. These are, but not limited to:

James Stockdale (look up the Stockdale Paradox and prepare to be amazed), Howard Stern (love him or hate him, he did what no one else has ever done in radio — against all odds), Seth Godin (marketing guru extraordinaire), Dogfish Head Brewing Company (an example of a company that isn’t trying to please everyone), Tony Hsieh (CEO of Zappos and gold standard when it comes to customer service).

Customer Service Obsession

I’m not sure if you’d call it a strategy, but one of our core values has to do with our obsession with customer service. For us, it’s not about just selling horror shirts. While that is obviously a large part of what we do, we are more focused on creating an experience for our customers. After all, we are horror fans too, so we are very community-driven in how we engage and interact with our customers. We also view each and every interaction with a customer (happy or angry) as a way to learn more about them and ourselves. In keeping with customer service, we are also very

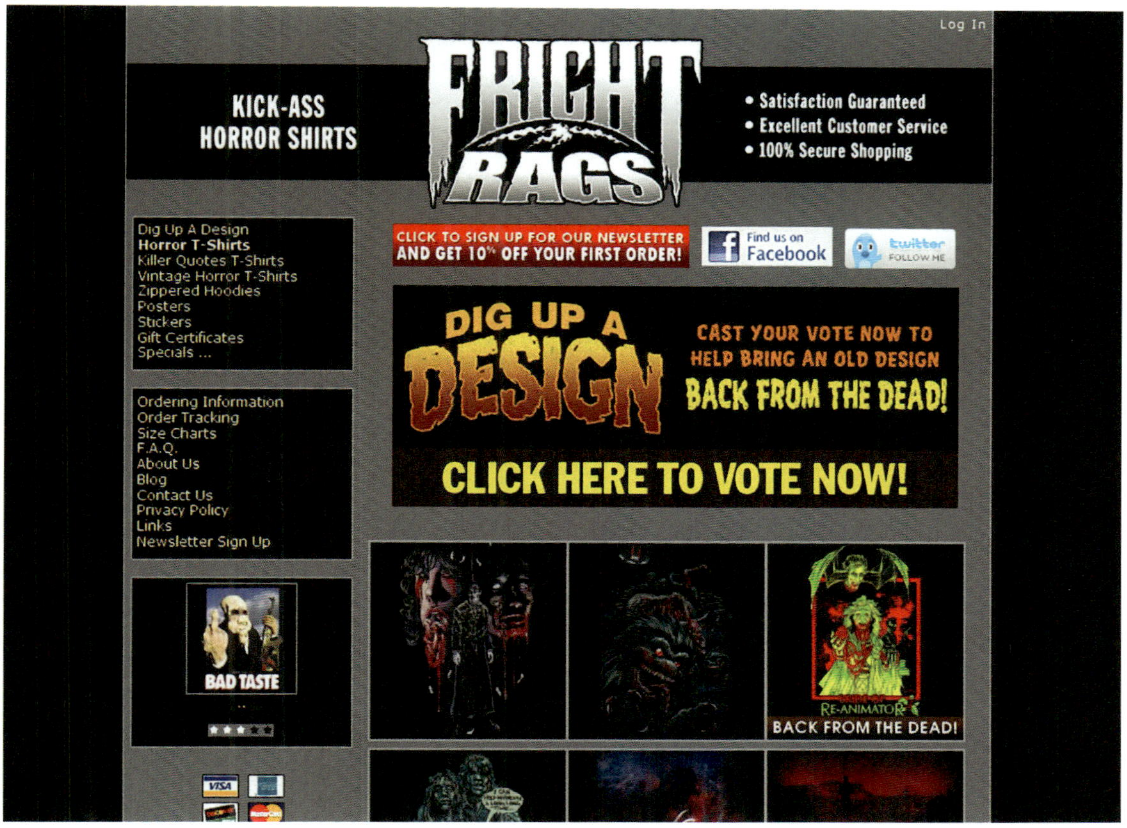

A screen-shot of Fright-Rags.com

focused on getting orders out as quickly as possible, answering questions immediately, and keeping the customer informed at every step of the process once their order is placed. I think we tend to stand out by doing these things because other people may not be doing them.

Self Promotion Ideas

In the early days of Fright-Rags, I always put extra stuff (stickers, pins, etc) into orders. We've kept this up but have also expanded it to include specialized trading cards, candy, and sometimes other items like DVDs. But my primary means of promotion has come from our newsletter list, and it's been that way for quite a few years now. I look at the people on our newsletter list as an extended group of friends, and I want to talk to them about how we're doing, what we're doing, and what we can do better. It's not about just sending out sales letters, it's so much more than that. I want to engage our customers and spark conversations with them. After all, they are just as passionate about horror as we are.

This shirt was a collaboration between Jeff Finley and Ray Frenden for Fright-Rags.

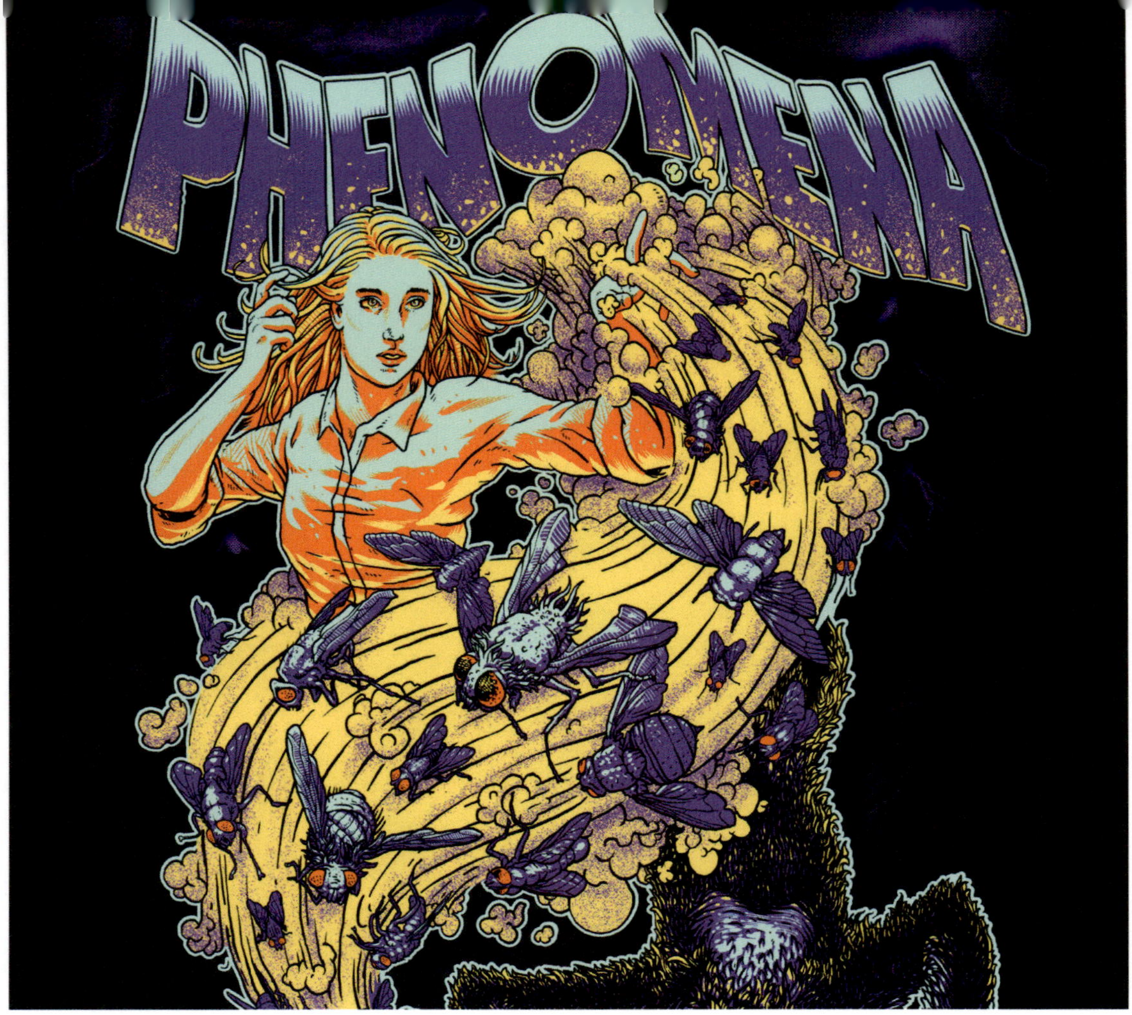

My Advice to You

Start. As simple as that sounds, it's the one thing that holds people back the most. They get caught up in minutiae like copyrighting everything they do, or getting a trademark, or worried about their ideas getting stolen even before they have sold a single t-shirt. So my advice is to start right now. Dive in and figure it out while you're in it. Hell, I didn't even have a DBA until I received a check for $12,000 from Hot Topic and couldn't even cash it because it had my company name on it!

Trend Watching

Well, I have to say that when I started out, horror shirts (or even horror-themed shirts) were in short supply. But since then I've seen zombies, robots, vampires, etc infiltrate just about every type of t-shirt company. Plus, t-shirts have gotten much softer and more comfortable. The trends have moved away from the 6.0 oz. heavyweight shirt to the lighter 4.5 ringspun cotton which was popularized by American Apparel.

My Secret to Success

Perseverance. While luck has a huge impact on our success, it was the perseverance to stick it out long enough that even gave us a chance to be lucky. That, and sticking to our guns. It's too easy to get caught up in all the things you can't do, and not focus on the things you can do well. And I find our best successes come from when we focus in on the things we know we can succeed at, which is usually what we're most passionate about. When those things align, magical things happen. And cutting out all the distractions helps you do just that.

Your Personality in your Brand

I truly feel that in order to stand out and move from a side project to a brand, you have to stick to what you're passionate about and engage your customers. I forget who said it, but the quote I like best to describe this is "People buy products from people, not companies." It's all too common for people just starting out to tout themselves as bigger than they are. They use terms like "we" when it's just one guy in his basement. I did the same exact thing... Ironically, as I really did become a "we," I gravitated to using my own name and identity with my brand. I personalized emails to my customers, and even shot videos of myself talking about how I got into horror and why it means so much to me. Little did I know, I was crafting the story behind our brand and putting a face and voice to the company so customers could relate to us.

I spend a lot of my time cultivating those relationships by doing things like sending surveys, allowing customers to vote on designs, showing them the process of taking a design from sketch to shirt, and even showing them how a shirt is printed.

The Brand Sells, Not the Design

Too many designers get focused on the "design" as a way to express their brand. To them, it's all about what the actual design on the shirt looks like... Of course, the design is important. But that isn't what sells. It's the brand that the design is representing that sells the shirt. So you must spend as much — or more — time crafting and developing your brand than you do on designing your shirts. If you do that, then the shirts will sell themselves since they will be coming from a place of passion and built on a foundation that expresses that passion in a way that others can relate to.

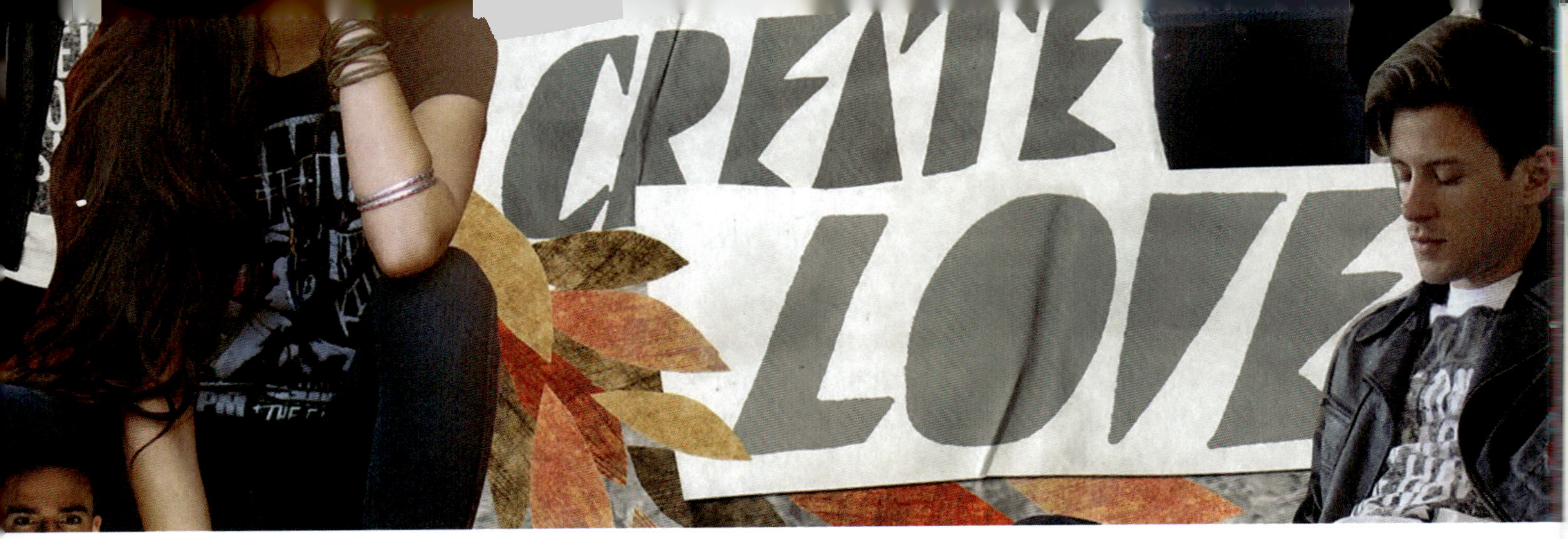

Glamour Kills is the successful clothing line of Mark Capicotto

Mark Capicotto

My name is Mark Capicotto. I am 24 years old and I am the owner and designer of **Glamour Kills Clothing**. GK has been in business since 2006. Basically I started the business when I was 19 or 20 years old. I was going to college at the time, freelance designing for bands, and working a pizza delivery job.

One day I was just sitting around talking with some friends while designing some merch and said I could do this myself and run and sell my own designs and business. With what little money I had saved up, I printed a few designs and stored everything down in my parent's basement. I had some html/web knowledge so I built my own site and Myspace and off I went. A few designs lead into a few more and then so on. Every time I sold more shirts I put all the money right back into the business (was still working the pizza delivery job as well for the first year) it wasn't until about the second year I was able to quit and barely make enough to live off of GK alone.

As the company grew so did I. I began getting more experienced with marketing and branding myself and started sponsoring bands, actors, friends, and anyone who would wear my clothes. The rest is pretty much history.

My Breakthrough Moment

I can't really pin point it to one moment. The day our brand was sold nationwide through the chain Zumiez would be one. The first time I saw my shirt on National TV. The first time I ran and paid for my first print ad in a national magazine. There are so many milestones, still to this day we do things and I smack myself and say is this real life?

My Inspirations

I grew up a huge fan of Rob Dobi. I think when I was about 13–14 I was first getting into design I was seeing a lot of band t-shirts and album packaging that really stood out and was so awesome. A friend sent me a link to Rob's site and I was in love. To this day Rob comes out with some of the best stuff I have ever seen.

Be Unique and Do Things First

Try and do something no one else is doing and introduce completely new ideas and techniques to designing clothing. Since day one I have prided myself on leading the pack in all things that are popular in our demographic.

When I was first starting out not a lot of people were using Myspace to promote their clothing companies on online social networking sites. For instance Myspace up until then only bands/musicians were using it to market and promote themselves. I, myself growing up in the music community, thought this was a no-brainer. Why not promote your clothing company via Myspace. Nowadays you can't step foot on Myspace without seeing a million clothing companies trying to make it.

Embrace Your Own Style

Figure out your style get to know it and embrace it, don't try and do things because you think other people will like it or because Johnny Cupcakes or Obey is doing it and it's popular at the moment. Find your niche and stick to it. Some of the best and long-running brands that have been doing this for years and years have their aesthetic, yet still roll with the times, never straying from their own unique style and vision for their brand.

Trendsetting

I started GK with intent of bringing a new style to this music scene (then it was all black band tees small print maybe one–two colors). Now everywhere you look it's neon colors thrown about. When I started GK I wanted to bring something fresh and new; our first few collections were very bright little did I know it would kick off such a huge trend. To this day I still keep the same aesthetic with off the wall and weird designs and inspiring quotes but I want to keep things fresh, new, and always moving forward. I never want people to become bored and expect the same ol'.

My Secret to Success

Hard work, hard work, and hard work. For the past two years of GK, I was able to save money by running the shop out of my parent's basement. I was a one man operation maybe working 10–14 hour days doing everything from packaging orders, designing, promoting my brand on Myspace, and answering emails (the list can go on). To this day I still have my hand in almost every aspect of the company. One thing you can't do is just assume you're going to have this successful brand right off the bat. Marketing, promoting, and building your brand is just as important as your designs. You could have the best-looking designs in the world but if no one knows who you are then it's pointless.

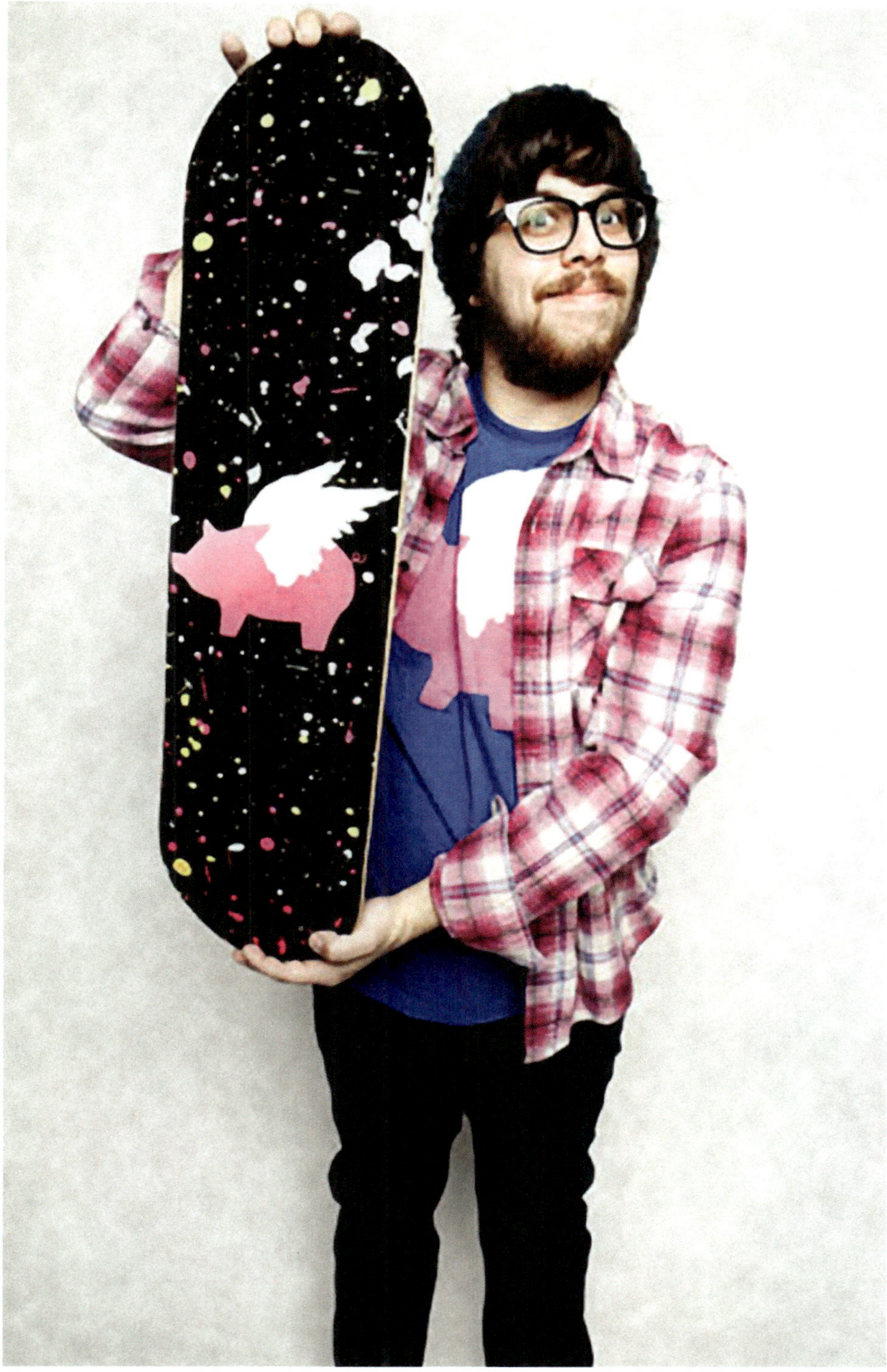

Justin Kamerer

My name is Justin Kamerer, aka Angryblue. I'm 30 and have been self-employed for about five years. I worked night hours on Angryblue while holding a day job for a few years prior to that. I've been interested in art as far back as I can remember. I got into it via comic books and album art. I went to a magnet high school to focus on art, but didn't think I could really pull off being an artist for a living and had the focus of most high school students, so other than enjoying dabbling in multiple mediums; I didn't put a lot of thought into it.

After high school, I stopped drawing for a few years. I had sketchbooks and journals

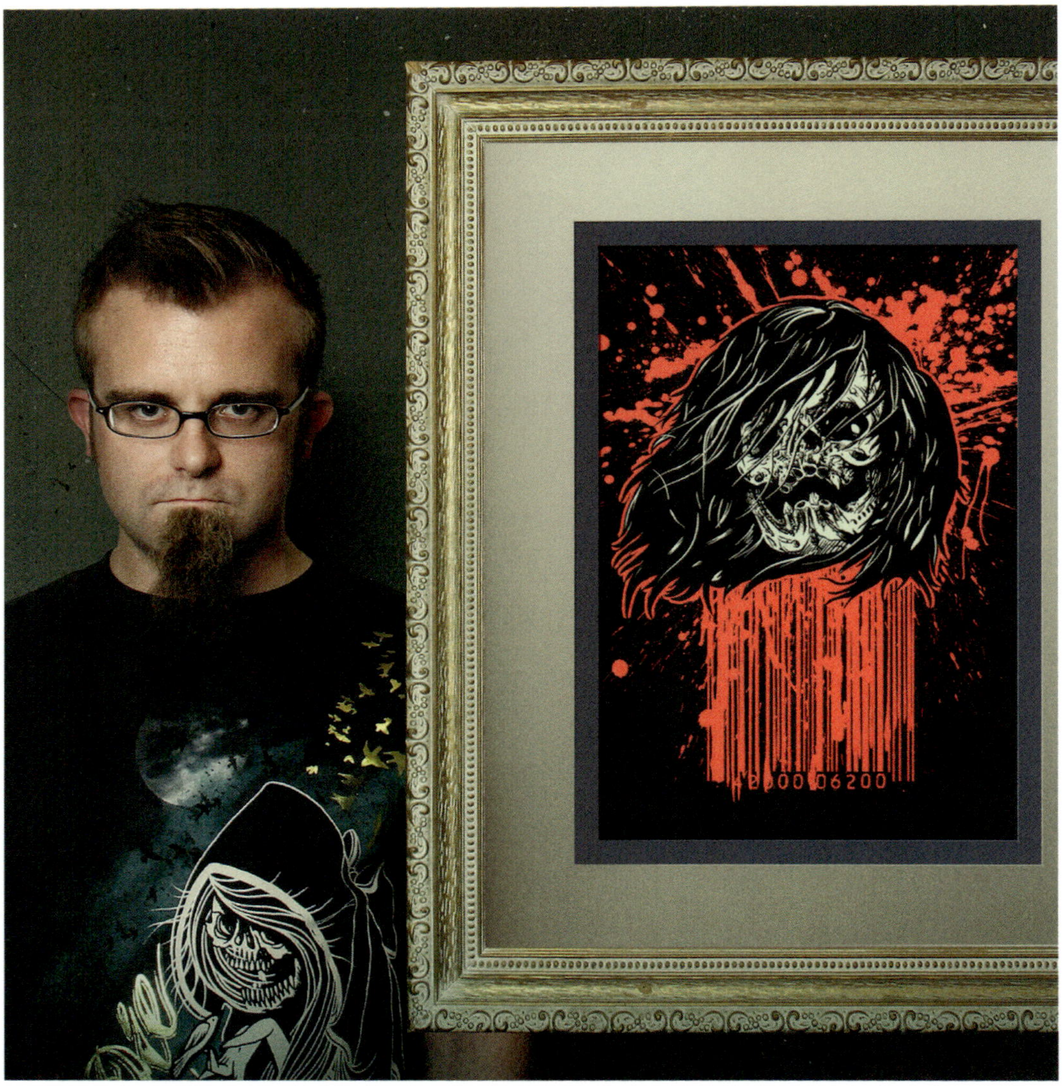

Justin Kamerer is a Weapon of Mass Creation

I'd occasionally scribble in, but nothing serious. I needed to figure out how to pay my bills and got a shitty job at a soup and sandwich place. After a week of that, I decided it wasn't for me, walked a few doors down to a sign shop and asked for a job. My logic was, "If I can't be an 'artist,' I'll see if I can pull off being a designer so I can do something creative." I got the job and the training was, "There's the computer. I'm going fishing for two weeks." So I had to figure out how to use this archaic vector program from the stone ages with a vinyl plotter.

"My approach is very iconic. If I can do an illustration and draw a circle around it, I'm happy." —JUSTIN KAMERER

After about a year, I got tired of that and dove into the web development world for about six years. Early in that, I was introduced to *Juxtapoz* magazine and learned about Derek Hess, pop-surrealist artists and the poster art world. I was hooked! I had friends in bands and started making flyers for them. Then I started talking the bands into letting me do some merchandise for them.

My schedule was: wake up at 7:00 for work, come home at 5:00, nap for an hour, work on art until 2:00 in the morning, sleep, rinse and repeat.

After a few years of doing web design and being told "make the logo bigger" from every client, I got really burned out on it and decided to venture out on my own with the few leads I had. I had really built my portfolio up and thought I'd see if I could pull it off.

My Breakthrough Moment

There might be two of them. One was my best friend (Jeral Tidwell of Humantree.com and co-owner of Crackhead Press) guilting me into quitting my day job and giving myself the chance to try to make it on my own. The other would be the first time I pushed a squeegee on the screen-printing press we put together at Crackhead Press. I was hooked.

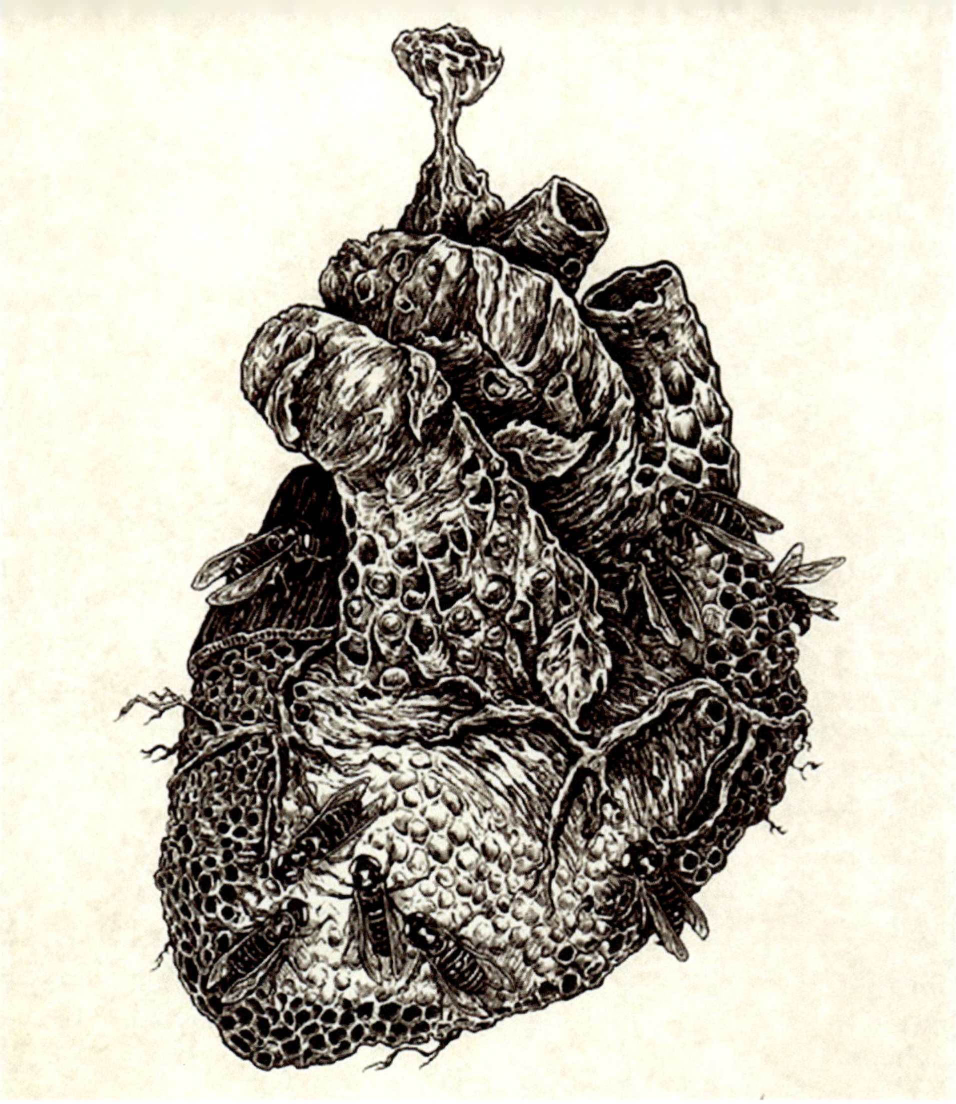

"The Hive"
by Angryblue

My Inspirations

Phew. Big list. Jeral Tidwell (man, I don't want to admit that in print), Derek Hess, Frank Kozik, Shepard Fairey, Wieslaw Walkuski, Franciszek Starowieyski, James Jean, Pushead, Craola, Chipp Kidd, ALL of my poster art friends (this sounds like a total cop-out, but the constant machine that is the poster art world keeps me constantly disarmed with clever approaches to imagery associated with bands and delivering information), Dave McKean, Rob Dobi, Jacob Bannon, Mike Sutfin, Aaron Horkey, Jay Ryan, Soviet and German propaganda, Sam Kieth, Alex Pardee, Michael Hussar, Michael Michael Motorcycle; just to name a few.

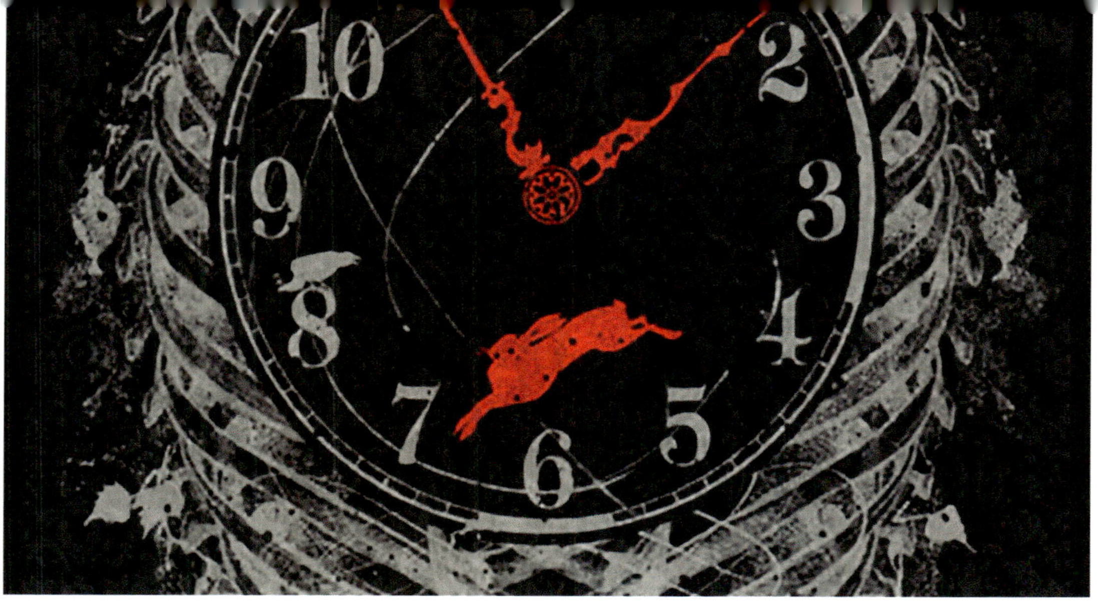

"You Are Safe" by Angryblue

Keepin' it Iconic

My approach is very iconic. If I can do an illustration and draw a circle around it, I'm happy. I mix design and illustration with nods to alchemy, religious iconography, cults and secret societies and anything else that might use an icon to communicate a message whether it's "don't touch that" or "these are all things that mean something to me."

My Simple Self-Promotion Strategy

I say that I'm an art whore. I assume I can handle any project handed to me and put my spin on it whether I've done it before or not. Beyond that, I do what I feel is the regular run-of-the-mill and ever evolving Internet-based pushing.

My Advice to You

Get to work. Your only limitation is you. Surround yourself with an overwhelming amount of inspirational materials. If you keep yourself in a constant state of brainstorming, some really cool things can happen.

Get out of your comfort zone. Yes, we know you can do that style and do it well. Do something that you've not approached before. I told one of my contacts at a major merchandising company that I wanted to try out anything she'd never think of me for. Trying out designs for Cher or Paul McCartney is obviously quite different than what you'd normally expect from me. I like to have the opportunity to problem-solve visually. It's a great challenge and will break you out of your usual slump.

Feedback is Your Friend

Find peers you can communicate well with. I think that the most important thing that has happened to me artistically is getting over worrying about a wounded ego. My partner in art-crime and I are really good at seeing a new piece and critiquing the hell out of each other. Even to the point where to someone else — it might sound vicious.

Obviously, the point isn't to figure out how to just tear someone down, but it's important to have someone say, "I see what you're going for, but this isn't working" or even, "You've already done this before a million times. Bring something new to the table." Sometimes, I'll work for a day on an illustration only to come back the next day and realize it's really awful. It's even worse when someone knows what you're capable of and doesn't say something for fear of hurting your feelings. One night, I was up until 5:00 in the morning working on a drawing. I thought I was really making this awesome masterpiece and it took showing it to another artist and having them say, "Really? That is just awful" for me to realize that. Even though I was really into it, I needed to re-approach it altogether. When I went back and started over from another perspective, it came together a lot better. Art is subjective. You are not a delicate flower. You're making a product that needs to be successful.

My Secret to Success

I'd like to be self-involved enough to think it's my personal style, but the real answer is probably consistency, meeting deadlines, research, and versatility. Those get you regular jobs that expand your portfolio. Most of my work comes by request through my website.

Research: Know Your History

When it comes to the merchandising stuff, it's important to research the band so you can figure out where they're coming from and who their target audience is. It's just as important to figure out how to make a shirt appeal to the hardcore Metallica fans who might get an obscure reference to a song lyric as it is to be able to successfully design something for Tina Turner's audience. Sometimes you can have a LOT of fun with a project. Sometimes, it's just a job. On both occasions, you can deliver something that has the right impact for the crowd you're catering to.

As goofy as it might sound coming from someone who might be recognized for drawing a lot of skulls and birds for metal bands: research is really important to me. It's important to understand the history of advertising from posters, to TV, to apparel.

As a designer, I think it's important to submerge yourself in pop-culture and the pop-culture from eras gone. Understanding what makes certain illustrations or typography represent an era and why is really valuable for having versatility in your portfolio. What makes those designs tick? What lettering styles made Soviet posters or French deco posters have that style only they have. Once you understand those, you can take them and pervert them for your own deviant needs.

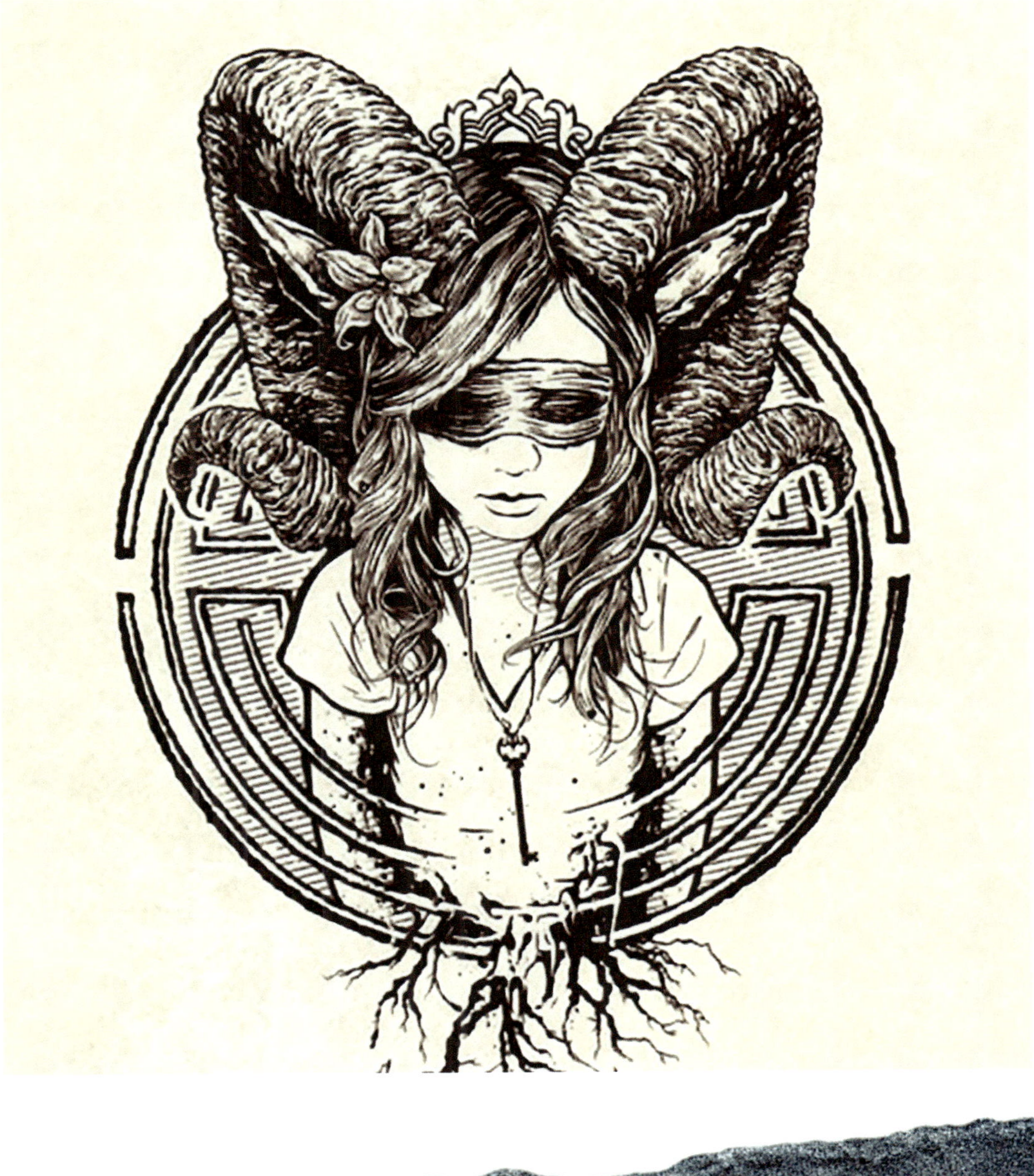

"Faun" by Angryblue

Brandon Rike

My name is **Brandon Rike**, and I have been in official business since 2002. At this point, I've been doing it for nearly nine years. I am 27, and I started doing t-shirt graphics for bands around the age of 19.

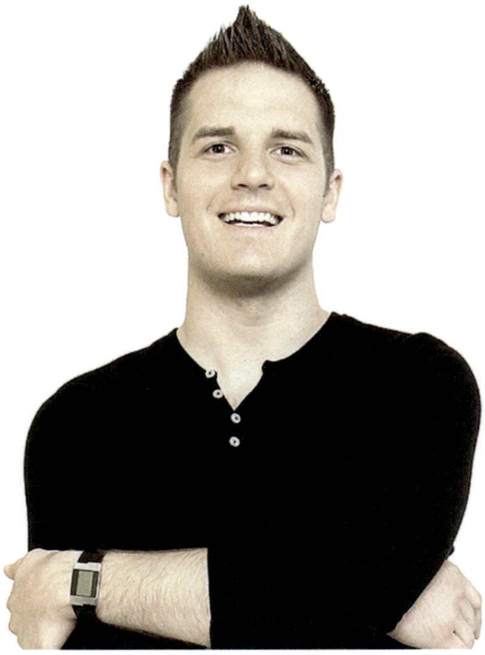

My First Band Logo

I've always loved art. I was always a kid who could draw. Drawing was what I did with most of my time. Around the age of 13, my friends and I started a band called Dead Poetic. When we made our first tape, I designed the jacket. It was a humble beginning, but I sketched for weeks on creating the perfect logo for us. Making all the letters work together, encapsulating it all into one solid shape, making sure there was good symmetry from side to side. I was using a pencil and graph paper while I was in math class. At this point, all I knew was that I was making a logo for our band. Nothing more, nothing less.

As time went on, I continued to design flyers for our shows, and jackets for our demos. As our band kept playing shows, we met other bands who I would design graphics for as well.

Skipping High School Art Class

Meanwhile, my high school art class had little to offer that interested me. At this age, I was over making clay pots and tie-dye, but I was not over creating art and graphics. I enrolled in a post-secondary program, in which I went to college for my junior and senior year. It was not until I got involved in this college's design department that I actually learned the term Graphic Design. I realized that I had been doing Graphic Design for years now, and now I could give it a name. I learned how to use Photoshop and Illustrator, and learned about what good typography really was, and how to create good composition. I took about half of an associates program, and never got a degree. Rock and Roll took over.

Move Over College, Here Comes Rock and Roll

My band did our first tour in 2001, and continued into 2002. In that year, while on tour, I designed graphics for bands that we had toured with, like Underoath, Beloved, The Uriah Omen, and Evelynn. While I had designed several graphics for bands the years before that, these were my first jobs that weren't just local friends. I was designing for bands who played a lot of shows, and sold a lot of merch.

As time went on, and we toured with more bands, it was a lot of, "Hey sweet shirts! Who designed them?" "I did." "Oh cool, do you want to do some for us?" That was the bulk of my business. It wasn't until we started touring with bigger bands, who gave my name to the global merchandise companies who they worked with. Then everything really started taking off. Now the majority of my business comes through these global merchandising companies.

My Breakthrough Moment

It was when my hobby turned into an income. I designed some shirts for a good friend's band. He asked me how much I charged, and I said $40 per approved graphic. His jaw dropped. He looked at me like I was a stupid child and said, "You have to charge more, way more!" By this time my graphics were as good as anything else out there. He explained to me that I wouldn't be truly taken seriously until I started charging the industry standard. Very reluctantly, I started quoting people the "standard," and the jobs kept coming through. Not only did they keep coming through, I was getting more work than ever. It was as if a light bulb had gone off, and not only was I being viewed as a top-level designer, but I put the time and effort into my work to really feel deserving of my new rate. It changed everything. It was like getting a new three-piece suit. I was respected as a good designer, and I worked harder than ever.

My Inspirations

My main inspiration was always Asterik Studio in Seattle. I was friends with Don and Ryan Clark, who now operate under the moniker of Invisible Creature. Those guys appeared to have such attention to detail, and were able to span from super evil art to happy kid toys. I ask them advice from time to time, and am always checking their site.

One of my favorite designers, these days, is Aaron Draplin in Portland. Aaron has a no-BS approach to art, and creates graphics with the bare essentials. I admire his simplicity, and hard work attitude.

"I want to be at the top of everyone's list because I am dependable and have a superior work ethic." —BRANDON RIKE

I'm also always checking out designers like Ames Bros, Morning Breath, Mike Giant, Shepard Fairey, House Industries, Aesthetic Apparatus, and Methane Studios.

I've found that FFFFOUND is a great resource of seeing art from so many designers compiled into one place. There are so many great designers that I feel like I could never touch — so it's nice to always be striving for that anyway.

Why Style Isn't Important to Me

Honestly, artistic styles come and go. So I have no interest in creating a style that people can point out as mine when they see it. I think too many designers are concentrating too much on putting their agenda into their client work. I want to stand out because I am versatile, and can meet the client's needs. More than that, I want to stand out because I work my butt off, and go to bat for my people. I want to be at

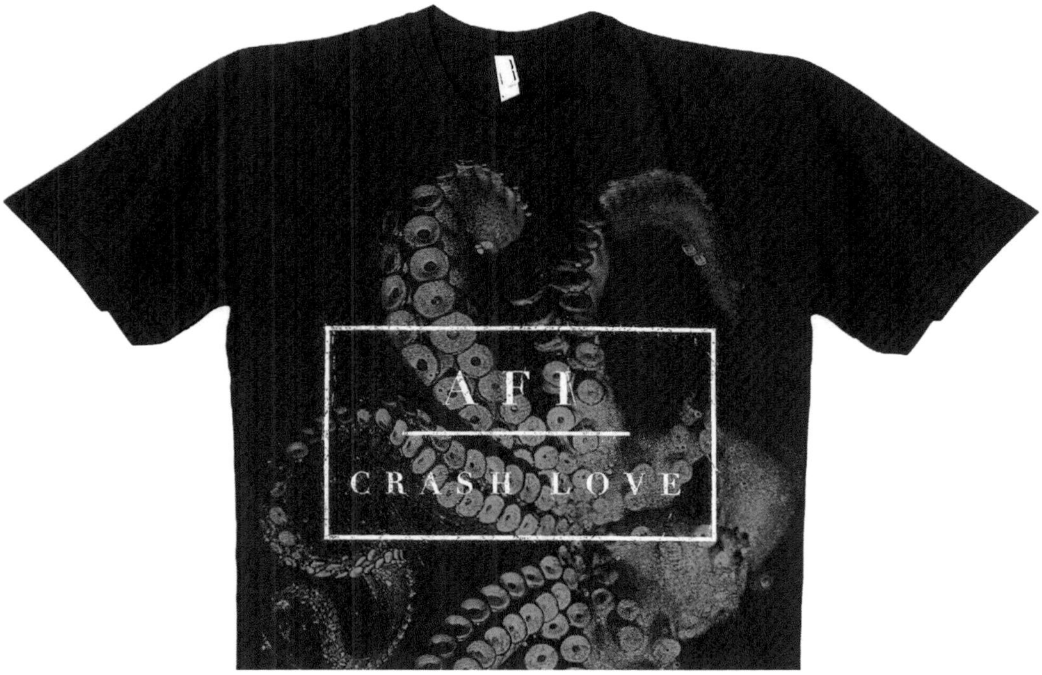

Shirt design for AFI by Brandon Rike

the top of everyone's list because I am dependable and have a superior work ethic. Talent took me a few steps, hard work is carrying me the rest of the way.

My Non-Promotion Strategy

I started with word of mouth, and it's taken me this far. I do want to focus a little more on branding myself, and keeping an updated website, but the good news is that I'm just too busy to devote any time to that.

My Advice to You

Get over yourself, and do the work. Don't be lazy. Laziness will not succeed. Hold a higher standard for yourself, and focus on doing great work. Talent only gets you so far, you have to be smart and hard working to actually make a living at this. Put up a site that easily displays your work, so that people will get who you are as soon as they're there. When you get the job — work hard at it. You are selling yourself to them as well as the art. Be good to people.

Trends I've Observed

Oh man. Well, I remember doing off-placement of prints around 2002, and thinking this was the coolest thing ever. That whole trend got out of hand. Neon got out of hand. Splatters and hand-drawn stuff got out of hand. Oversize prints also got out of hand. I've tried to stick to my guns, and always be able to come back to a good solid classic graphic (which has also always been in fashion). It's nice to roll with the trends in order to push yourself to get out of your comfort zone, but it's also nice to know what good design is, and to be able to implement solid principles amidst the trends.

My Secret to Success

Hard Work. Period. I go to bat for my clients, I work my butt off to make sure they are satisfied. This has enabled me to build great rapport with the people I work with, enabling me to remain around the top if their list. It's much easier to get asked to do one project than it is to be someone's go-to designer. Being a go-to guy happens when you never miss a deadline, and always go above and beyond expectations. Slackers and lazy designers will not succeed in this industry.

I love what I do. I adore what I do. When I am not designing stuff, I want to be designing stuff. I fall asleep thinking about what I'm working on the next day, and I wake up excited to create it. I have been extremely blessed to do, not only what I love for a living, but also what I am best at. I am also blessed to make a good income doing it. But it doesn't come without hard work. It doesn't come without an obsession for good design, and the desire to continue seeking out good art that inspires and excites you. You have to love doing this. You have to find ways of always keeping it fresh, and always looking for where the industry trends are going next.

With band graphics, you have to be able to know the visual connection to the music these bands create. You have to be able to see colors and images when you hear their music. You have to be able to create art that looks like the band sounds. The marriage of music and art is a sexy one, and I love constantly figuring out how the two work together.

On a more practical side, you have to be able to work quickly. Many of these deadlines are one–three day turnarounds, and you have to be able to accommodate. I've been doing it for so long, that I really only allow myself two–four hours to do an entire batch of graphics.

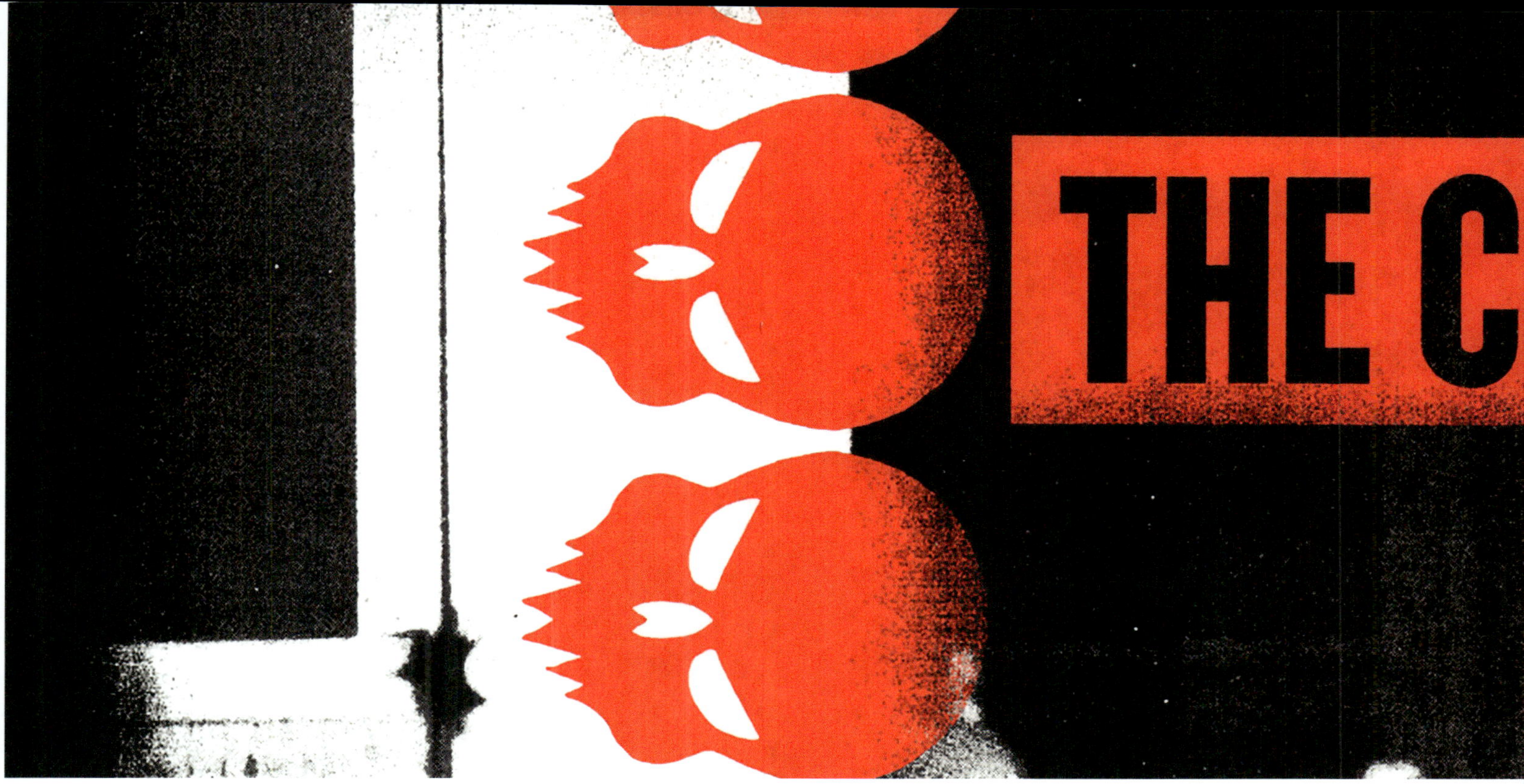

Design for The Chariot by Brandon Rike

With the quick deadlines, comes mastering another skill. How good can you be under such restraints? You may only be able to give about 60% of yourself to a given project, so is your 60% good enough? I believe great design come from restraints, so working so quickly can only make me better.

Overall, I often feel like the luckiest guy in the world. I get to make band t-shirt graphics for a living, and I have no intention of stopping any time soon.

Maxx242

I'm Maxx242, I'm 35 years old, and I've been designing professionally for about 13 years. How did I get to where I'm at today? That's a long story, but I'll break it down to several words: family, friends, sacrifice, commitment, drive, dedication, and will. Oh, and Redbull. I would say meeting Risk One was one of my breakthrough moments, but there were a lot of moments that got me here.

My Inspirations

My Mom really inspired me, but as far as artists go, Jeff Soto, OG Abel, Regino Gonzales, Armando Huerta, Francisco Rivera, Aurthor Adams, Dave Stevens, McFarlane, Campbell, Turner, Keith, John Connell, Jason Gallo, Mr. Cartoon, Mear One, Slick,

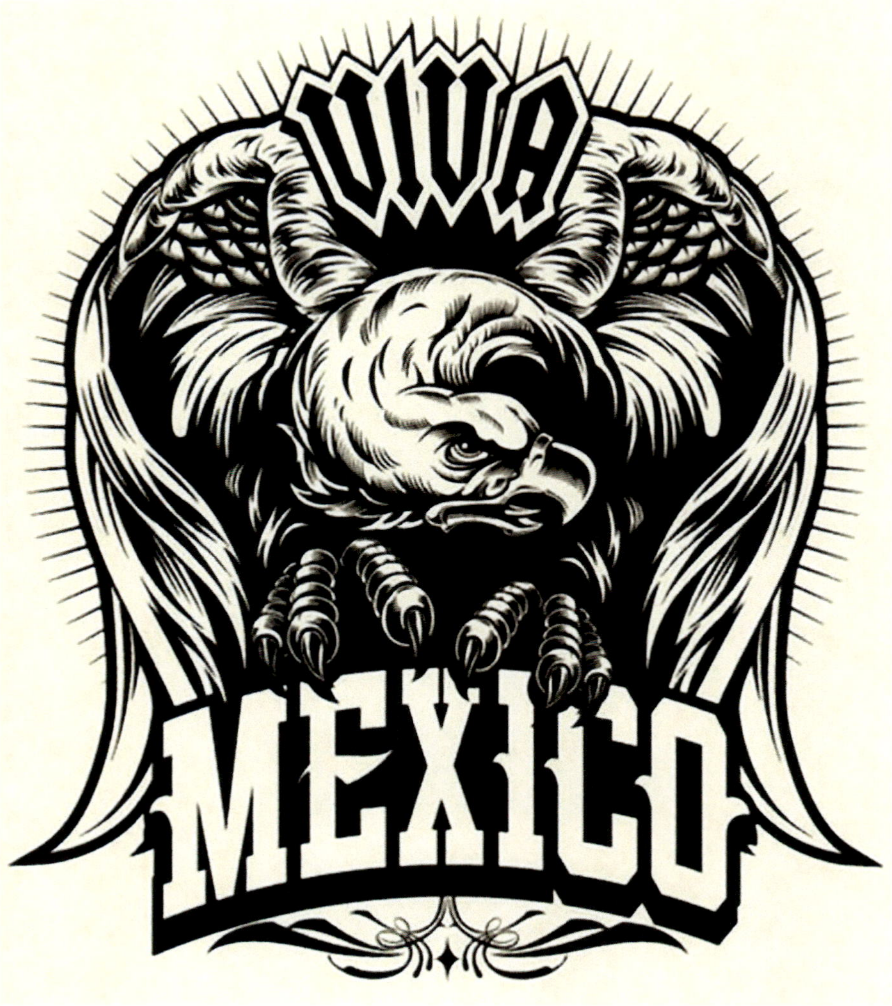

"Viva Mexico" by Maxx242

Craola, Frazetta, Jim Phillips, Mike Giant, VCJ, Coop, Ryden, Giger, Dali, this list gets long, but those are some main ones there.

My Strategy to Stand Out

I don't really have a strategy, I feel like I've been very fortunate in what I do and when I did it. I draw what I like and what I grew up with I guess. With that said I feel that refining your art, marketing, and promotions, and the right relationships will help you stand out as an artist. I've been lacking in promotion, I need to work on it. However, promoting yourself is very important. Having a good website is key; a home base to drive people to. Other than that, really work on refining your art. Promotional items and the right relationships are important. Do what you love, always.

Trends

There have been a lot of trends over the last ten years, don't even know where to start. I've seen the fall of the skate industry to it rising again, and then falling again. Moto, retro, choppers, Dover clip art, get money, skulls (but those are always in), MMA, licensed products, tattoo art, street wear, shoes, denim, sunglasses, west coast, east coast, etc.

My Secret to Success

Success all depends on what your definition of the word is. Be true and committed and everything else will fall into place. My faith, my family, and my commitment I believe have given me my success.

Be Dedicated and Committed

In the end I have to say that the key is dedication and commitment, there are weeks that in five days I'll get about ten hours of sleep. I try really hard not to let a lot of distraction come along. I don't drink or smoke, I don't go out a lot. If I'm not at my desk drawing or in front of my computer, I'm spending time with my family. Do what you love, and do it a lot. Always look for artistic growth, we all having growing to do.

Jon Kruse

My name is Jonathan Kruse. I'm 26 and I have owned my own clothing company called Mediocore Clothing for a little over two years. I also run the website **howtostartaclothingcompany.com**.

I graduated from California State University Northridge in 2007. It was right in the beginning of the recession before they were even calling it a recession and there weren't many jobs out there for designers. I ended up getting a job at a place that did movie posters in Hollywood. All I did was clean images and any other work other designers didn't want to do. Even though it was what I worked so hard in school to do, I didn't want to be in a 9 to 5 job commuting two hours every day to Hollywood.

Getting Out of Hollywood

I told myself this was the only time in my life that I would be able to start my own business and I went for it. It was rough in the beginning because I had no idea what I was doing. I had some friends in the business and they helped me out so much in the beginning and I wouldn't have been able to do it without them. I've stuck with it and made plenty of mistakes but I've learned from it and I am going to keep on pushing forward.

My Breakthrough Moment

I've had a couple. The first was being in a newspaper article in England where they talked about my "shark week" shirt. Next was doing amazing at Renegade SF selling almost $3,000 of shirts in two days. I was published in a Computer Arts Magazine writing an article about e-commerce design. Finally I am getting published in a book called *Torso* that came out in September 2010.

Also it's cool to have Jeff Finley ask me to write this. He has been someone I've always looked up to in the design community.

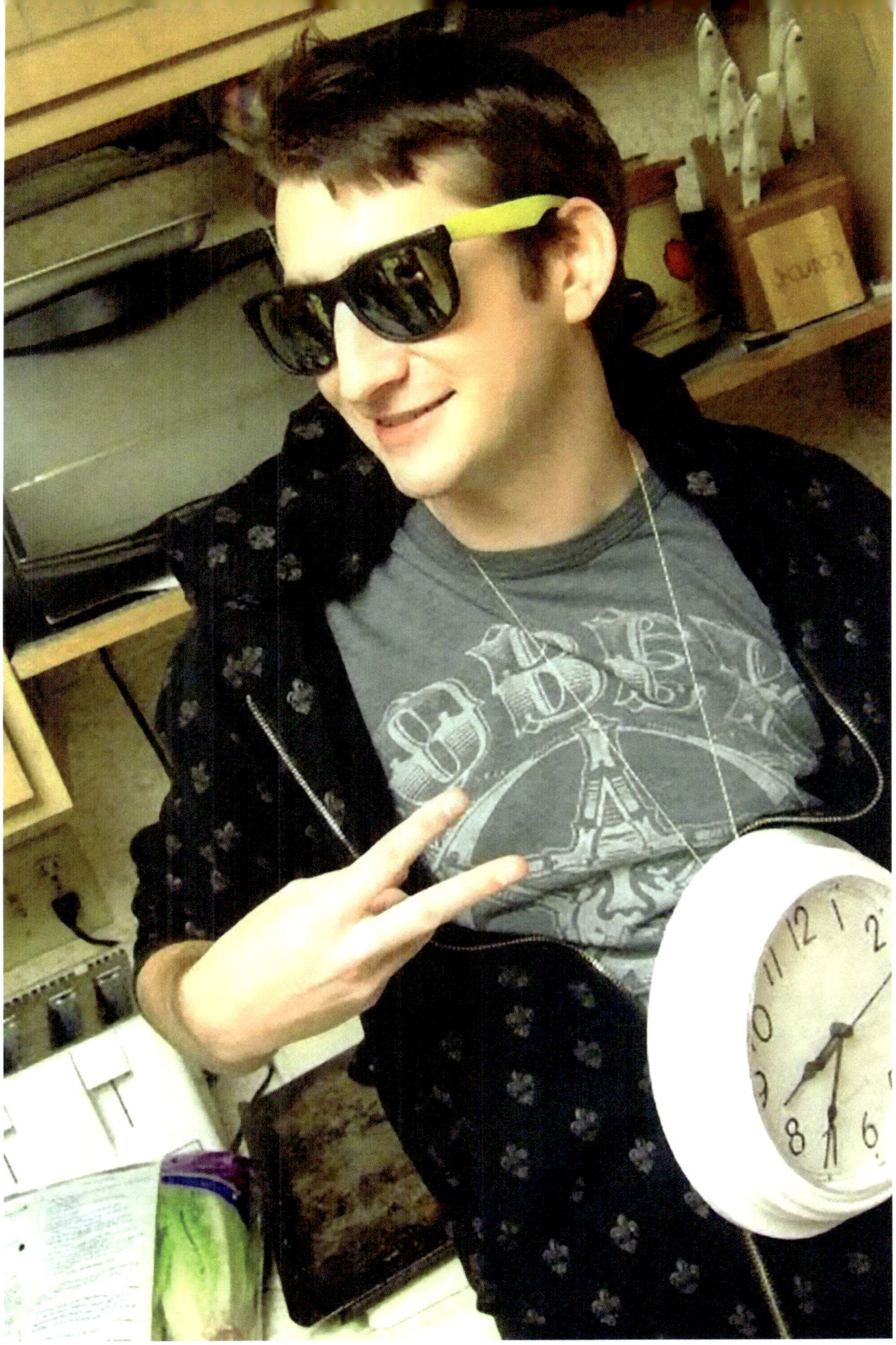

Jon Kruse is a designer and brand owner who writes about the business of running a clothing company.

My Inspirations

Banksy changed my life. I remember being in design class bored about dealing with just the aesthetics of design and his work opened my eyes. Soon after I was wheat pasting my own clever things all around school. I ended up going from graduating with honors to barely passing some of my classes the last semester because I was so consumed with work outside of school. In the end what I did outside of school with wheat pasting is a lot closer to my job now than school was.

How Ideas Can Set You Apart

The first shirt design I did was from this crappy hand-drawn flyer I did. It said, "Missing Turtle. Answers to Michaelangelo. His favorite food is pizza, but he hates anchovies. He has an orange blindfold cut out for the eyes. Keep an eye out at the clubs and bars because he's a party dude. Be careful because he has nun-chucks. His owner really misses him. Call splinter at 555-4372"

For this design, I really liked the subtlety of it. People could walk by and glance over it but only those that stopped to read it and were fans of TMNT would get it. You need to make people think to get the joke, you can't spell it out for them or it's not funny.

Self Promotion Tips

This isn't unique but I make friends with blog owners and have them get the word out for me. Each of these people gets thousands of visitors to their t-shirt blogs every month and by just sending them an email about a new shirt or sale I can spread the word quickly.

If I Could Do Things Differently

The thing I wish I had done from the start was run my clothing company as more of a business. In the beginning I was designing, printing, and shipping all the shirts. Now I don't do any of that. I know designers that are better than me that I get to design my ideas. I have a printer that can do amazing detail with a lot of colors and still keep it soft. I also get my brother to ship shirts for me. I still manage my company and do a lot of work but by hiring out talent, my company looks a lot better. It's hard to let go of some of the creative control but if you want to grow you need to do it.

My Advice to You

Just do it. Go out there and try. Fail and learn from your mistakes. Succeed and figure out what made it succeed. I get a lot of people that ask me questions about starting a clothing company and many times it's very apparent that they haven't even tried yet, they are just looking for all the answers. You'll never have all the answers.

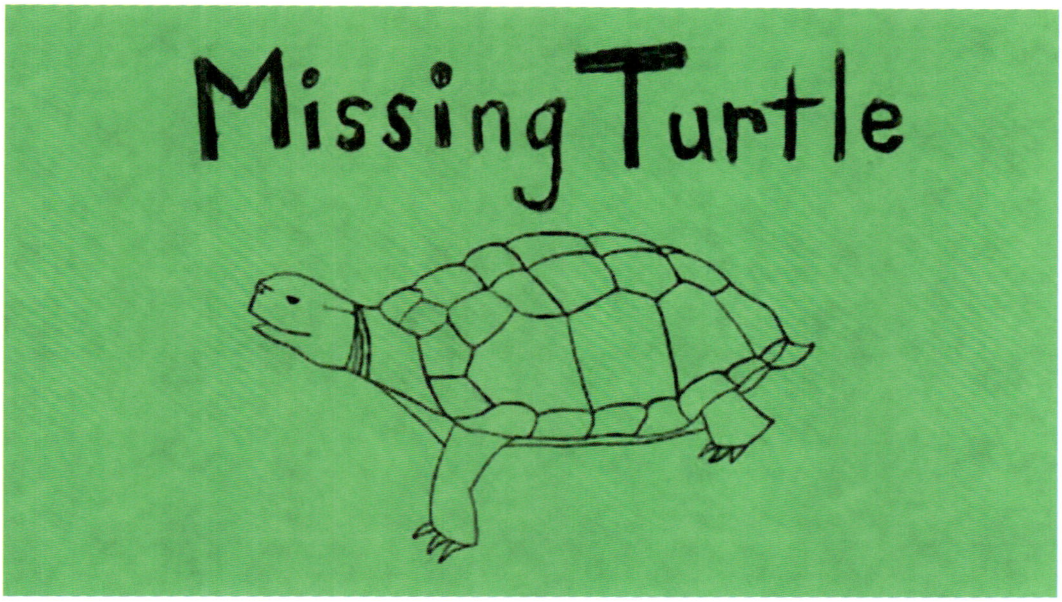

"Missing Turtle" by Jon Kruse

My Secret to Success

I've never rushed anything. The big jobs and big names just come to me because I put out high quality work. I'm in the web design field making websites for clothing companies but this applies to all design jobs. I've done things differently than the rest of my competitors and have created a name for myself for always trying to be ahead of everyone else.

Fin

Stop reading this, and get out there and make something happen!

Lightning Source UK Ltd.
Milton Keynes UK
UKIC01n2338120815
256861UK00003B/3

* 9 7 8 0 6 1 5 5 2 3 4 7 7 *